ON THE LINE

ERIC RIPERT

ON THE LINE

CHRISTINE MUHLKE

ARTISAN

Published by Artisan
A Division of Workman Publishing Company, Inc.
225 Varick Street
New York, NY 10014-4381
www.artisanbooks.com

Library of Congress Cataloging-in-Publication Data
Ripert, Eric.
On the line / Eric Ripert and Christine Muhlke.
p. cm.
Includes index.
ISBN-13: 978-1-57965-369-9
1. Le Bernardin (Restaurant). 2. Restaurant management. I.
Muhlke, Christine. II. Title.

TX945.5.L37R57 2008
647.95747'1—dc22
2008005930

Design by Helicopter
Printed in Singapore
First printing, October 2008
10 9 8 7 6 5 4 3 2 1

Editor's Note: We have used the generic "he" throughout this
book to avoid cumbersome constructions. It is by no means
an editorial comment; in fact, though women are still only a
fraction of the workforce in the high-end restaurant industry,
their numbers are growing at Le Bernardin.

CONTENTS

INTRODUCTION

Since it opened in 1986, Le Bernardin has received nothing but the highest praise, from diners and critics alike. The brother and sister team of Gilbert and Maguy Le Coze turned a room on the ground floor of a midtown Manhattan office building into a restaurant that caused a shift not only in how New Yorkers perceived French restaurants, but also in how Americans ate fish. Using experience they had gained from their successful Paris restaurant of the same name, plus talent and a considerable force of personality and will, the siblings created something entirely new: a four-star restaurant with soul.

Yes, the service was formal and the wood-paneled space had a boardroom feel, but between the revolutionarily simple and fresh seafood that Gilbert was sending out and the charge of French sexiness that Maguy gave to the dining room, Le Bernardin had a modern esprit that New York's other La's and Le's (Le Pavillon and other such landmarks) couldn't touch—and haven't since. In the ensuing decades, even after Gilbert died at the age of forty-eight in 1994, and Eric Ripert assumed command in the kitchen, it has maintained the quality of food and service, making it one of only three New York restaurants to earn three stars from the Michelin Guide. (With most magazines and newspapers, four stars is the highest rating. Michelin, however, tops out at three.)

It's one thing to get a good review. But how does a restaurant stay on top for more than twenty years? If the food, service, and overall experience at every table are to be memorable for every diner at every meal, that means that experience has to be repeated almost 150,000 times a year. Multiply that by twenty-two years, and logistical vertigo occurs.

This book provides a snapshot of how Le Bernardin works on a meal-to-meal basis: the whos, whats, wheres, whys, and, most important, the hows. There is so much that diners are unaware of as they enjoy their meal—namely, the fact that each meal is a precarious balance between discipline and chaos. The kitchen is a fraction of the size of other four-star kitchens, with few of their bells and whistles. The plumbing is old and faulty. The building management controls both the heating and air-conditioning for the room. And yet . . . That a meal at Le Bernardin continues to be a magical experience is a testament to what Le Coze and Ripert, through hard work and fierce discipline, have built together. That so many of their staff stay with the restaurant for years, even decades, is further proof that perfection has its rewards.

ERIC RIPERT
A PASSION FOR FOOD

My mother was a very good cook, very French. She was born in Morocco, which influenced some of her cooking. She cooked a little Vietnamese, too. The French food she did was slightly too refined for everyday meals at home and she was obsessed with having a great table set for lunch and dinner—tablecloth, porcelain, silverware—so I was eating in a very sophisticated environment without even knowing it. I loved being in the kitchen with her. Not necessarily for the cooking—though by the age of four I was baking breadsticks. What I liked was the ambience: picking at things and eating them right off the stove.

"My role model was Paul Bocuse: Before him, chefs were really in the background; the maître d's were celebrities. I know you shouldn't be looking at becoming a star—you should be looking at the craft—but I must say I was tempted to become recognized."

—Eric Ripert

When I was twelve, I decided to become a chef. I stole a book from the library about the greatest restaurants in France. I'd flip the pages and dream. I should return that book to the library some day....

I was a pretty terrible student, so at fifteen I was sent to a professional college. I studied cooking, but the food we cooked was boring; I ate better at home. Let's just say I was a very good waiter. When I graduated, I wrote to all eighteen of the three-star Michelin restaurants in France looking for a position. I got only one response, a "no" from Maxim's. And then, one Friday a couple of months later, La Tour d'Argent called and asked if I could be in Paris that Monday.

When I was fourteen, a psychic gave me the cross of Carabaca, a Spanish saint who grants miracles (I still wear it).

She then described the first restaurant where I'd work. A few years later, I was emerging from the Métro on the way to my first day at work at La Tour d'Argent and I realized that it was exactly the place she had described. I don't know how much protection the medal really provided, since the first minute there I cut my finger. Then my chef asked me to do a hollandaise and I told him the stove was too hot and there were too many eggs in his recipe. He said, "Okay, go pick the chervil." And I said, "What's chervil?" I couldn't even use a knife properly! On my lunch break, I'd run home to practice julienning carrots. I eventually moved to the fish station, which was my favorite, and then to pastry, until they kicked me out for eating so many petits fours one afternoon. I stayed at the restaurant for almost two years, and I learned that it's

Eric Ripert
Le Bernardin

very hard to work in a kitchen.

The chef sent me to work at Joël Robuchon's restaurant Jamin, which turned out to be the most stressful job I've ever had. Joël was really tough, but he's a genius. I spent two years making my way up the ranks, then Robuchon found me a job cooking with Jean-Louis Palladin, who was the chef at the Watergate Hotel in Washington, D.C. I was twenty-four and I spoke no English. I went from working in a structured kitchen with the best equipment to something totally rock 'n' roll. I had a really tough time assimilating, and Jean-Louis didn't like my attitude at first. Robuchon had taught me technique and discipline and levels of excellence that you can rarely duplicate anywhere, but I was very, very scared of making mistakes, because you were seriously punished. Jean-Louis really freed my mind. He said, "Cooking is fun: You can create, and if you fuck up, you start again." He had a huge influence on my vision today by saying that if the product is beautiful, you don't have to do very much to it, you just enhance its qualities. If you have a beautiful leg of lamb, don't do a square of this and a square of this; just slice the leg of lamb and it will be beautiful.

In September 1990 I moved to New York to work with David Bouley, whom I'd cooked with at Jamin. After six months, out of the blue, Gilbert Le Coze called and said, "Jean-Louis said you were a very good chef. I need someone to replace my chef, so you come tomorrow." I was like, This guy's nuts! I told him I'd committed to a year at Bouley, so I wasn't available. He said, "Okay, I see you tomorrow," and hung up. I never went. Jean-Louis told me I was crazy, that it was the job of the century. I was so ignorant that I had no idea what Gilbert's reputation was, or what Le Bernardin was. Three weeks later, Gilbert called back and said, "Come see my kitchen, we'll have breakfast." I went, and we had an incredible connection right away. That was January 1991, and I told him I wasn't available until June. He said

"Before I started working at Le Bernardin, I took a vacation in Italy and Spain. Gilbert joined me in Barcelona, and we went to San Sebastián and Madrid together. We partied like maniacs and talked about everything from cooking to the meaning of life. When I started at the restaurant, he gave me so much power and support. I didn't realize at the time how young I was to be taking over such a big kitchen. Being so naive was a good thing, because I didn't feel the pressure. Gilbert let me make mistakes; he let me be, basically. But he always said, 'Think Le Bernardin philosophy: The best fish, prepared simply.' He also prepared me for the media attention he knew was coming: "Hopefully you'll see good articles in your life and have positive write-ups. But be sure you read them only once and look at your picture only once. Because if you go back, you're screwed.'"

—Eric Ripert

RIGHT:
A young Eric cooking at an anniversary dinner at La Tour d'Argent.

OPPOSITE:
Eric in the Le Bernardin dining room soon after he took the reins in the kitchen.

he was willing to wait. By April, I was chef de cuisine at Le Bernardin. I was twenty-six.

At the time I started, the mood at the restaurant was low. Maguy was taking care of their satellite restaurant in Miami, and she was missed. Gilbert wanted to dedicate his life to the business side rather than cook; he was still involved with the kitchen, but it wasn't with the same intensity. And then, in July 1994, Gilbert collapsed at the fitness center downstairs from the restaurant and died soon after. He was forty-eight years old. I got the news while cooking a dinner at the James Beard House, but I didn't tell anyone; I saw the meal through, took my bow after dessert, and told the guests I was sorry that Gilbert couldn't be with them that night.

The restaurant didn't close for a single day. Emotionally it was very difficult because I lost someone who was a great friend and almost like family. In the kitchen, it wasn't that much of a challenge; for me it was the same job as before, except I didn't have Gilbert's support. Maguy pushed me to create a new menu. She said, "I don't want any

more Gilbert dishes. You do an entire menu, and I want it to be completely yours." I took a two-week break with my wife, and then Maguy and I changed ninety percent of the menu. I didn't feel the stress—I was so focused—but at the same time, there wasn't a good vibe. The team was down, and the restaurant wasn't busy.

Ruth Reichl, the restaurant critic of *The New York Times*, waited nine months before reviewing the "new" Le Bernardin. She visited at least eight times before deciding that we could keep our four stars, beginning her review with, "Four stars are easier to get than to keep." Gilbert's protégé was "having wonderful fun in the kitchen," she wrote; she talked about how we stripped each fish to its most basic elements and dressed it up to emphasize them, such as a delicate halibut simply poached in saffron broth. The review was very liberating, and suddenly Le Bernardin was back. It created a huge interest for the clientele and press, we were kicking again, and, soon after, Maguy made me a partner.

If Maguy and I had a mantra, it would be "Be yourself." I like to think we're ourselves, but at the same time we're sensitive to changes, and we're not blinded by our egos. We still cultivate that sense of awareness of what the clientele needs—despite the trends, despite the fashion. Our dishes are still relatively simple, focusing on deep, true flavors rather than elaborate presentation. I'm always seeking inspiration, but the fish will always be the star here.

We finally have this place running at the level we want it to be. I have an incredible team, both in the kitchen and on the management side. When I was a line cook, I loved the rush, the adrenaline of service. I still take great pleasure in cooking, but I envision my role as being the eye for the kitchen. I learned that from Robuchon, who never cooked. When I asked him why, he said, "My role is to make sure everybody executes for everybody in my dining room, cooking as perfectly as the way I would do it."

In 2000, the team went to a management seminar. We were astonished to find out we were managing in a dictatorial way. So instead of being involved in opening and closing every day and taking full responsibility for the kitchen, I thought I have such smart people around me, why not put some of the burden on them and try to make them more wealthy?

Wolfgang Puck is a great inspiration to me. He has my friend Lee Hefter as his executive chef, and Lee takes most of the burden for the kitchen and the cooking, and Wolfgang takes care of all the business. I presented this model to my chef de cuisine, Chris Muller, and promised to surround him with the right team to make it work. I was Chris for many, many years; until maybe three, four years ago, I had total control of the kitchen. Now I'm the palate. And I'm the inspiration—I hope—of the team. But I've given all my executive responsibility to Chris so I can focus on the business. This year I asked him to use more sous-chefs to expedite the food so he can be more free to walk around and see what's

wrong. It's a constant evolution. And I think today we are finally ready to do business beyond Le Bernardin because we have that system working.

I never thought I'd become so interested in the world beyond the stove. At the beginning Gilbert said to me, "Sure, now you're obsessed with your little sauce and everything, but one day you'll see: You'll be passionate about the human aspect." I thought, There's no way I won't be running the kitchen! I was obsessed from the first dish to the last dish. And now, as with so many things

at Le Bernardin, I see Gilbert was right. I've never had so much fun interacting with all of the people. I especially love mentoring, helping cooks develop their palates and their careers.

Here's a secret: The lease on Le Bernardin runs out in 2011. I hope we can successfully renegotiate, but the one thing Gilbert didn't leave us is a crystal ball, so we have to prepare. That's why I wanted to publish this book, as a tribute to the incredible people who make this one of the best restaurants in New York every meal, every day.

PART ONE

THE
HISTORY

To the diner's eye, Maguy Le Coze is the elegantly dressed woman who glides through the dining room, perching on the chairs of favored guests and keeping a well-made-up eye on the tables. But ask anyone who has worked at Le Bernardin—or, for that matter, anyone in the industry—about her, and they will tell you that she is the soul of the restaurant.

The first Le Bernardin was opened in Paris in 1972 by Maguy and her brother, Gilbert, who grew up in their parents' restaurant in the seaside village of Port Navalo in Brittany. The two, who were incredibly close, had always had a taste for food and nightlife: In their teens, they opened a disco in the village. When they reached their twenties, they decided it was time to conquer Paris. They scraped together money to rent a small restaurant on the Quai de la Tournelle on the Left Bank, naming it Le Bernardin, after a song that their father used to sing to them about an order of food-and-wine-loving monks.

"It was a little nothing bistro with Gilbert and a dishwasher in the kitchen, and me in the front with one waiter," says Le Coze. "The menu was the simplest you could imagine: oysters, mussels, and three or four fish dishes my brother had learned to cook during summers

at my parents' restaurant. It was the absolute bare minimum. Our background wasn't very professional; having a little restaurant in Brittany has nothing to do with running a restaurant in Paris."

The first few years were very difficult, but they were fortunate in that it was the dawn of nouvelle cuisine. "There was a revolution going on," says Le Coze. "The chefs were upending classic techniques to do absolutely whatever they wanted. It was a great opportunity for Gilbert; he started using his imagination to create dishes." The Le Cozes became part of a group of young chefs, including Alain Senderens and José Lemprera, who worked and went out together. Finally, in 1976, the restaurant was given one Michelin star. Thanks to Gilbert's charisma and Maguy's style, Le Bernardin became popular with the fashion crowd. But they still weren't financially secure, so they took a consulting job with Prunier, one of the oldest restaurants in Paris (and a fish restaurant as well). "We advised them for a year, and when we saw their finances we said, 'Oh la la, it's even worse than our place!'" Le Coze recalls.

Even so, they decided to open a bigger restaurant. In 1981 they relocated to a space on rue Troyon, near the Arc de Triomphe, and soon earned their second Michelin star. "Everything was going well," says Le Coze, "and then the American press discovered us. Suddenly, it was the American invasion. We were happy because people were writing in to request reservations, but soon eighty percent of our clientele was

American, and our French customers began to desert us a little. They all preferred the old restaurant on La Tournelle."

Seeing all those Americans made Le Coze wonder if she and Gilbert couldn't make it in New York, too. Although she'd spent only a week there in the 1970s, Maguy persuaded her brother to visit to see whether it would work. But he was frustrated by the lack of quality ingredients. "He tried to find fresh fish, fresh herbs—things like basil and cilantro," Le Coze recalls. "One day I asked a friend, Adrienne Zausner, whom I'd met through the food writer Gael Greene, if she had any basil, and she brought us a tiny bunch from her garden. Gilbert was furious."

But Maguy wouldn't let it go. She found ten investors to put in $100,000 each, and located a space on Third Avenue in the Fifties. The building owner put in money, and negotiations went on for eight months before they fell apart. A year later, she was looking for investors again. And then one day, six years after she had initiated the idea, she met a friend of a friend who was close to Ben Holloway, who was then chairman of Equitable Life's real estate group. "She told me he was looking for a restaurant for his new building. We were on the plane the next day! Ben took Gilbert and me for pizza—not an auspicious start—but that night he invited us to his apartment to shake hands over Dom Pérignon, which made Gilbert much happier."

Six million dollars later, the Le Cozes opened Le Bernardin at its present location in January 1986. By April they

had four stars in *The New York Times*—a restaurant first. (Restaurant critic Bryan Miller wrote, "A **** is born.") Soon they were getting twelve hundred calls a day for reservations.

What Gilbert was doing was radically different, says Le Coze, and not just because he was the first French chef to serve only fish. ("At the time there were two fish restaurants in New York, both Greek, and they served it either broiled or fried. French restaurants served fish from France, and the quality suffered during transport.") But finding good, fresh seafood proved to be an incredible challenge at first. Gilbert decided that since they were in America, and since New York wasn't far from the sea, he was going to serve only American fish. He was the first chef to buy his fish directly from the Fulton Fish Market—no easy task considering he didn't speak a word of English—and sent out dishes that

had never been put on a restaurant table before, such as skate, monkfish, and sea urchin. "People didn't even know what they were," recalls Le Coze. He found much more tuna at the market than they were used to in France, but every way he tried to cook it, it was a catastrophe. When Maguy suggested just serving it raw, he added a little salt, lemon, a few shallots, and chives, and voilà—a dish that came out of her imagination became a staple at the restaurant, and soon at restaurants around the country as well.

Maguy returned to run the Paris restaurant while Gilbert labored in New York, taking care of business and public-relations requests before heading into the kitchen for a double shift. Finally, at the end of 1986, after almost fifteen years, they sold the Paris restaurant to Guy Savoy, who was looking for a larger space, and Maguy officially moved to New York.

OPPOSITE, TOP:
Maguy and Gilbert, ages eight and seven, in Port Navalo, France.

OPPOSITE, BOTTOM:
Gilbert and Maguy at their second Paris location, on rue Troyon.

ABOVE:
Le Bernardin, c. 1987.

ABOVE:
Maguy and Gilbert
photographed in
Central Park for
People.

OPPOSITE:
Maguy and Eric at a
benefit in 1996.

*"Maguy is the inspiration and
the driving force, the living
soul of Le Bernardin. She's
the eyes and the palate of
the client, but better. To be
Maguy means no compromise.
You do it the way it's
supposed to be done."*

—Eric Ripert

Several years later, Gilbert expressed
an interest in serving *"maman's
cooking"*—bistro food, traditional
French cuisine—in other restaurants.
They were contractually forbidden to
open another restaurant in New York,
so they took one of two proposals they
had in Miami in 1991 and opened the
first Brasserie Le Coze in Coconut
Grove. Next they opened in Buckhead
in Atlanta, in January 1994. Gilbert was
negotiating another space in Charlotte,
North Carolina, and Maguy had her eye
on Las Vegas—"not that I'd ever been
there," she says, "but everyone told me
that there weren't any good restaurants
there besides Wolfgang Puck's." Gilbert
gave her the go-ahead; they were in
negotiations with a hotel when Gilbert
suddenly died.

A devastated Maguy abandoned the
Charlotte deal, moved from Atlanta
to New York, and sold the restaurants
in Miami and, later, Atlanta. She
leaned on her young executive chef,
Eric Ripert, who had been with the
restaurant for three years, to help her
through. "With Eric, the restaurant
blossomed more than ever, because we
really concentrated on it," she says. "The
first thing I told him was to change the
menu completely, except for the raw
dishes that were Gilbert's signature.
Like Gilbert, he kept the food simple
and respected the ingredients, which is
the key to Le Bernardin. I stayed very

close to him for a while to help him get
ahead and support him; he was so young.
Eventually he became more comfortable
in his role, and at that point I made him
a partner. Now it's I who lean on him.
It's a rare occurrence in the business,
but Eric is a rare and special man. You
don't meet people like him every day.
He's extraordinarily loyal and sincere."

Le Coze's role has changed
completely over the years. She and her
brother had been the personality of the
restaurant, and she knew every client,
right down to what they liked to eat. But
she has gradually become more involved
in operations, going over the profit-and-
loss report daily and troubleshooting
problems, from overcharges to
employee satisfaction. "No matter
where I am in the world, I'm closely
involved in everything that happens
in the restaurant," she says. "If there's
a blocked drain in the kitchen, I know
about it—and there isn't a single day
when there isn't a technical problem.
Sometimes it will be calm for a day or
two, and then all hell breaks loose."

Whenever she's at home in New York,
she spends a few hours in the dining
room each evening after she's finished
in the office. She feels her strength
is her ability to see details—the little
things that no one else notices—so it's
important for her to be there as often as
possible to see that everything is running
smoothly. "So many restaurateurs
who have expanded no longer have a
presence in their restaurant," she says.
"Eric and I make sure that one of us is
always there."

As for keeping those stars, "I think
it's a question of maintaining the same
quality: quality in the kitchen, quality in
the reception, quality in the service," she
says. "We're able to stay constant because
people have been with us for such a long
time, so they know our standards. And
at the same time we're always evolving. I
do this by discreetly changing something
in the room every year, whether it's the
frames on the paintings, the color of the
walls, or the fabric on the chairs. It never
ends, and for that I'm grateful."

THE RESTAURANT TODAY

Le Bernardin is a very interior space. Unlike slick decorator-stamped restaurants of its caliber, there are no flourishes to hold the diner's attention besides the food.

After the first course, few people remember that they are eating on the ground floor of a fifty-five-story building that occupies an entire block of midtown Manhattan, a few hundred yards from some of the most powerful media companies in America, and a few hundred yards from tourist-thronged Broadway. The restaurant's discreet curtained windows tell little of what's happening inside; and out on the street, the only thing you notice is a jumble of suited businessmen maneuvering around tourists heading down the street to the matinee of *Mamma Mia!*

Through a glass foyer, two women open the doors of the main entrance onto a small, five-seat bar, where once a week for more than twenty years, a local poet has come to dine and write. The eye is drawn to the left down a long, soaring space, paneled in warm teak and beige fabric, with latticework along the windows, all designed by Philip George. Behind the maître d's podium is a heavy glass screen, behind which are the two most popular tables in the house. Throughout the room, the thirty tables are spaced to allow for private conversation; it's almost impossible to eavesdrop, which is a draw for some regulars but disappointing for those who want to hear them.

Once the diner has settled in, the outside world, even the neighboring tables, fade away. The room never tries to compete with the food, except perhaps for the towering, exorbitant flower arrangements that punctuate it. Art has

been a focal point of the room since it opened. The building, which was known as the Equitable Building when it was constructed in 1985, was designated as a showcase for American art by its owners, exhibiting works in its public spaces and a 3000-square-foot gallery. As a condition of occupying space in the building, the Le Cozes were told they had to hang important art on the walls. With a budget from building management, Maguy combed galleries, flea markets, and auction houses for nineteenth-century oil paintings with marine themes, such as a seafood market in Brittany or the portrait of a fisherman (Maguy and Gilbert's grandfather) that hangs over the bar. Several years ago, Le Coze and Philip George changed the heavy gilt frames for ones that were lighter and simpler. Le Coze also added two vibrant, Modigliani-like paintings by contemporary Mexican artist Abelardo Favela and works by Colombian artist Valentino Cortazar to inject more color into the space.

At the far end of the dining room, a stairway to the right leads upstairs to Les Salons, a kind of miniature Le Bernardin, where up to 90 people can dine privately during lunch and dinner. Accordion-pleated partitions can be lowered from the ceiling to create up to three private rooms or raised to create a party space, as it often is for corporate celebrations, birthdays, and other events. The Salon, as it's called among the staff, has its own kitchen, also a miniature replica of downstairs, with a menu and service identical to those in the restaurant.

That Le Bernardin always feels calm and the service personal while the restaurant serves up to 300 people each weekday, plus as many as 90 upstairs, is a testament to the discipline and structure created and imposed by Le Coze and carried out by the maître'd, Ben Chekroun. The fact that the kitchen can prepare its food quickly and at a consistently high level is a testament to the system that was set in place by Gilbert Le Coze and evolved by Ripert and now his chef de cuisine, Chris Muller. Together, they work to create a unique New York restaurant experience, one that is purely in the service of the food.

> "You must always evolve. If the restaurant were still like it was the day we opened, it would be old! You must always change—but subtly."
> **—Maguy Le Coze**

UPSTAIRS DOWNSTAIRS: THE LAYOUT

Operating a restaurant in a midtown office building has its logistical challenges. Most New York restaurants have their (small) offices, prep kitchens, and locker rooms in the basement, with their main kitchen up a short flight of stairs.

At Le Bernardin, the basement offices are almost a half block from the restaurant.

This cramped area—four small rooms off a narrow hallway, plus a tiled alcove with a sink for the fish butcher—is overseen by the porter. Here, fish is filleted, dry goods and truffles are stored, cardboard boxes are broken down, and silver is burnished in a special machine on Saturdays. There's also a dedicated refrigerator for City Harvest, which picks up leftovers daily for distribution to the city's hungry. Once the fish butcher leaves at 1 P.M., cooks use his counter space to make ravioli and do other prep work. The loading dock is underground; all deliveries arrive there in the morning, to be distributed upstairs via a small, slow elevator. All staff members arrive there, too, passing from the locker room or offices to the upstairs via the elevator, which can barely fit six and tends to break down. Like so many other aspects of the restaurant, faith is required.

PART TWO

IN THE KITCHEN

The team is big by New York restaurant standards: a staff of forty cooks for a hundred-seat restaurant. The compact kitchen, however, is only average by four-star standards, without much of the cutting-edge equipment and gadgets of newer restaurants. (When you mention Le Bernardin to chefs who have visited the kitchen, they almost always whistle and say, "I can't believe he serves three hundred meals a day in that place.") Between lunch and dinner, and tasting menus at both, it sends out up to twelve hundred dishes a day—as many as a restaurant twice its size. During the heat of a meal service (and it *is* hot), an order is called out to be fielded by one of the cooks every fifteen to thirty seconds, while a food-laden tray is carried out to the dining room every sixty to ninety seconds—an impressive pace for such finely tuned food. Pulling this off requires intricate organization and a regimented hierarchy that leaves little room for error, much less elbows.

Executive Chef
Eric Ripert is the face, the eyes, and the palate of the kitchen.

Chef de Cuisine
Chris Muller has total control, from a managerial perspective, of the food that enters and leaves the kitchen.

Executive Sous-Chef
Eric Gestel is Ripert's other right-hand man in the kitchen; in addition to helping Muller run meal service and inspect plates, he cooks wherever Le Bernardin's food is needed off-site.

Executive Pastry Chef
Michael Laiskonis creates and plates the restaurant's clean, straightforward, contemporary sweets, which won him a James Beard Award for outstanding pastry chef in America in 2007.

Pastry Chef
Jose Almonte manages both lunch and dinner services and oversees all special projects, from birthday cakes to desserts for outside events.

Pastry Sous-Chef
Ricardo Guaman is in charge of making all of the cookies for lunch and organizing the dessert *mise en place* for dinner the next day.

Sous-Chefs
These five people help the chef de cuisine keep meal service running smoothly by expediting orders and jumping in to help cook where needed.

DECODING THE LANGUAGE OF THE KITCHEN

Understanding the special language of the kitchen is a prerequisite to understanding how the whole operation works. It's a vocabulary filled with a shorthand that is based largely on classic French culinary language but even borrows some terms from the military. The intensity of lunch and dinner service means that all communication must be brief, and the noisiness means it must be shouted. Because food can be ruined in a matter of seconds, there's no time to explain or repeat oneself.

Le Bernardin Glossary

BACK WAITER: Six waiters who serve as the liaison between the dining room and the kitchen (see page 116).

BRIGADE SYSTEM: A kitchen organization system institutionalized by legendary cook Auguste Escoffier requiring that each position have a station with a set of defined duties.

CALL OUT: To read aloud an order ticket to the cooks, thereby placing an order for the item(s) to be prepared. In order to prove that they heard the order, the cooks must then respond with "Oui!"

COOK: A person just out of culinary school or with only a few years' hands-on experience. Also called *line cook*.

COVER: One guest, as in "Saturday we did two hundred covers for dinner."

A (FAIRLY TYPICAL) DAY IN THE LIFE

6:30 A.M.
Porter arrives in his basement area, checks kitchen inventory and garbage pickup. Saucier, garde-manger manager, lunch cooks, and fish pass begin prep work for lunch service; produce and dairy delivery

7:00
Morning saucier arrives

7:15
Delivery from Blue Ribbon Fish arrives: black bass, cod, fluke, halibut, monkfish, organic salmon, sea urchin, skate, snapper, squid, striped bass, oysters, jumbo lump crab, turbot

7:20
Fish butcher arrives

7:50
Porter stocks the kitchen with dry goods

7:55
Linens are delivered (10 tablecloths short)

ENTRÉE: Main dish, in the American usage.

EXPEDITE: To oversee the kitchen's output during mealtime.

FIRING A TICKET: Cooking an order.

FRONT WAITER: Six waiters responsible for delivering the food from the bus station to the table (see page 116).

LINE: A row of stoves along which the cooks are positioned. At Le Bernardin there are two lines: one for appetizers and one for entrées.

MISE EN PLACE: Literally, "put in place" in French. All the ingredients each cook will need during service—from salt and Espelette pepper powder to oil and vinegar, from diced shallots to julienned shiso. ("Everybody check your *mise en place*: service starts in twenty minutes.") Each cook prepares his own based on the dishes he's responsible for, a process that can take up to four hours. Often shortened to *mise*.

PASS: The counter on which prepared dishes are placed to be inspected, and frequently tasted, by the chef de cuisine. The back waiters take the dishes from the pass and deliver them to the dining room. "In the pass" refers to a dish that is ready to be served: "Pounded in the pass in thirty."

(Translation: The tuna appetizer will be ready in thirty seconds.)

PLATE: To assemble a finished dish to be served: "Before you plate the turbot, make sure the potato foam is warm."

SERVICE: The period of meal preparation. There are two services daily, lunch (noon to 3 P.M.) and dinner (5 to 11 P.M.). ("I get in to prep at seven A.M., but lunch service doesn't start till noon.")

SOUS-CHEF: A cook with considerable experience on the line who now has a supervisory role in the kitchen, overseeing line cooks.

STATION: A cook's position in the kitchen—both where he stands and what he prepares. ("What station are you working?" "Today I'm on canapé.")

TOURNANT: A relief chef (usually an experienced cook) who jumps in to help the stations in need rather than having a fixed station. Also known as *chef de tournant*.

WALK-IN: The refrigerated room and adjoining freezer where the day's ingredients are kept on metal shelves and in plastic bins. There are three walk-ins, one for the kitchen, one for the pastry department, and one for fish.

The Stations

In the regimented world of the kitchen, a person's position is also the name of his station, which is both where he stands in the kitchen and the job that he performs: Think of a shortstop in baseball. An entry-level cook with one to two years of experience, known as Level One, starts at garde-manger, gradually making his way up the line, position by position, until he reaches the sauce station.

FISH PASS

Before each meal service, this person is responsible for killing and cutting up lobsters; cleaning hundreds of pounds of shrimp, langoustines, scallops, sea urchins, and calamari; and making the calamari stuffing, tomato confit, and vegetables for the market salads. Then, during lunch and dinner service, each time a fish order arrives in the kitchen, he removes the required fillet(s) from the refrigerator compartment at the end of the garde-manger line and quickly walks it over to the sauté station, where it is left to come to room temperature. He also prepares oysters to order, and after service he cleans and reorganizes all the walk-ins.

GARDE-MANGER

Garde-manger, which means "pantry" in French, is where everyone, regardless of experience, starts in Le Bernardin's kitchen. Neophytes—culinary-school grads and those with at least one year of restaurant experience—develop their knife skills, identify ingredients, and work efficiently in a small space. To keep

---

8:00
First container of filleted fish sent upstairs to walk-in

8:15
Chicken and veal stocks put on stove

8:41
Delivery arrives from Browne Trading in Maine: cod, fresh seaweed, halibut, jumbo scallops, monkfish, sea urchin, skate, white tuna, wild Alaskan salmon, peekytoe crab, Italian organic caviar, langoustines

8:45
Reservationists arrive

8:47
First reservation made

9:30
Florist creates floating flower arrangement for each table

9:40
Back waiters set 30 tables in dining room

10:10
Tuna arrives from Japan via FedEx

10:50
Bread arrives from Tom Cat Bakery

Continued ⟶

things simple and to avoid error, each of the three garde-manger cooks (more during high season, from September to January) has at most two dishes to prepare during each service.

The menu's eight cold appetizers come from the garde-manger. The garde-manger line has eight refrigerator compartments, which store prepped and portioned ingredients for each of its assigned dishes. For efficiency purposes, the popularity of an item determines where the cook making it stands. The most popular dish—the pounded tuna carpaccio, for example—is made the closest to where the chef de cuisine stands. This cuts down on cross-traffic.

VEGETABLES AND HOT APPETIZERS

The restaurant's nine cooked appetizers are prepared on these two stations. Dishes are grilled, sautéed, or poached on one side, then finished at the counter behind the cooks, which contains the necessary garnishes. This line is also where the calamari is fried during dinner, when it is served as a canapé. Because these appetizers are more complex than cold ones, requiring cooking and saucing, only

a Level Two cook may work here, after being promoted from garde-manger.

VEG: After someone has worked on garde-manger for at least eight months or has at least two and a half years of kitchen experience, he moves over to the veg station, where he is responsible for the single vegetable-based hot appetizer on the menu (usually sautéed mushrooms).

CANAPÉ: *Amuse-bouches* such as lobster cappuccino are served to guests only in the evening (at lunch, tables receive salmon rillette). So every day at four o'clock, a steel cart the size of a typing table is wheeled out and tied to the side of the pass (there's no room for it anywhere else), and an experienced garde-manger cook makes up to three hundred of the evening's canapés.

HOT APPS: Once someone has at least three years of kitchen experience, he progresses to cooking small pieces of fish and meat, learning to work on two or three dishes simultaneously. The three hot app (appetizer) cooks prepare everything from fried calamari to sea urchin ravioli with caviar.

ENTRÉES

In a space the size of a minivan, four cooks squeeze together over extremely high heat to prepare the restaurant's delicately complex dishes at a pace that would impress a short-order cook. The pressure is so intense that only a Level Three cook— someone who has at least four years of kitchen experience—is thrown onto the entrée line.

MONK: Called the poaching station in other restaurants, it's where fish is poached and some of the less complex fish entrées—such as skate, striped bass, and monkfish (hence the name)—are plated and sauced. This is the beginning of the line (also known as downtown); a cook makes it here after four to five years of kitchen experience.

SAUTÉ: Almost all of the fish is seasoned and cooked here on six burners and two flat tops (flat, griddle-like surfaces that are hottest in the center, allowing the cook to "play" the heat) and in one oven— up to seven pieces at a time— at dizzying speed. This one-man show is the fastest-paced station, and the one that sets the rhythm for the rest of the kitchen. If the sauté

cook is backed up, the entire kitchen must slow down, as everything depends on the fish. To add to the stress, he also has to scrape out all the cast-iron pans with a wire brush and briskly rub them clean with a towel after each use. A cook moves here after at least five years in a kitchen, and quickly has the burns on his forearms to prove his status.

SAUCE: This is the front of the line (also known as uptown), where twenty sauces are made twice daily and more complex—or costly—dishes, such as lobster and Kobe beef, are prepared. After more than a year in the kitchen, a cook can make a six-month commitment to learn the craft of saucier, the most difficult skill to master. (Vincent Robinson, the daytime saucier, has cooked here since the restaurant opened, and Ripert is careful to keep him in good spirits, which means the junior saucier works the long evening shift.) During service, a back sauce—someone who's been promoted from sauté and will soon move to sauce—helps cook and plate.

10:55
Forty-five lobsters arrive from Jordan Lobster

11:00
Five sous-chefs arrive for lunch service; review notes from chef de cuisine regarding VIPs, special deliveries, meals in the Salon, etc.

11:15
Staff meal is served: tacos, rice, and salad

11:30
Garde-manger setup is completed

11:45
Sauces completed by saucier, tasted by sous-chef; waitstaff arrives

11:55
Busboys begin toasting bread for salmon rillette. Chef Ripert arrives in kitchen to greet staff and taste sauces

12:00 NOON
Restaurant opens for lunch. Chef de cuisine and executive pastry chef arrive to oversee service

12:15 P.M.
City Harvest picks up leftover produce and fish for soup kitchens for the homeless

12:20
First cold appetizer order comes in

PASTRY

With just four burners, a small oven, an ice cream maker, and a microwave oven for melting chocolate, this 10-by-14-foot area at the rear of the kitchen manages to send out more than 500 complex desserts, 1500 cookies, and 1250 petits fours every day, plus whatever else is required in the Salon upstairs. Organization is key: Each of the ten desserts on the menu has at least five components, which are made and portioned in the morning, ready to be assembled once the orders print out from the dining room. In addition, the full-time staff, including three production employees who spin the twelve ice creams and sorbets daily and make the dessert components, must make two kinds of cookies for lunch, five kinds of petits fours for dinner, three kinds of pre-desserts for tasting menus and VIPs, cookies for sorbet, VIP chocolates, cheese sticks for the bar, and birthday cakes. At this point, they know each other so well that they barely speak as they send out a dessert every minute during the rush.

DISHWASHERS

It takes a team of fourteen to keep pace with the dining room, with its thirty-five different pieces of white china (ten just for canapés), and with the kitchen, which goes through pots, pans, and utensils at a pace that can be hard to keep up with during service. Two to three men run the main dish area, which houses a single conveyor-type dishwashing machine. In a separate alcove just off the kitchen, one man washes pots and pans, and another washes glasses (very carefully) in the back of the kitchen, where he shares space with prepping cooks. During dinner service, there's one person on staff just to dry glasses. "They're doing the most difficult job in the house, and they're often the least recognized in the industry," says Ripert. "We're lucky that they're so dedicated; many of them have been with us a long time."

The Kitchen at a Glance

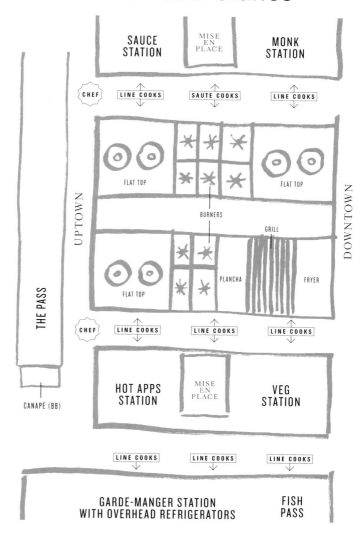

SAUCE STATION — **MISE EN PLACE** — **MONK STATION**

CHEF — LINE COOKS — SAUTE COOKS — LINE COOKS

FLAT TOP — FLAT TOP

BURNERS

GRILL

FLAT TOP — PLANCHA — FRYER

CHEF — LINE COOKS — LINE COOKS — LINE COOKS

UPTOWN — DOWNTOWN

THE PASS

CANAPÉ (BB)

HOT APPS STATION — **MISE EN PLACE** — **VEG STATION**

LINE COOKS — LINE COOKS — LINE COOKS

GARDE-MANGER STATION WITH OVERHEAD REFRIGERATORS — **FISH PASS**

12:25
First cold appetizer is sent out

12:30
Sommelier places first wine order with barman

12:40
First entrée order arrives in sauté station; by 1:19 one entrée order will arrive every 30 seconds

12:47
First entrée is sent out

1:05
VIP walks out because another VIP is at his favorite table

1:07
Miss Le Coze sneaks into walk-in with toast for salmon rillette snack

1:08
One cold appetizer order will arrive every 15 seconds

1:09
Miss Le Coze's second rillette snack

1:10
Maguy's third rillette snack. ("Every day for twenty years, it is my habit.")

1:15
First dessert order comes in

Continued ⟶

BB Canapé: Short for bread and butter plates, which is what canapés are served on.

Behind!: What one yells while walking behind anyone and everyone in the kitchen to prevent spills, burns, and chaos. Kitchen veterans abbreviate further, fluttering their lips and saying, "Brrr!"

Downtown: The position on a station farthest from the pass.

Giuliani: Julienne, a cut that produces uniform thin matchstick strips. (Yes, it's a reference to New York City's former mayor.)

Ouai! (pronounced "Waaaay!"): A bastardization of the French *oui*, shouted by cooks to show that they heard the order that was just called out by the chef.

Oven down: Open oven.

Ravs: Ravioli.

Uptown: The position on a station closest to the pass.

VIP: A dish that requires extra attention.

Very VIP: A dish that requires close scrutiny from the cook to the sous-chef, sous-chef to the chef de cuisine, back waiter to the station, front waiter to the table. ("Ordering two fluke, very rush, very VIP.")

The Indispensables: What Every Cook Needs

TASTING SPOON: Everything that leaves the kitchen is tasted at different stages by several cooks, which is why small plastic spoons are available all over the kitchen.

LARGE METAL TABLESPOONS: Used to stir sauces, sauté vegetables, even peel ginger.

TURNING SPATULA: The curve of this slotted spatula, also called a fish turner or Peltex, helps cooks flip delicate pieces of fish.

METAL SKEWER: The best way to tell if a piece of fish is done. The cook inserts the skewer into the middle of the flesh for a couple of seconds, then places it on his upper lip, or just beneath the lower lip. If it's warm, the fish is done. If it's hot, it's most likely overcooked.

WHISK: Used at almost every station to revive vinaigrettes and froth sauces just before plating.

SQUEEZE BOTTLE: Everything from oil to vinegar, ponzu sauce to caramel sauce, goes in these bottles, which allow for precise plating.

SKILLET: Fish is cooked on three types of skillets—cast iron for skinless fish that will be finished in the oven (striped bass, turbot, cod, monkfish, and red snapper), Teflon for fish with skin (black bass), and grill pan for grilled items such as escolar.

KNIVES AND SHARPENER: The most commonly used knives are a paring knife for garnishes, an 8-inch knife for prepping vegetables and aromatics, and a slender fish knife. Each cook has his own knife kit and constantly sharpens his knives throughout prep and service.

CRABBO: The plastic pint container that fresh crabmeat arrives in, reused as everything from a measuring cup ("Give me a crabbo of jus") to a soft-drink container during mealtime.

1:17
First dessert is sent out

1:32
Escolar is returned to kitchen: not well-done enough for the customer

1:34
Well-done escolar is returned to the customer

1:35
Fish butcher finishes 800 pounds of whole fish

1:45
Dinner cooks arrive to prep

2:45
Sous-chef orders micro greens for new menu item

3:35
Maguy, Eric, David Mancini hold profit-and-loss meeting with accounting

4:00
Waitstaff breaks for staff meal: spaghetti, garlic bread, and salad

4:30
Porter leaves

4:45
Waitstaff returns to dining room; captains and front waiters set tables; back waiters clean glasses, fold napkins, and polish and sort silverware

MISE EN PLACE: Each cook has his own *mise en place*, organized in compartmentalized bar trays for speedy use during service.

IMMERSION BLENDER: Used for fast, in-the-pot pureeing and sauce-foaming. A giant one hangs on the wall for larger tasks such as making shrimp stock.

DISH TOWEL: Used as a pot holder (even for 500-degree ovens) and plate cleaner.

GOOD SHOES: Slippery floors, spilled grease, and endless hours spent standing require tough leather with good support, plus a slight heel. Leather clogs are popular, as are Blundstone boots, Mephistos, and even postal-carrier shoes. You won't find any Crocs in this kitchen.

THICK SKIN: A must. The ability to work fast on your feet in a small, hot, windowless space for twelve hours a day while being teased and simply yelled at by your colleagues demands it. Youth and a sense of humor are also pluses.

"When you're on sauté, you have to learn so many things: Where the hot spot is in the pan. How to rotate the fish, turning the pan from left to right to cook it evenly. Where you put your pan in the oven to finish cooking—do you put it on the top rack or the low rack? So you're learning tricks as you're cooking. And you're learning them at a fast pace and you know that it's not gonna get easier, it's gonna get harder, because the more you learn, the more they put on you." **—Sous-chef**

ABOVE: Hot apps and veg cooks assemble their dishes on the "piano," the shallow stainless steel counter that abuts the flat top.

4:46
Reservationist checks availability for last-minute requests; four calls on hold

4:50
Waitstaff meets to review training manual

5:00
Restaurant opens for dinner first seating

5:35
First dinner order arrives in the kitchen

5:45
Chicken and veal stocks taken off stove in the Salon

6:15
Stocks brought downstairs to kitchen in elevator

7:00
Sommelier pours small glass of La Tâche from a customer's half-finished bottle for Chef Ripert to taste

7:05
Kitchen is calm; cooks refresh their *mise en place*

7:40
Chef Ripert greets customers in the dining room

Continued ⟶

The Résumé

A candidate must have been at each previous job for at least one year, preferably in quality restaurants. Culinary school education is increasingly common but isn't as important as on-the-job experience. Chef de cuisine Muller likes to have a few "school of hard knocks" cooks to keep things balanced, and a kid or two to remind the other cooks what they used to be like. Ripert is looking for someone who'll be a good team player and who can handle strong discipline ("I dance around them a little at the interview").

The Trail

A candidate is asked to do a trail, or follow a cook for a shift. Muller responds best to those who look clean (long hair in particular drives him nuts), stand straight, keep their mouths shut, move food in and out of the oven with grace, and have what he calls kitchen presence and kitchen awareness. "We don't want a bunch of cacklebirds walking around, or a bunch of dirty people," he says. The ones who are asked back are "the people who are intense and looking for it and ready to go. I'll say, 'Can you do me a favor and cut up three onions?' And then I see: Did they find the cutting board themselves, or did they have to ask someone? If they had to ask, that's fine, but if they waited a half hour and didn't get it 'cause they were too scared and too stupid to ask for one . . ."

The Skills

Ripert has four requirements:
1. "First, how delicate are they with their knife skills? It's super-important, because a piece of shallot cut one way or another makes a huge difference when you bite into it."
2. "Then it's about taste. When they cook, you see if they have those taste references, because with a shallot, if you sweat it halfway or fully or not properly, it's a very different flavor. A cook is going to compensate: If it's too sweet, he'll add a little lemon juice or sometimes a little touch of other vegetables. If it's too oniony, he should have the patience to know that nothing's going to save it."
3. "Next we look to see if they're organized and clean in their stations."
4. "The last test is plating, where you really see if they can domesticate their hands and, when they're under pressure, be able to do something . . . artistic is not really the word, but something clean."

The Keys to Quality

TRAINING. All cooks, no matter how experienced, must work on every station in the kitchen, beginning at garde-manger. This allows them to understand the restaurant's style and philosophy. If their previous job was sous-chef at Daniel for five years, they're still starting with salads.

ORGANIZATION. Each cook might only work in a two-foot-wide area, but it contains everything he needs so he doesn't have to stop to think in order to execute a dish. Chef Muller demonstrates in garde-manger: "One refrigerator, one dish. Order comes in for fish. Pull out the fluke, pull out the bowl from the refrigerator. Season the fluke, ding ding ding. Then you have the garnish. Done, and I didn't even have to move my feet. Everything's right here. How can you forget what you need?"

DISCIPLINE. "Without it, we can't do anything," says Ripert. "The team must have discipline and be considerate, because there are so many at work on the line."

RESPONSIBILITY. Every cook does his own prep work, arriving four hours before the meal to begin cutting and portioning out the vegetables and garnishes

7:55
Miss Le Coze walks through the dining room to greet customers and check service

8:15
Woman dines alone at the bar, reading *Power and Organizations*

8:40
Second-seating orders start arriving

9:00
Night cleaner arrives to help dishwashers

9:14
Kitchen is firing on all cylinders

10:00
Chef de cuisine leaves; closing sous-chef takes over

10:30
Late night dinner orders start arriving; night porter arrives

10:45
Three of five sous-chefs sent home

required and assembling all the components needed for the dish he'll be making. This guarantees uniformity and ease of preparation under pressure, and it reduces waste. Doing one's own prep work isn't a common practice in the industry, but Ripert has philosophical reasons for the system: It isn't cost-effective, but it gives cooks a sense of ownership, of responsibility for their dishes, from start to finish.

MENTORING. Before a cook can progress to the next station, he must train his replacement. (Says Muller, "I try to stress to the cooks that their success depends on the success of the person they're training.") After a cook has learned all eight stations, Muller will ask whether he wants to continue at Le Bernardin or move elsewhere to learn another style of cuisine. Those who show leadership or organizational skills are invited to become sous-chefs, which requires a one-year commitment. If they want to move on, "Chef has friends everywhere, so I call them up," says Muller. Sous-chefs, who have been at the restaurant longer, are asked if they want to open their own restaurant, move elsewhere, or continue at Le Bernardin in another capacity, such as at Ripert Consulting, and are then helped along with the necessary connections.

TEAMWORK. "You can't be an individualist in this kitchen," says Ripert. "One day you'll get hit by the rush and it will be too intense, and your friends will help you. And you have to help your friends when they need it."

QUALITY CONTROL. Before service starts, sous-chefs are required to check every station for quality of *mise en place,* and to taste every sauce at the sauce station. Then, during service, before a dish leaves the kitchen, it's inspected by the cook who has assembled it. Either the sous-chef who's running the line or the chef at the pass will pull off a tiny piece with a plastic spoon and taste it, then check the temperature with a metal skewer.

"The ones with a clear vision stay a year, a year and three quarters. You get the occasional guy who does three to five, and suckers like Eric Gestel and me who are here for a long time. Most former sauciers and sauté cooks are running a restaurant now."
—Chris Muller

WHAT THEY DID BEFORE

Garde-manger Richard Bard:
Car detailer

Sous-chef Jennifer Carroll:
Pre-law before attending culinary school

Morning sauté Will Cox:
Business school to cooking school

Hot apps Erik Fricker:
Chemistry lab research assistant at Rutgers University

Saucier Joe Palma: Economics and philosophy student

Sous-chef Matt Schaefer:
Taught English

Garde-manger Josh Thomas:
Finance degree from University of Miami; worked for business firm. ("It was the sitting-down part that got me. It's like, how can I possibly do nothing and be more tired sitting down than standing up?")

Garde-manger Stacia Woodrich:
Legal secretary for a Fortune 500 company, then culinary school

---

11:30
Orders for lobster and Kobe tastings continue to arrive

11:45
Orders are sent out; kitchen is scrubbed and mopped, starting with garde-manger

12:15 A.M.
Kitchen staff clean their stations and stoves, then go home. Closing sous-chef checks the walk-ins, fills out overtime forms

12:20
Night cleaner cleans ovens and hoods; hoses down kitchen floor mats with power hose

1:00
Pastry staff clean their stations and go home; remaining dining room staff go home

1:30
Dishwashers sweep and mop before going home

THE CHEF DE CUISINE

Until 2002, Chef Ripert was still calling out orders and working with his chef de cuisine, Chris Muller, on the day-to-day operation of the restaurant. But as he began looking more closely at the kitchen structures of other restaurants at his level, he realized that the company would be stronger if he gave Muller almost total control, leaving himself free to see the bigger picture of the restaurant.

"It's not that common to experience the best the world has to offer in terms of ingredients and people who are interested in learning the craft and exploring the craft. You come to work and there's a guy who wants to know what's in your brain— that gives you a great deal of satisfaction. Plus, who gets better scallops than I do?"

—Chris Muller

So Muller, who started at Le Bernardin at about the same time as Ripert, is now responsible for everything from ordering approximately six million dollars' worth of food every year to calling out orders to the cooks during service to making sure that every dish that's sent out meets the standards set by Ripert.

Ripert still visits the kitchen daily, tasting each of the twenty sauces before service and sticking a spoon in numerous pots and plates. He'll also jump in to help run service or cook for a VIP on busy nights. "Our kitchen and those of Daniel, Jean-Georges, and Thomas Keller are very similar in terms of organization," he explains. "They have a strong management, and then on top of that they have someone who's in charge of the physical aspects of the kitchen. Here it's Chris."

It's because of Muller that Ripert has been able to take the kitchen to the next level. "We have a lot of communication, level. "We have a lot of communication,

a lot of discussion; he's very close to me," says Ripert. "Together we're really progressive in thinking about how we can be even more efficient, more inspiring, more creative. It's terra incognita: Basically every day we discover something and try to go in a new direction."

Muller is Ripert's opposite. A native of Dickeyville, Wisconsin, who started as a fry cook in his parents' restaurant at the age of ten, he's the fast-talking all-American bad cop to Ripert's suave, easygoing Frenchman. He has the boyish looks of a high school football player who's actually kept in shape (standing on your feet all day for three decades will do that; he's also active in coaching his sons' football teams on weekends). He can be tough on cooks in the old-school tradition, breaking them down in order to strengthen them. Ripert is more in favor of fostering harmony and calm in the kitchen. But the young cooks do come to realize that Muller is able to

maintain the restaurant's standards under the relentless, crushing pressure of the kitchen—every single one of the twelve hundred dishes made each day must be flawless—by using his knowledge and twenty-five years of experience to make split-second decisions that can affect an entire evening, not to mention Le Bernardin's reputation. They also see how much time he spends at the restaurant ("I drive from my garage in Jersey to the garage here. I haven't parallel-parked in years") and how personally he takes what's on every plate. It makes his occasional bullying easier to take.

Q: What's the biggest challenge you face in the kitchen on a daily basis?
Chris Muller: Consistent quality. One day the tuna is perfect, the next day the tuna sucks. We have to make a decision: Either we use our skill to make it right, or

we say we can't serve it and try to get it from somewhere else. The margin is big. The difference between what you think is good and what I think is good is huge because I've been here so long.

Q: How stressful is it to make sure every dish is the best people have had?
CM: You can't really think about it that way, or it drives you crazy.

Q: How often do people send things back?
CM: Most people that send stuff back do so because it's too salty. I always taste it, and sometimes they're right, but I usually think it's underseasoned. We're not perfect all the time. Nothing is ever perfect, period. You can have a new guy, an old guy, things happen. But we like to think that fewer things happen here than at other places. That's the goal.

Q: How do you define success in the kitchen?
CM: Success for me is everyone comes in, they prep their items, they sell all their items, there are no tragedies, no plates come back, no fights between the guys—that's success. That's ninety-five percent of the time. Maybe we average eight plates a week sent back to the kitchen—eight out of six thousand. That's not so bad. We're not machines. And the clients, too—everyone has different taste buds. Some people want piping-hot fish; to me, piping-hot fish is well-done fish.

Q: What's the average age in the kitchen?
CM: I like to have a mix. I like to have a couple guys in their early twenties. Kids add a dumbness to the kitchen, which you need because it grounds people. You got a guy who's been cooking for twelve years and he thinks, yeah, I'm hot shit!

And then he sees a kid like that and he's like, wow, that's what I was ten years ago. Plus, when you start someone out in a career who really wants to do something like this, it's a good payback for yourself. We take some guy who didn't know how to hold a knife and help him develop a profession, a career, a skill he'll have for the rest of his life. We have at least two or three of them out of forty cooks.

Then you go to people in their middle twenties for their ability to work the long hours and stand on the line without killing somebody. Their aspirations are lower: They want to learn flavors, learn skills, and then they want to party. They'll cook all day, then they'll go to a bar and talk about work, talk about food, or they'll try to get laid and they'll go to bed at four in the morning, get up at ten-thirty, eleven, and come to work. New York is a great place for that.

Then you have the experienced guys in their thirties who want to be chefs. Not that the twenty-year-olds don't want to be chefs, but they want to get more experience and learn a couple of cuisines first. The thirty-year-olds want to take my job, which is what you want at a certain stage. That's a good asset for me to have, so I can distribute my work. Otherwise I couldn't stand here and talk to you.

Q: How do you manage everyone?
CM: We try to manage individually, not blanket manage. If you feel sick, tired, have an emotional problem, you won't cook good food. We try to put people in a situation to be happy. Chef calls that the temperament of the kitchen, the ambience of the kitchen.

Q: How is someone different after he's cooked here for a year?
CM: A Level One cook should have a good foundation of basic cooking and working principles: how to work clean, how to work smart, how to get something done. But not how to make a sauce or cook a piece of fish—no way. Level Two will have exposure to extreme organization, professionalism, to different types of cuisine and a good grasp of skills, but not perfecting them. Level Three will have all of the above, but they also got to work on the sauce station, so they developed a skill that they can put in their back pocket for the rest of their life.

"Because I'd suffered psychologically in the kitchens I had worked in before, I take pains with the management about being kind, human, and civilized. I put a lot of pressure on guys like Chris to create an environment where people are happy to work, or at least not uncomfortable or afraid. And it's a challenge because every day at twelve o'clock and eight o'clock, it's war."
–Eric Ripert

THE OTHER RIGHT HAND
THE EXECUTIVE SOUS-CHEF

There's another Eric in the kitchen, one who's been there almost as long as Ripert. Eric Gestel, also known as Coco, is a key player, expediting with Chris Muller during service; serving as Le Bernardin's traveling ambassador at charity events, photo shoots, and off-site meals; and helping to train kitchen staff at satellite restaurants.

"The one thing that keeps the kitchen from disintegrating into chaos is teamwork. Also, we use the French brigade system. It's like the chef is God. The chef says, so you do."

—Adam Plitt, sous-chef

A native of Martinique, Gestel, thirty-nine, first worked with Ripert at Joël Robuchon's Jamin in Paris in 1988, where Ripert was a line cook and Gestel was an apprentice cook. They ran into each other years later at a Meals on Wheels benefit in Chicago, where Gestel was working. "I told him I was going to go back to France, and he told me to come here to New York," recalls Gestel.

Gestel is responsible for making sure the food is up to Le Bernardin's standards wherever it's required—a segment on *Martha*, a photo shoot for *Food & Wine*, a private dinner for twenty in a residence at the Ritz-Carlton in the Cayman Islands—no matter what the kitchen situation. (He's made do with a hot plate and a cooler.) "Le Bernardin is a brand name, so we try to use mostly our own products." That means a lot of FedExing and checking in duct-taped coolers filled with fish, herbs, olive oil, knife kits, CO_2 dispensers, Maldon salt, and more. "When you do the same food without our product, it doesn't work," he says. "If we have to substitute, we try to work with the local product, like on Grand Cayman Island, where we'll use their fish and fruit. But we keep the same principles and techniques." Increased airport security has changed the way Gestel and his team transport food to events. "We used to take a lot of things with us on the plane," he says. "Now we put everything in a cooler, package it well, and ship it via FedEx. If it's in the United States it's okay. Outside the country we try to have a backup, just in case it gets stuck in Customs."

Gestel's friendly demeanor can hide just how focused he gets during his long days. "I'm not comfortable until the party is done," he says. "When you relax, you don't think about details." The younger cooks make fun of the checklist he constantly refers to, but his meals turn out pretty perfectly in the end. "As long as you know what to do, it doesn't matter where you do it."

THE ONE TRUE STAR
FISH

Fish has always starred at Le Bernardin, and some players have never left the stage. Lobster, snapper, black bass, striped bass, cod, skate, turbot, halibut, salmon, and tuna were the most consistently high-quality East Coast fish that Gilbert Le Coze was able to find at the Fulton Fish Market in the 1980s, and they still are today.

"You can't serve something old, and that's why we have trouble serving Hawaiian, Japanese, and European fish," says Ripert, who buys primarily from East Coast distributors. "Fish from Portugal is great, but it goes to the supply house, the importer, the distributor, and then to us—six days out of the water is too old for us. At the end of the day, we use American fish."

Gilbert Le Coze's favorites remain on the menu to this day, though Ripert has an on-again/off-again relationship with turbot, salmon, and lobster: "Turbot has its moments. And at one point I took the salmon off the menu because I was so tired of eating it and seeing people eating it," he says with a laugh. "But then with the wild salmon that we're able to get from Washington State and the way we cook it, I'm excited again. Lobster we took out at one point, too. It was lousy and expensive. Even recently, the price has increased sixty percent while the availability has decreased fifty percent."

Other fish have fallen out of favor because they've become endangered, such as Chilean sea bass, cobia, grouper, and, at one time, swordfish. Now that cod populations are said to be dwindling, Ripert buys only line-caught, not net-caught. He and Chris Muller follow the guidelines of the National Resources Defense Council endangered list, but they also keep in mind that boycotting a particular fishing industry can put tens of thousands of families out of work.

Because the restaurant uses only fresh fish, it's at the mercy of the previous day's catch. Its purveyors, such as Rod Mitchell at Browne Trading Company in Portland, Maine, buy the best of the auction lot for Le Bernardin, but some days Mitchell doesn't deem it good enough. "There'll be times where Rod will call me on Sunday and say 'I got five thousand pounds of monk and there's nothing.'" The restaurant must quickly contact other sources to find supplies for the next day's service. "We have a quality that we accept," explains Muller. "That was brought to us, and to the fishermen, by Mr. Le Coze. He grew up fishing with his grandpa, who taught him to say, 'Why is this fish healthier than this? They're both fresh, they're both six pounds, both caught in the same water. Look at the eyes, look at the gills. Feel it.' He taught our purveyors what our specs were, he taught Chef what those specs were, and we carry on that tradition. That's why he's credited with changing the way Americans eat fish—and I think that's justified."

It's clear that Ripert has taken Le Coze's teachings to heart when he says, "We have an opinion on every fish here. For some reason, I believe that every fish has a personality. Each fish has a category in my head."

Salmon

Wild salmon to me
is the best in terms
of flavor and consistency
— Chef Ripert

Scallops
They have a natural sweetness
but they don't absorb anything,
not even salt, especially if
they are fresh

Sea Urchin

Has a wonderful texture, almost silky with the fresh, sweet flavor of the ocean

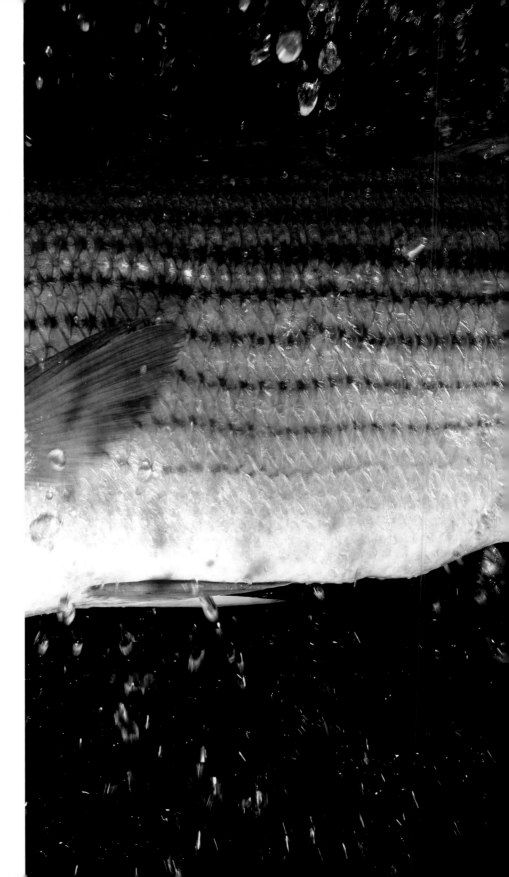

THE SECRET INGREDIENT

One of the more surprising findings in the storeroom is the boxes of Wondra. Primarily associated with fried-chicken-making Southern housewives, a light coating of the supermarket staple is the restaurant's secret to crisp, evenly browned fish. "It's a finer flour; it won't cake," explains Muller. "You won't get the feeling of something breaded, like with all-purpose flour. It also gives you a crispier texture and better definition in the mouth. Regular flour will give you a gummy feel—not that crispness that you're looking for." Start dredging—and be sure to blow off any excess.

A SAMPLE WEEK
OF STAFF MEALS

	LUNCH
MON.	Lobster Pasta
TUES.	Grilled Chicken Fajitas
WED.	Sausage and Peppers with Roast Potatoes
THURS.	Burgers and Fries
FRI.	Fish Fry with Remoulade
SAT.	---

	DINNER
MON.	Steak Tacos
TUES.	California Burger with Fries
WED.	Lasagna
THURS.	Chicken Curry and Rice
FRI.	BBQ Pork and Beans
SAT.	Pizza

striped Bass

Not too refined. It's more... plain
It's slightly drier than
black bass & there is a lot of
blood between the skin & fillet
which is very fishy — you
have to take the skin off
very carefully.

THE "WOW" EFFECT

First-time diners are usually surprised by how simple some of the dishes appear, whether it's a bowl of lightly dressed crabmeat and a few pieces of shaved cauliflower, or thinly pounded tuna with foie gras and chives. But a considerable amount of thought and hard work goes into every dish in order to create a depth of flavor. Even the sautéed mushrooms have a surprising secret.

"It's about harmony," explains Ripert. "It's that link, flavor-wise, which is not visible, not touchable, between the ingredients and the flavors. If we succeed, it's going to have a 'wow' effect on you."

"There are some things that taste really good, but you can't quite put your finger on it," says Muller. For example, the foie gras scraps left over after trimming it into rectangles for the pounded tuna appetizer are melted into chicken stock to make the snapper sauce, as well as to sauté the pea shoots and wild mushrooms.

"You don't feel the foie gras, you feel the depth of flavor," Muller says. Or the octopus appetizer, which gets three drops of sweet Solera vinegar on its legs that adds "that twist, that depth." And the crab-cauliflower dish? The peekytoe and jumbo crab meats are dressed separately because they warm at different rates and require different amounts of salt and pepper.

Lobster
If you cook it in advance and refrigerate it, you lose all the flavor — it must be cooked à la minute

51

Red Snapper
Less refined, more flaky,
and tender

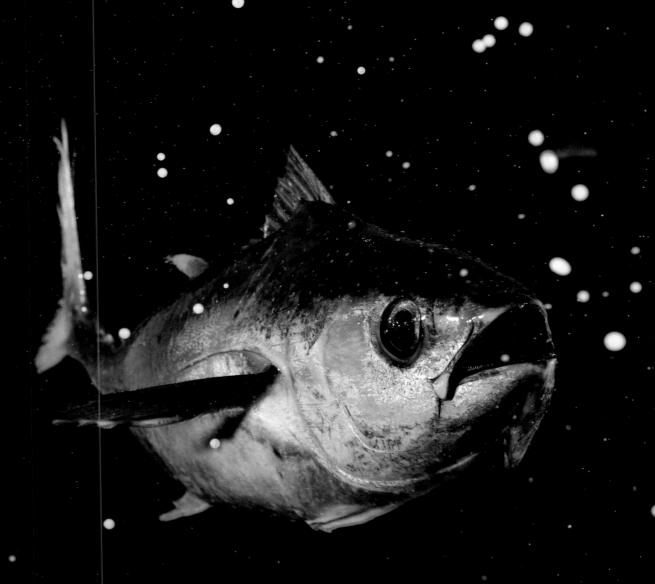

Tuna
Great seared or raw
with a rich meaty flavor

Monkfish

Monkfish loves to be treated like meat. It can handle a lot of spice. Also called poor man's lobster

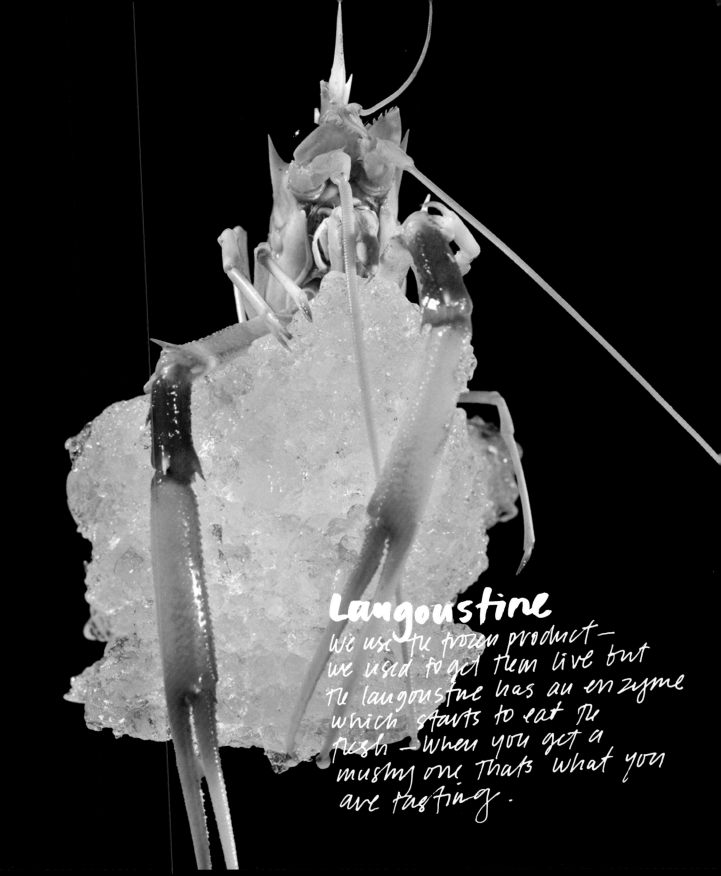

Langoustine

We use the frozen product—
We used to get them live but
the langoustine has an enzyme
which starts to eat the
flesh—when you get a
mushy one that's what you
are tasting.

BLACK BASS IN A FLASH

1:15 P.M.
Order for black bass arrives in kitchen; fish pass brings a piece to the sauté station and places it in a tray on the sauté cook's shelf, where it can begin to come up to room temperature before being cooked

1:33
Canola oil is poured into preheated pan

1:34
Sauté cook takes piece of fish from tray, blots dry on towel, seasons, dusts with Wondra, blows off excess

1:35:07
Places fish skin side down in pan

1:35:20
Presses fish down with metal spatula

1:35:40
Presses down again

1:36:30
Takes off heat, agitates pan, returns to heat

1:37:33
Pulls off heat, puts on lower heat on back burner

1:37:54
Flips fish

1:38:05
Saucier removes papaya duck salad from refrigerator and shapes in ring mold on plate

1:38:11
Cook pulls fish off heat, blots on towel, checks for doneness, returns to pan

1:38:45
Blots and checks again; puts on top of papaya salad

1:38:50
Cook takes dish to the pass

Black Bass
It's more refined than striped bass. It's not fishy. You cook it with the skin and it becomes very crispy.

THE FISH BUTCHER

Every day in his small alcove in the basement, next to what's basically the restaurant's loading and delivery area, Justo Thomas transforms eight hundred to a thousand pounds of fresh fish into pristine fillets in under six hours.

TOOLS OF THE TRADE

Boning knife

Filleting knife

Thin 10-inch knife for skinning small fish

Thicker 10-inch knife for larger fish

Knife sharpener (he sharpens after each fish)

Metal fish scaler

Needle-nose pliers and tweezers for bones

A digital scale to weigh each portion

Plastic wrap to cover the tiled walls, which get flaked with scales ("It's easier to take down plastic every day than it is to wash the walls.")

Thick rubber gloves

3-by-5-inch piece of cardboard (to scrape down the scales that collect in the sink)

Wooden crate to hold towels

Bottle of ginger ale

"He's incredible; I've never seen anyone so fast and precise," says Ripert. "Whenever he's on vacation, it takes two guys twice as long to do his job."

Thomas, forty-nine, a native of the Dominican Republic, has been at the restaurant since 2003. He was a butcher at a restaurant adjacent to Le Bernardin when his cousin, who had the job, moved to Boston. "I like working with fish," he says. "When people say they don't like it, I don't understand."

Thomas always knows where to make the first incision (some fish, such as snapper, have veins near the gills that can spoil the flesh if cut), where the bones are hiding, and how to get twenty-five portions out of thirty pounds of striped bass. According to the kitchen's specifications, each piece has to have a consistent thickness so that one side doesn't cook more than the other. That usually means that after Thomas has skinned, cleaned, and deboned a whole fish, he cuts off the curved edges to create a rectangle from which to work. Then, after he fillets and weighs each piece on a digital scale (when he's not on target, he's off only by a few grams), he arranges each piece on a plastic-wrapped sheet tray in order of size—generally the order in which he cut: "You don't want to get a table of six ordering the same thing and wondering why someone else got a bigger piece." The smaller pieces are used for tasting-menu portions. Whatever remains is picked up by City Harvest; snapper bones are taken upstairs to be made into stock. "There's a lot of waste," he says with a shrug. As soon as he's filled a tray, he wraps it with plastic, marks a piece of masking tape with the name and date, and runs the tray upstairs to the fish walk-in.

When a new dish appears on the menu, Ripert or Muller will come down and demonstrate how he'd like the fish cut. Thomas butchers the same types of fish, Monday through Friday. "You come here in the morning, the fish, it's like a river!" he says. And yet, as he points out, it never smells fishy because the product is so fresh. Twice a week, after he's taken the last tray of fillets upstairs to the kitchen at around 1:30 P.M., he has to prepare a few pieces of filet mignon to be used for stock. "I don't like to do meat," he says, wrinkling his nose as he removes pearly strips of sinew. "All that blood . . ."

THE NUMBERS

A typical weekly fish order for the restaurant

Baby octopus	40 lbs.
Black bass	500 lbs.
Cod	200 lbs.
Conch	30 lbs.
Escolar	200 lbs.
Fluke	120 lbs.
Halibut	300 lbs.
Hamachi	120 lbs.
Italian organic caviar	2 lbs.
Jumbo lump crab	120 lbs.
Jumbo scallops (in shell)	300 lbs.
Langoustine	120 lbs.
Lobster	600 lbs.
Monkfish	500 lbs.
Organic salmon	250 lbs.
Oysters	800 pieces
Sea urchin, in winter (in shell)	100 lbs.
Shrimp	150 lbs.
Skate	350 lbs.
Smoked salmon	10 lbs.
Snapper	400 lbs.
Squid	200 lbs.
Striped bass	500 lbs.
Tuna	300 lbs.
Turbot	250 lbs.
Wild salmon	180 lbs.

THE PORTER

All the restaurant's deliveries are made before nine A.M.—
any later and crosstown traffic becomes hopelessly
snarled—so porter Fernando Uruchima is the first person
to appear at the restaurant. At 6:30, he arrives at his
basement office from his home in Queens, puts on a crisp
white jacket, and grabs his clipboard.

THE NUMBERS

Standing weekly orders

Fresh black truffle (December to April)	6 lbs.
Canned black truffle (May to November)	7 12-oz. cans
Micro herbs	10 lbs.
Artisanal cheese	15 lbs.
Milk	30 gals.
Garlic	60 lbs.
Shallots	100 lbs.
Wild mushrooms	100 lbs.
Artichokes	120 lbs.
Baby vegetables	140 lbs.
Butter	250 lbs.
Domestic mushrooms	250 lbs.
Tomatoes	300 lbs.
Flavored vinegars	3 gals.
Extra virgin olive oil	14 gals.
Brandy	23 bottles
White wine	12 double bottles
Red wine	24 double bottles

He'll spend the next eleven hours making sure that all of the deliveries have been received and counted; that the newly arrived fish, produce, and dry goods are put away; that all of the lightbulbs in the dining room are checked; and that many more, less easily definable tasks are tended to. Calm, friendly, and fiercely efficient, he is a very important and popular figure at Le Bernardin—and not just because he's one of the only people with the key to the truffle fridge. ("I have the key for everything, so it's always, 'Fernando, bring me this. Fernando, open this,'" he says.)

The thirty-four-year-old Ecuador native began working at the restaurant in 1992, when his brother, Lorenzo, a captain in the dining room, got him a job as a dishwasher. (Their cousin, Segundo, runs garde-manger in the kitchen; both he and Lorenzo have been with the restaurant since it opened.) Within six months, Ripert recognized Fernando's potential and promoted him to porter.

A look at the items in his tidy glass-fronted office, located across from the elevator that is the lifeline to the restaurant, shows just how organized he is: schedules; lists of phone numbers for purveyors, staff, and emergency repairs; restaurant-supply catalogs; a knife on a string; a photo of Ripert receiving an honorary degree at the Culinary Institute of America in 1999; a Relais & Châteaux guide. He keeps a running to-do list that grows and shrinks throughout the day—"Check yogurt. Change lightbulbs. Light conference room. Skewers. Antonio Cervales call 8:13—coming in 10 minutes late (8:17). Order more verjus for Monday."

There are a daunting number of details that go into running this level of restaurant, but after so many years, much of the information is in Uruchima's head. He can tick off the order from the linen company without a single *um*: "Fridays we order double, so napkins, 1300. Tablecloths, we do three sizes: 54, 72, 62, and 90s for upstairs. We get 250 of those. Fifty pounds of rags, 350 kitchen towels. Uniforms we get on Monday. We dry-clean the chefs' coats: size 44, 100; 38–40, 40; size 36, 40; 52, 6. There are two big guys, one in the kitchen. Pants? 28 waist, 20; 30 inch, 25; 32 by 32, 30; 34 by 32, 30; 36 by 32, 40; 42 by 32, 40. Aprons, 200."

"I like the job because I'm always doing something different," says Uruchima. "I'm never in a bad mood. Five months ago they gave me a phone," he says, looking down at the cell phone clipped onto his belt. "So now they can reach me at any hour."

WHAT'S IN THE PANTRY?

The dry goods for the restaurant are stored on wire shelves in a small room in the basement between the box-compacting room and the fish-butchering area. Some of the items are used daily, others are seasonal, and still others are purely for experimentation, especially those on the pastry shelves.

PASTRY
Nut and praline pastes
Chocolate and neutral glazes
Glucose
Trimoline
Fondant
Malt, milk, and egg-white powders
Stabilizers
Leaf and powdered gelatins
Isomalt
Sansho powder
Elderflower
Maple sugar
Carob powder
Monk's pepper
Menthol crystals
Kola nut
Keltrol xanthan gum
Microwave popcorn
Powdered butterfat
Versawhip
Panda black licorice
Mini marshmallows
Carrageenan powder
Black beans
Sprinkles
Fireweed honey

KITCHEN
Power painter
Carta Vieja Chilean wine
6 Grapes Porto
Domino sugar
Rice flour

Hart canned corn
Palm sugar
Grandma's molasses
Wondra
Bascom's tapioca
Imbert candied chestnuts
Bazzini nuts
Candied cherries
Pam
Heinz white vinegar and ketchup
Hunt's tomato paste
Indigo crushed tomatoes
Libby's sauerkraut
Wolffer Estate verjus
Minus 8 vinegar
Maggie Beer
Sangiovese verjus
Setia olive oil
Puglia olive oil
Les Moulins
Dorés Bordeaux vinegar
Jerez vinegar
Melfor honey vinegar
Aji-Mirin
Bombay mango pickle
McCormick spices
Piquillo peppers
Maille Dijon mustard
Kirsch
Brandy
Vermouth
SerendipiTea teas
Quaker oatmeal
Maldon sea salt
Kosher salt

WHAT'S IN THE WALK-INS?

If you're walking through the kitchen toward the dining room, you'll often hear a muffled knocking coming from the left. That's the signal that someone is about to push open the heavy door to one of three walk-in refrigerators, their arms full of ingredients. There's a walk-in for fish ("the fish box"), one for pastry, and one for the kitchen ("the veg box"). Each compartment is filled with Lexan containers, neatly organized and labeled with the date the food arrived. (The oldest ingredients—which usually means yesterday's—are always used first.)

FISH BOX
Oysters in stacks
  of two (Pine
  Island, Kumamoto,
  Skookum)
Smoked salmon
Wild salmon
Organic salmon
Live scallops
Live lobsters
Caviar
Crabmeat (jumbo,
  blue, peekytoe)
Conch
Skate
Snapper
Black bass
Striped bass
Turbot
Monkfish
Halibut
Fluke
Cod
Escolar
Sides of tuna
Hamachi
Octopus
Shrimp
Langoustine
Kobe beef
Veal jus
Pot-au-feu sauce
Chicken stock
Clam stock
Mushroom stock
Coq au vin sauce

PASTRY COOLER
Marked and dated
  tubs of: ginger,
  caramel, yogurt,
  rhubarb compote,
  soufflé base,
  financier base,
  chestnut tuile base,
  chestnut wafers,
  praline cream,
  vanilla emulsion,
  chocolate ganache,
  corn base, praline
  base
Fruit purees for
  sorbet (apricot,
  blood orange,
  raspberry, coconut)
Blood orange juice
360 brown eggs
442 white eggs
22 quarts heavy
  cream
12 gallons milk
Oranges
Kumquats
Hollowed eggshells

PASTRY FREEZER
Sorbets
Macaroons
Lemon meringue
  base

VEG BOX
Artichokes
Romaine hearts
Mesclun
Frisée
Parsnips
Bartlett pears
Asian pears
Turnips
White beans
Wax beans
Fava beans
Sea beans
Haricots verts
Fennel
Asparagus (jumbo,
  pencil, white)
Chayote
Celery
Japanese
  cucumbers
Sugar snap peas
Snow peas
Peppers (baby bell
  red and yellow,
  Holland red and
  yellow)
Yukon A potatoes
Brussels sprouts
Heirloom carrots
Butternut squash
Granny Smith
  apples
Mangoes
Grapes
Green papaya
Sweet 100s
  tomatoes
Sweet white yams

Mushrooms
  (maitake, oyster,
  porcini, shiitake,
  chanterelle)
Radishes
Broccoli rabe
Napa cabbage
Spanish onions
Scallions
Ginger
Jalapeños
Baby leeks
Rosemary
Parsley
Basil
Purple basil
Chives
Chive buds
Dill
Chervil
Lemongrass
Shiso
Thai chiles
Thyme
Tarragon
Lemons
Limes
Olives
Avocado
Micro greens
Crème fraîche
Dijon mustard
Butter
  (salted, sweet)
Yogurt
Gruyère
Parmesan
Mozzarella
Goat cheese
Giant tub of house-
  made mayonnaise

THE PASTRY CHEF

In the midst of the clanging and shouting that goes on in the kitchen during the heat of service, there's a 10-by-14-foot patch of quiet. This is pastry, where even when all six employees are elbow-to-elbow, sending out a complex dessert every minute, there is what executive pastry chef Michael Laiskonis describes as "the calmness of our chaos."

"For me it's just about refinement, cleanliness of flavor, and enjoyment. Refinement is a word that Chef Ripert uses over and over. So if something's crunchy, how can I make it crunchier? If it's thin, how do you make it thinner?"

—Michael Laiskonis

Everything is so precisely organized in this pristine area, from the list of components for each dish printed above the stations to the clearly labeled and dated squeeze bottles of sauces and syrups, that chaos comes only from the volume required of them. "We're making more desserts than we have guests," explains the thirty-five-year-old Michigan-born pastry chef. "A lot of à la carte restaurants are happy if they do fifty percent desserts. With our prix fixe and pre-dessert, I think we sometimes do about one hundred ten percent desserts." And then there are the sweets that they produce for meals upstairs in Les Salons, adding up to an extra ninety plates (plus petits fours) per service.

Laiskonis, who has no formal training, embodies the focus and organization that are required of him. Slim, and pale from spending up to six days a week indoors, he has dark circles under his eyes from staying up late in order to "have a real day" with his wife, a restaurant manager whom he met when they were both working at Tribute restaurant in Detroit. He spends his mornings in his basement office in the restaurant, catching up on e-mail or printing out his recipes to add to the fat binders he has kept since the late 1990s. (Each recipe is identically formatted, ready for reprinting in any magazine or book.) Then he makes his way upstairs to begin the crush of production. The printout for the first order of the day is usually spit out at around 12:50; by 1:30, all hands are on deck.

Laiskonis has a chef de cuisine—Jose Almonte, who has worked in pastry for fifteen years and who receives well-deserved billing on the dessert menu—as well as four production assistants and an extern or two from the nearby Institute of Culinary Education who do most of the execution, from spinning ice cream to making batters,

baking petits fours to plating dishes. But Laiskonis is hands-on, whether it's plating desserts during the rush, warming miniature madeleines and pistachio financiers to send out with coffee, running upstairs to send out sixty chocolate tarts, or writing "Happy Birthday" in tight chocolate script on a plate. Once it calms down around three o'clock, he begins experimenting with new ingredients and techniques, from xanthan gum to freeze-dried corn. He has a whole box in the pantry marked THE EXPERIMENTAL STUFF. "A lot of times I find something cool, and they get wind of it over there"—he motions to the kitchen—"and eventually use it. They say, 'Go see Michael for some of the magic powder.'" (For example, the xanthan gum that he was playing with now gels the white soy in a fluke appetizer.)

Laiskonis has pushed the boundaries of pastry further than any of his predecessors, including François Payard and Florian Bellanger. While chocolate desserts will always sell—and Laiskonis's two chocolate offerings outsell other desserts by double—he challenges diners with a composition of chocolate and corn: chocolate ganache with hazelnut and freeze-dried kernels, corn sorbet, and a paper-thin tuile made from freeze-dried corn pulverized in a coffee grinder. Taking inspiration from a pastry tour in Japan, his panna cotta is made from black sesame paste and paired with a rich soy caramel in an elegant and relatively simple presentation, in the Le Bernardin style.

"I'm more satisfied with three ingredients perfectly combined than twenty that are standing on their end," he says. "At this level—I don't know if I'm putting my own maturity or evolution into it—I'm finding that when I'm constructing a dish, I'm constantly stepping back and saying, 'What can I take out?' It's more like sculpting, more of a subtractive thing. I'll put a dish on the menu, and after a couple of days

that little sprinkle of whatever is totally unnecessary."

It's an approach that has earned Laiskonis the James Beard Award for Outstanding Pastry Chef in 2007—not bad for someone who got his start a mere twelve years earlier as a "vegan punk-rock anarchist guy" who took a job at a Detroit-area bakery during a break in college, where he was studying photography, and never went back. He created a position for himself as a night baker, working from 6 P.M. to 10 A.M. and reading old culinary school textbooks in his free moments. He knew he wanted to pursue this as a career when he locked the owner out of the bakery one day because he didn't want him to come in and mess everything up. He created a pastry department at another restaurant before moving to the newly opened Tribute as a line cook in 1997. Two years later he was their pastry chef, spontaneously sending out seven-course dessert tastings to the many chefs who ate there when in town. One of them was Eric Ripert, who lured him to New York in 2004.

The dish that most impressed Ripert—and has since dazzled countless diners at Le Bernardin—is Laiskonis's "egg": a hollowed-out shell filled with milk chocolate crème brûlée, liquid caramel, caramel foam, two drops of maple syrup, and a few flakes of Maldon sea salt (see page 210 for the recipe). It quickly became his signature. Today the restaurant makes about ninety per day, served as a pre-dessert.

Laiskonis isn't resting on past accomplishments; after the elation of the restaurant's earning three Michelin stars wore off, he realized that the stakes were even higher, since a Michelin inspector could return any day, every day. Instead, he's intent on refining his palate and technique. "Over time my desserts have gotten smaller because I want people to want one more bite," he says. In the end, though, "it's just about making people happy."

TOOLS OF THE TRADE

Chilled plates: a must for ice cream

Convection oven: five racks for baking every cookie and dessert base

Digital scale: for weighing everything (flour, sugar, butter, etc.) to the correct decimal

Ice cream spinner: the department's first new ice cream machine since the 1980s

Microwave oven: for melting chocolate

Miniature spatulas: for precise plating of narrow desserts

Parchment paper: to put on baking sheets for easier cleanup

Ring molds: many sizes, for tarts

Silicon molds: for painting geometrically precise rectangles of sauce and ganache bases onto chilled plates

Squeeze bottles: for precision saucing

Tablespoon: for shaping sorbet quenelles (first warmed against the back of the hand)

A DAY ON THE PASTRY LINE

6:30 A.M.
Head production person arrives to set up the *mise en place* for lunch, preparing dessert bases, sauces, coulis, and garnishes for the 10 menu items

7:00
Two production people arrive; one begins spinning 12 ice cream and sorbet bases, the other helps out with dessert components

9:00
Five trays of chocolate-corn ganache are finished; 100 black-sesame panna cottas are poured into molds

10:00
Twelve desserts and sorbets are finished and stored in the pastry kitchen freezer

10:30
One hundred dozen almond cake and pistachio financier petits fours are finished for lunch

12:00 NOON
Executive Pastry Chef Michael Laiskonis and Pastry Chef Jose Almonte arrive to check out the setup for lunch service and begin working on special projects

12:45 P.M.
First dessert order comes in

12:47
First dessert order goes out; by 1:40 one dessert order will go out every minute

1:30
Sous-chef Ricardo Guaman arrives to help with service and begins working on the *mise en place* and petits

fours for dinner service, including *pâtes de fruits* (fruit jellies), chestnut creams, *diamants,* and *macarons*

1:45
Laiskonis and production person go upstairs to the Salon to make 40 chocolate-corn desserts for private lunch

2:00
Two night production people arrive and start working on chocolate caramel petits fours and chocolate "eggs" for dinner

3:00
Ninety eggshells topped and cleaned for chocolate eggs

3:15
Pastry production takes over the Salon to make cheese sticks for the bar; 15 sheets of puff pastry cover every available flat surface

4:00
Morning production people go home

5:15
Chocolate eggs are finished

5:30
Ten dozen cheese sticks are shaped and put in walk-in until ready to bake

5:45
450 chocolate caramels finished

6:00
First dessert order comes in

6:04
First dessert order goes out; by 6:30, one dessert order goes out every minute

8:00
Orders stop at end of first seating; prep and replenish for second and third seatings

8:55
First dessert order for second seating comes in

9:00
First dessert order goes out; by 9:15 one dessert order will go out every minute

10:30
Fifteen-minute break in service before the third seating

12:00 P.M.
Laiskonis and Almonte leave

1:00 A.M.
Production people send out last desserts, clean department, and leave

ERIC RIPERT
THE BIRTH OF A NEW DISH

For the past two years, we've made the sous-chefs part of the creative process. We break them into three teams of two and give each team a dish to work on between lunch and dinner service. It could be based on something from my notebook, a cookbook in the library, or an update of a dish that's been on the menu for too long. Sometimes it takes just a few days for them to get it right, sometimes months.

Sometimes we abandon it altogether and move on. If a dish makes it onto the menu, the sous-chefs get a bonus. It's been exciting to see them learn to think more creatively (at first they were scared to speak up) and to be more involved, to have this interaction instead of just executing dishes.

It took the longest time to get to this point. For twelve or thirteen years, I was the only one who was developing the dishes on the menu. And then obviously, after a certain point, I was like, *pffft!* Enough! We needed to have some new sources of ideas. In a way, getting the sous-chefs involved is a way for me to mentor.

I'm teaching my philosophy to help them create, and hopefully they can eventually develop their own style. I didn't have that experience with the chefs I worked for, with the exception of Jean-Louis Palladin. They were like, "You do that, you shut up."

And now I understand why. Creativity is one of the most difficult things to teach. To create dishes in our style isn't easy. But it's been great watching some of these cooks evolve. And we've gotten some great dishes out of it. Soa Davies came downstairs one day with a dish that was absolutely untouchable: an appetizer of wild and smoked salmon, apple, and jalapeño

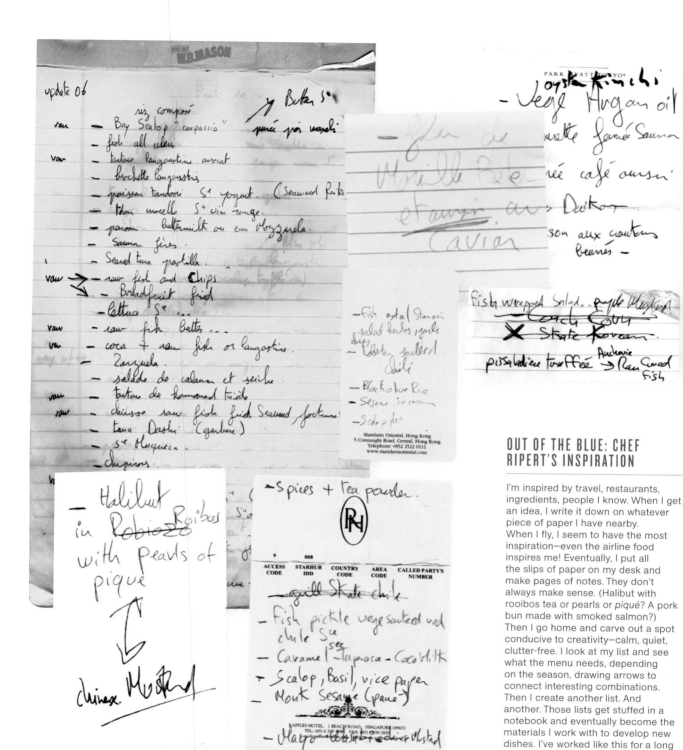

OUT OF THE BLUE: CHEF RIPERT'S INSPIRATION

I'm inspired by travel, restaurants, ingredients, people I know. When I get an idea, I write it down on whatever piece of paper I have nearby. When I fly, I seem to have the most inspiration—even the airline food inspires me! Eventually, I put all the slips of paper on my desk and make pages of notes. They don't always make sense. (Halibut with rooibos tea or pearls or *piqué*? A pork bun made with smoked salmon?) Then I go home and carve out a spot conducive to creativity—calm, quiet, clutter-free. I look at my list and see what the menu needs, depending on the season, drawing arrows to connect interesting combinations. Then I create another list. And another. Those lists get stuffed in a notebook and eventually become the materials I work with to develop new dishes. I've worked like this for a long time. It's served me well.

emulsion. She also created an escolar with red wine béarnaise that went straight onto the menu. We were so impressed with her style that we promoted her to the consulting and menu-development side of Le Bernardin.

When I'm developing a new entrée, I always remember Gilbert's advice: "To really succeed in fish, you need contrast: acidity, spice, texture." That's why every fish dish on the menu will have a balance between crisp and unctuous; exotic spices tempered with a dash of acidity, best seen in dishes like the lobster in grapefruit juice, or even the surf-and-turf, which pairs rich Kobe beef and escolar with lemon brown butter sauce and spicy kimchi. I haven't quite gone in for the gels and foams that are trendy at the moment. I'm more curious about Eastern and Caribbean flavors—the tamarind paste in a lobster sauce, the coriander, star anise, Thai chile, and fish sauce in a verjus sauce for halibut.

Tasting by Committee

Almost every day, at five o'clock, the sous-chef teams bring a tray containing the elements of their creations into Ripert's tiny office or the conference room, which contains a wall of cookbooks and several dry-erase boards filled with ideas for new dishes.

DISH #1

Grilled Bacalao Salad

THE COOKS:

Adam Plitt [AP]
Matthew Schaefer [MS]

THE TASTERS:

Eric Ripert [ER]
Chris Muller [CM]

ER: Okay, guys! Let's go. First off, we've got to get into the habit of putting back the cookbooks.

AP: This is the same curing that we tried before, twelve hours. This is haddock from Blue Ribbon purveyors, served with finnan haddie sauce.

ER: I like the flavor very much. Maybe we don't let it be so hot. We've had grilled bacalao served with a salad on the menu for a year and a half, but it needs something new. It's not clean enough, in terms of the flavor or the presentation; there are too many elements on the plate.

CM: Let's replace the dish altogether. That's why we're here with smoked haddock and crème fraîche. Our flavors now are avocado, tomato, sherry vinegar. Let's look for another flavor to complement the fish.

MS: We brought the existing garnishes for the cod dish downstairs to see if we could try a new presentation. One thing we found about the cod finnan haddie was that if you cut it clean like this—three precise slices as opposed to a whole piece of fish—you lost a bit of the smokiness, since you didn't have as much surface area.

ER: The idea was to do fish that's cured, not cooked. Grilled very lightly. The sauce brings richness and more smokiness to it. We can try it with caviar, but if we do, it's going to be too luxurious. And one caviar dish on the menu is enough. We don't want too many people requesting supplements. We tried salmon eggs, which were too mushy, and trout eggs, which were crunchy and playful. The idea now is to add an illusion of freshness, so we're trying to incorporate something crunchy like a Japanese cucumber without overwhelming the flavors of the cod. Do you think we should put the eggs on the fish or in the sauce? I think they should be in the sauce. It's gonna be cute, but it brings . . . maybe it's a bit too cute.

CM: We like to be French, but we don't want to be too French.

ER: We don't want to be too . . . obsessive. We don't want to do cute cuisine. If we put this sauce on in the kitchen, it's going to look like hell by the time the waiter brings it out. By putting it on at the table, it's going to interact. It doesn't look too precious, does it? It needs a little spiciness—black pepper. In terms of salt, we're going to have a lot of problems with that dish.

AP: Do you think it needs any acid, Chef?

ER: Definitely. It's too rich.

AP: I was thinking a pickle, like a sherried shallot. The sherry would go well with the smoke.

ER: The cucumber and a shallot pickle is a good idea. The sauce has eggs in it, and the cut of the shallots is a fine dice. It has to be almost like a mignonette for oysters.

CM: To advance this dish, we'll go thinner on the slice. Three slices per portion? Did you weigh this?

ER: I'd love to give four slices. I'm afraid we look skimpy if it's three.

CM: We're happy with the trout eggs. We like the cucumber. We'll keep the spicy daikon sprout.

ER: Let's work on the pickled shallot. If we can sweat shallots before the vinegar, almost like a marmalade . . . put them on slow so they become dark—sweet, sweet marmalade of onion. Then deglaze with vinegar. Not too much.

AP: I was thinking sherry.

ER: Sherry and cider. Cider could be cool. Do one base of shallot and try different vinegars. And try to get a longer piece of fish and cut it against the grain. We're close on that dish, eh? If the pickled shallot doesn't work, we go back to the lemon juice.

Okay, thank you, guys! Who's next?

Postscript: The team worked on this dish for three months, but it never made it onto the menu.

DISH #2

Escolar with Red Wine Béarnaise, Potato Chips, and Green Salad

THE COOK:

Soa Davies [SD]

THE TASTERS:

Eric Ripert [ER]
Chris Muller [CM]

SD: The salad is romaine and sea beans, and that's it.

ER: It's great, Chris.

CM: I concur.

SD: The fish gets a little bit of that mignonette of tarragon and shallot.

ER: It's very simple, the presentation, but it's our style.

CM: I agree. We just have to find out how to get it more precise, cleaner. It'll come when we start to do it.

ER: Where do we put the sauce?

SD: Tableside.

ER: But the potato's going to lose the crunch. Two seconds in the sauce, and then . . . I like that simplicity. You can't do simpler than that.

SD: The two taste really good together. Or do you want the potato right on top of the salad?

ER: It would be okay, but the captain is going to do that.

SD: I think just scatter the chips all over the dish. More haphazard, like this. The sauce is a red-wine brown butter.

ER: I want Maguy to taste this, because I think we've got it. [*Leaves room.*]

CM: We've given this to Miss Le Coze like four times already. The combination of the sauce and the tuna is foremost. And everything else, it doesn't reach the level of the sauce and the tuna. We once did a salmon with purple mustard and butter in phyllo with a piece of truffle in between. We worked for like a year to add a vegetable to it. Finally we said the hell with it, 'cause nothing else came close to achieving the height of the rest of the dish.

ER [*returning from Maguy's office*]: She liked it! We're done. Nothing to change. Simple.

SD: The chips haphazard like that?

ER: Is that a pain in the neck to do?

SD: Not really.

ER: I like the salad, but it's a bit too acidic. I would like to have it emulsified. The dressing needs a little help, but we have a dish, we have a presentation.

SD: The salad is just an afterthought. It's something light and refreshing that's next to it.

CM: When I taste that, the salad's not bringing anything, 'cause it's not reaching the level.

ER: It's a bit off, the dressing. If it's better, it will complement the rest of the dish. Make the dressing slightly softer. The garlic has to marinate more. It's really important to have the garlic and vinegar interacting together, then you add the mustard and emulsify and salt and pepper. So we have a dish, done deal.

Postscript: This dish made it onto the menu after three weeks, minus the romaine salad. (See the recipe on page 158.)

Le Bernardin's Current Menu

ALMOST RAW

WE'VE ALWAYS SERVED GREAT OYSTERS PLAIN →

OYSTERS
Single Variety or Assortment of Oysters (Six Pieces)

HAMACHI
Marinated Hamachi Vietnamese Style; Nuoc Mam Vinaigrette

TUNA
Layers of Thinly Pounded Yellowfin Tuna, Foie Gras and Toasted Baguette, Shaved Chives and Extra Virgin Olive Oil

WILD SALMON
Wild Alaskan and Smoked Salmon; Apple, Celery and Baby Watercress; Jalapeño Emulsion

KANPACHI
Kanpachi Tartare Topped with Wasabi Tobiko; Ginger-Coriander Emulsion

FLUKE
White Soy-Yuzu Marinated Fluke; Seaweed and Spiced "Rice Crispies"

BLACK BASS
Black Bass Tartare Mediterranean Style; Olives, Citrus, Fennel and Marjoram

SCALLOPS
Flash Marinated Scallop Slivers; Shiso "Pesto"; Yuzu and Pink Radish

FINALLY A GOOD FARM-RAISED CAVIAR →

CAVIAR
Organically Grown Farm-Raised Osetra   ($90 Supplement per ounce)
Wild Iranian Osetra Caviar   ($200 Supplement per ounce)

CONCH
Thinly Sliced Conch Marinated Peruvian Style; Dried Sweet Corn

MESCLUN SALAD
Salad of the Day's Market Herbs and Vegetables with Balsamic-Shallot Vinaigrette

BARELY TOUCHED

ESCOLAR
White Tuna Poached in Extra Virgin Olive Oil; Sea Beans and Potato Crisps; Light Red Wine Béarnaise

CALAMARI
Sautéed Calamari Filled with Sweet Prawns and Wood Ear Mushroom; Calamari Consommé

LOBSTER
Spicy Lobster Curry; Heart of Palm Meunière; Mango Chutney

LOOKS LIKE A SNOWFLAKE →

CRAB
Warm Peekytoe-Maryland Lump "Crab Cake"; Shaved Cauliflower; Dijon Mustard Emulsion

TUNA
Seared and Marinated Yellowfin Tuna Tartare "Sandwich"; Ginger and Lime

BACALAO
Grilled Salted Cod Salad; Avocado, Romaine, Aged Jerez Vinegar and Extra Virgin Olive Oil

LANGOUSTINE
Warm Langoustine Carpaccio; Young Ginger-Matsutake Mushroom Salad; Vanilla-Citrus Oil

OCTOPUS
Braised Baby Octopus; Black Trumpet-Truffle Purée; Herb de Provence Infused Red Wine-Ink Sauce

SCALLOP
Ultra Rare Charred Scallop; Smoked Sea Salt and Dried Olives

GOOD OPTION FOR THOSE WHO DON'T WANT ALL SEAFOOD →

MUSHROOM
Slowly Braised Porcini and Oyster; Asparagus and Baby Leek

LIGHTLY COOKED

RED SNAPPER
Pan Roasted Red Snapper; Crispy Papadum and Preserved Tomato Chutney; Thai Basil infused Kaffir Lime Broth

SKATE
Grilled Skate; Mango-Jalapeño Salad; Bourbon, Lime and Guajillo Pepper Broth

SURF AND TURF ←
White Tuna and Seared Japanese Kobe Beef "Korean BBQ Style"; Fresh Kimchi; Lemon Brown Butter Emulsion

CODFISH
Sautéed Codfish; Stuffed Sweet Pepper and Celery-Tandoori-Yogurt Sauce

MONKFISH
Pan Roasted Monkfish; Celeriac Emulsion; Red Wine-Brandy Sauce

WILD SALMON ←
Barely Cooked Wild Alaskan Salmon; Daikon and Enoki Salad; Baby Leek-Wasabi Sauce

HALIBUT
Poached Halibut; Marinated Grapes and Cherry Tomatoes, Pickled Shallot; Verjus-Lemon Grass Infusion

WILD STRIPED BASS – LANGOUSTINE
Baked Langoustine and Striped Bass; Confit Tomato Agnolotti; Bouillabaisse Consommé and Curry Emulsion

LOBSTER   ($12 Supplement)
Baked Lobster; Wilted Romaine, Squash and Candied Ginger; Port and Tamarind Reduction

BLACK BASS ←
Masala Spiced Crispy Black Bass; Peking Duck-Green Papaya Salad in a Rich Ginger-Cardamom Broth

GROUPER
Florida Grouper; Shiso-Matsutake Salad; Lemon-Miso Broth

RED SNAPPER
Whole Red Snapper Baked in Rosemary and Thyme Salt Crust, Extra Virgin Olive Oil and a Casserole of the Day's Market Vegetables (Please Allow 24 Hours Notice; Two Person Minimum)

Le Bernardin will not serve Chilean Sea Bass, or Blue Fin Tuna in support of NRDC and Sea Web's educational efforts to speed the recovery of these endangered species.

> GOOD HARMONY
> BETWEEN
> THE FISH
> AND THE KOBE

> WILD SALMON
> IS A
> REAL DELICACY

> I
> LOVE
> THIS ONE

> A SMALL EFFORT
> TO EDUCATE
> OUR CUSTOMERS

UPON REQUEST

SQUAB
Pan Roasted Squab Stuffed with Truffle, Soft Polenta, Armagnac Scented Jus

LAMB
Pan Roasted Rack of Lamb; Sunchoke Purée; Natural Jus

KOBE BEEF   ($150 Supplement)
Seared Japanese Kobe Beef; Truffled Herb Salad   (8 Ounces)

PASTA
Buffalo Mozzarella Tortellini; Wild Mushroom Consommé; Nettle; Parmesan Emulsion

PRIVATE ROOMS AVAILABLE

PRIX FIXE $107   CHEF: ERIC RIPERT

CHRISTINE MUHLKE
A NIGHT ON THE LINE

After I'd been observing the restaurant for a few weeks, Chef Ripert announced, "To really get the experience, you need to work on the line one night." "Great idea," I replied, terrified.

Chris Muller reluctantly agreed. "I'll put you with Eddie Dollinger on monk. But not too much yapping. Wear your whites—and comfortable shoes."

The monk station is in an awkward spot, set at the far end of the wickedly paced sauté and sauce stations. All of the other cooks face east or west; the monk guy faces the pass and blocks the narrow path that both the kitchen dishwasher, laden with baskets of hot, dirty pots and plates, and the fish pass, carrying trays of fish to the sauté station, are constantly rushing across to and from their areas near garde-manger. The twenty-four-year-old Dollinger, who's six foot two (not a small kid), was constantly being asked to move. (In kitchen lingo, it's not "Excuse me" but a loud "Bee-hind!") But if he stepped aside to the right, he'd be in the spattering path of the sauté cook, who regularly dumps out the grease from his pans before cleaning them in the corner.

Dollinger showed me his temporary domain: two stockpots filled with simmering poaching liquid, a few small saucepans for heating sauces *à la minute*, metal canisters filled with truffle emulsion that will accompany the fish, and a metal canister of utensils (whisk, spoons, fish skewer, a slotted spatula to gently lower and raise fish).

At 5:30, the orders started raining in. Every few minutes, Dollinger gingerly dropped a piece of halibut into the poaching liquid, pulled a plate from above the line, and threw it into the oven below ("Plates will never be hot enough—ever"), and grabbed a plastic-wrapped garnish plate from the stack in the nearest fridge. He dumped that plate's contents into a small metal bowl, added salt, pepper, and oil, and tossed it with his fingers, then ladled two scoops of verjus sauce into a small pot to warm. Next he carefully removed the fish from the liquid, pulled the now blistering plate from the oven with just a folded dish towel to protect his hand, and inserted a metal skewer into the fish for a few seconds before pressing it against his lower lip to see if it was warm. He then quickly but lightly arranged the dressed vegetables on top of it: half a cherry tomato here, half a grape there, a sea bean connecting the two, some turnips. He poured the warm sauce into a porcelain beaker and handed me a kitchen towel.

"Want to take it to the pass?"

I grabbed for the plate and pitcher with the thin towel, burning my hand. At the pass, Muller looked at the plate with resignation, rearranged a dislodged sea bean, wiped the rim of the plate and pitcher clean, and put it on a tray for a back waiter.

"Pretty fun, huh, Muhlke?" he chuckled.

By now it was so busy with the pre-theater rush that sous-chef Jennifer Carroll was helping out on sauté, sliding down onto her knees beneath Ed's legs like a heavy-metal guitarist to pull some plates out of the oven. Everyone was cooking and plating so quickly, there was no time to think, just do.

By 7:05, things got eerily calm. The cooks restocked their garnish plates from the walk-in, refreshed their *mise en place*, and wiped their stations clean. I caught a glimpse of my face in the office window and saw that I had the "tan" that comes from standing next to open flames and 500-degree ovens.

Dollinger and sauté cook Ron Hsu started joking around in their private language, developed from months of intense nights on the line together. "People say your personality comes out at night," said Dollinger. "It's a long day, and you just come up with stuff to get you through. Ron, did we dominate, or were we dominated?" he asked Hsu about their performance during the rush.

"I'd say it was fifty-fifty," Hsu replied, his forearms and hands covered with burns and scars. "I was flawless on the black" (aka black bass).

Muller tried to talk to Dollinger about his sons' little league baseball, much to the young cook's surprise—forty-five minutes earlier, there hadn't been many friendly words directed his way. I asked Dollinger what he hopes to get from his time at Le Bernardin. For the Johnson and Wales culinary school graduate, who deferred payment on his student loan, the stakes are high. "I want to be exposed to a lot of different things," he said. "We get to do really cool things here, like with fresh truffles. It's only made me a better cook. Eventually

I want to be a chef and maybe own my own restaurant. For now it's see what you can see. I really like working here, but there are highs and lows. It's really intense because we have standards to uphold."

At 8:40, Muller called out to fire two black bass. Hsu took down the fillets that the fish pass had put on his shelf when the order first came in and sprinkled them with kosher salt from shoulder height to distribute it more evenly. He dusted the fillets with Wondra, blew off the excess, and pressed them down into the waiting pan.

The kitchen was a barely contained storm of activity until ten o'clock, when Dollinger decided it was safe to ask me to help plate halibut. After ten tries, I started to get the hang of setting the sea bean at just the right angle. I "progressed" from saucing to squirting out truffled potato emulsion from a drop-on-the-floor-hot CO_2 canister, slicing mushrooms for turbot (too thick), julienning herbs for skate (not uniform enough), putting sautéed pea shoots into a ring mold (not as easy as it looks), even poaching a piece of halibut (a triumph). In the literal heat of everything, I realized why each cook does only two dishes max and has prepared all of the ingredients beforehand: You're a food-making machine. There's no room for creativity, let alone thought. If you begin to think about the fact that you must make every dish four-star perfect, you will lose your mind, beginning with your sense of humor.

At 10:45, there were still fifteen tables to feed. "Fifteen tables at ten-fifteen. Sure we're in a fucking recession!" said Muller. "At ten o'clock it's painful because you're exhausted, but we find ways to make it easier: beers at midnight, a late supper—right now we're into chopped salad." At 11:30, orders for Kobe and lobster tastings were cooked by the punchy staff. At 12:15, cooks soaped down and scrubbed their stations, while saucier Joe Palma cooked off the Kobe trimmings for the kitchen.

The dishwasher area, by now a subtropical climate, was overflowing. Dollinger snuck me a piece of truffle. Station by station, the kitchen was cleaned. A back waiter was sent downstairs for beers. At 12:30, we gathered around the pass, red-faced and filthy, silent with exhaustion. It was hard to believe that these people were going to do it all again later the same day, for a salary of about $30,000 a year.

"Cheers," said Muller, raising a pilsner.

THE DISHES

Below, and throughout this section, are play-by-plays of some of Le Bernardin's most popular dishes, from the moment the order is placed until it's set on the waiter's tray.

THE STATION: GARDE-MANGER

The Cast
Chef: Eric Gestel
Cook: Victor Panora

The Duration: 2 minutes

The Mise en Place

FOIE GRAS TERRINE	EXTRA VIRGIN OLIVE OIL
BAGUETTE SLICE, TOASTED	SHALLOTS, MINCED
TUNA	CHIVES
SALT AND WHITE PEPPER	LEMON

The Action

Gestel:
"Order in pounded tuna!"

Panora:
"Yes, Chef! Goin' in."

Panora:
• Takes chilled plate out of the reach-in.
• Takes a piece of sliced foie gras terrine out of the reach-in. ("Door!")
• Spreads foie gras on the toast.
• Places the toast in the center of the plate.
• Takes a tray of pounded tuna out of the cooler. ("Watch your head!")
• Peels plastic from one side of the tuna and centers the fish, plastic side up, over the foie gras toast on the plate, then removes the second piece of plastic from the top of the tuna.
• Seasons tuna with salt and pepper, brushes with olive oil, sprinkles with some finely minced shallot, adds sliced chives on top, and wipes off excess ingredients from the plate.

Panora:
"Pounded in the pass?"

Gestel:
"Let's go!"

Panora:
• Squeezes fresh lemon over the dish and brings it to the pass.

Tuna
Carpaccio

RECIPE ON PAGE 148

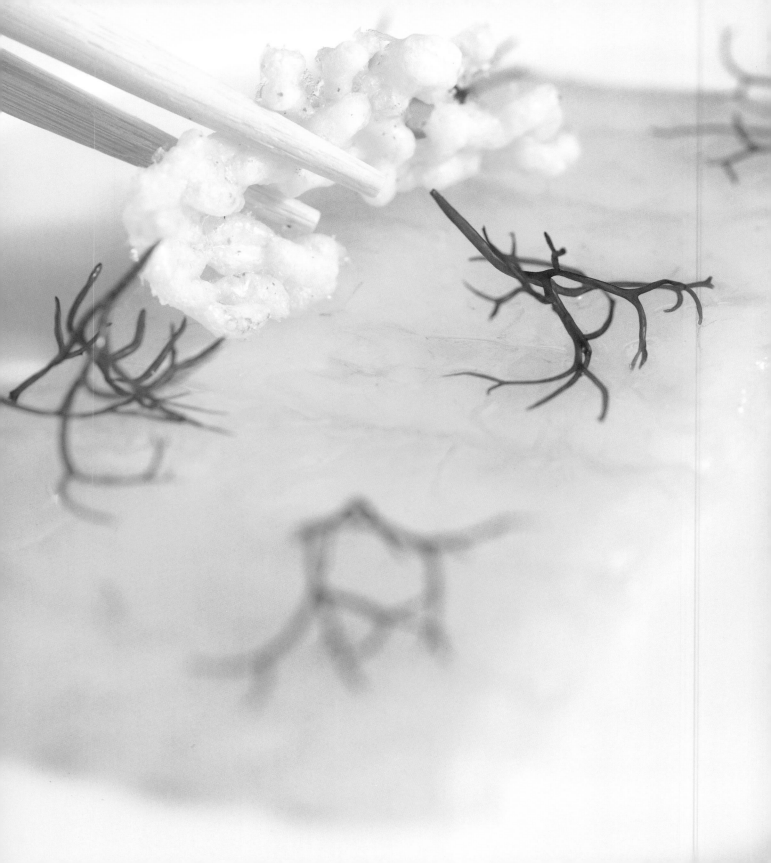

Fluke
White Soy

RECIPE ON PAGE 147

Fluke
Four Ceriches

RECIPE ON PAGE 152

Salmon
Jalapeño Emulsion

RECIPE ON PAGE 146

Kanpachi
Tartare

RECIPE ON PAGE 151

Escolar
Béarnaise

RECIPE ON PAGE 158

THE STATION: VEG APPS

The Cast
Chef: Eric Gestel
Cook: Marino Castillo

The Duration: 5 minutes

The Mise en Place

ESCOLAR
  (CALLED WHITE TUNA
  IN OUR KITCHEN)
OLIVE OIL POACHING LIQUID
RED WINE BÉARNAISE
  (MADE BY SAUCIER
  JOE PALMA)

SHALLOTS, MINCED
CRACKED BLACK PEPPER
TARRAGON
SEA BEANS
POTATO CRISPS
SALT AND WHITE PEPPER

The Action

Gestel:
"Fire one white tuna!"

Castillo:
"Yes, Chef!"

Castillo:
• Seasons fish and places
in a pan of olive oil to poach.
• Places small saucepan
of red wine béarnaise on
the heat.

Gestel:
"How long on the white
tuna?"

Castillo:
"White tuna in two!"

Castillo:
• Takes fish out of the
poaching oil (usually
cooked medium rare),
places on a cutting board,
makes 5 slices, and plates.
• Seasons the eye (inside)
of the fish and adds shallots,
cracked black pepper, and
tarragon in a line on top.
• Flashes the plate (puts
it in the oven for less than
a minute).
• Places sea beans and
potato crisps around
the fish.
• Pours hot béarnaise
sauce into a gooseneck
(a white porcelain sauce
container).
• Brings the finished plate
and sauce to the pass:
"Behind down the line!"

Hamachi
Tandoori

RECIPE ON PAGE 159

Oysters
Baked
RECIPE ON PAGE 162

Caviar—Sea Urchin

RECIPE ON PAGE 174

Caviar-Pasta

RECIPE ON PAGE 164

Bacalao

RECIPE ON PAGE 168

Langoustines

RECIPE ON PAGE 170

Lobster
Cappuccino

RECIPE ON PAGE 165

Octopus
Black Olive and Preserved Lemon

RECIPE ON PAGE 166

Striped Bass

RECIPE ON PAGE 186

THE STATION: MONK

The Cast
Chef: Chris Muller
Monk Cook: Ed Dollinger
Sauté Cook: Ronald Hsu

The Duration: 6–7 minutes

The Mise en Place

STRIPED BASS	TOMATO AGNOLOTTI
CONSOMMÉ	ONION AND FENNEL COMPOTE
SALT AND WHITE PEPPER	CURRY EMULSION
LANGOUSTINE	MICRO CHIVES
CANOLA OIL	

The Action

Muller:
"Fire one striped bass!"

Dollinger:
"Stripe!"

Hsu:
• Puts seasoned piece of striped bass in a buttered pan, adds just enough water to cover the bottom of the pan.
• Puts the pan on the fire and brings to a simmer.
• Puts the pan in 500°F oven.

Dollinger to Hsu:
"How long on the fish?"

Dollinger:
• Puts saucepan of consommé and a small Teflon pan on the flattop to heat.

Hsu:
• Opens the oven, turns the fish over, and puts the pan back in the oven: "Three minutes!"

Dollinger:
• Seasons a langoustine tail, adds canola oil to the hot Teflon pan, and puts in the langoustine.
• Grabs an order of agnolotti and drops into boiling water.
• Puts a bowl in the oven for 30 seconds.

• Flips the langoustine.
• Drains the agnolotti.
• Takes a hot pan of fennel and onion compote (kept hot during entire service) down from the shelf over the flattop.

Hsu:
• Takes pan of fish from the oven, checks the seasoning, takes fish out of the pan, blots it on a towel, and places in center of the shallow bowl: "Fish on the plate!"

Dollinger:
• Checks the langoustine for doneness, blots it on a towel.
• Plates the agnolotti around the fish, spoons a teaspoon of compote on top, and puts the langoustine on top of the compote.
• Pulls the simmering consommé off the heat, pours the consommé into one gooseneck (porcelain sauce container), and ladles the curry emulsion into another.
• Garnishes the top of each agnolotti with a micro chive. Grabs sauces and bowl: "Coming down the line, behind!"

Monkfish
Red Wine – Brandy Sauce

RECIPE ON PAGE 176

Halibut
Beets

RECIPE ON PAGE 180

Surf - and - Turf

RECIPE ON PAGE 198

THE STATION: SAUCE

The Cast
Chef: Chris Muller
Sauté Cook: Ronald Hsu
Saucier: Joe Palma

The Duration: 5 minutes

The Mise en Place

ESCOLAR (CALLED WHITE TUNA IN OUR KITCHEN)	SALT AND WHITE PEPPER
KOBE BEEF	KIMCHI MARINADE
NAPA CABBAGE LEAF	YUZU-BROWN BUTTER EMULSION
BUTTERNUT SQUASH	BARBECUE SAUCE
ASIAN PEAR	CHIVES

The Action

Muller:
"Fire one surf-and-turf!"

Hsu:
"Yes, Chef!"

Hsu:
• Drops an order of escolar in the grill pan.

Palma:
• Puts a piece of seasoned Kobe beef on the flattop.

Hsu:
• Puts one piece of cabbage, 3 butternut squash bâtonnets, and 4 Asian pear bâtonnets in a bowl, seasons with salt, pepper, and kimchi marinade.

Palma:
• Flips the Kobe beef. "How long on the white?"

Hsu:
Turns the escolar.
• "Forty-five out." (45 seconds to the plate).

Palma:
• Puts the bowl of vegetables on a shelf above the flattop.
• Puts a saucepan of yuzu–brown butter emulsion on the heat.
• Places line of barbecue sauce down the plate, places caggabe on the plate, plates the Kobe beef (cooked medium) toward the center bottom.

Hsu:
• Plates the grilled escolar to the side of the seared Kobe beef.

Palma:
• Places the pear and butternut bâtonnets over both the escolar and the beef.
• Pours the sauce into a gooseneck (porcelain sauce container) and brings the dish and gooseneck to the pass.

Salmon
Sweet Pea – Wasabi Sauce
RECIPE ON PAGE 202

Black Bass
RECIPE ON PAGE 200

Chocolate–Peanut

RECIPE ON PAGE 212

"Egg"

RECIPE ON PAGE 210

Lemon

RECIPE ON PAGE 216

Rose — Raspberry

RECIPE ON PAGE 214

Chocolate — Corn

RECIPE ON PAGE 206

PART THREE

THE DINING EXPERIENCE

One of the things that diners remark upon after eating at Le Bernardin is that the service is almost invisible. By the end of the meal, you've been helped by as many as seven people, but you can't quite identify them. Although friendly and available, they work out of your field of attention so that you can focus on the food, and companions, in front of you.

While it might seem effortless, it's a rigorous ballet that requires training and focus. The men—and, increasingly, women—juggle a plethora of details in their heads while projecting an air of gracious calm.

This calm disappears the second they set foot in the tiny bus areas set around the room, like actors stepping offstage. (You won't find any actors here, as waitstaff are hired only full-time.)

Like other four-stars in New York, the restaurant will fill each table about two times over the course of dinner service (five to eleven P.M.); lunch, served from noon to two P.M., has only one turn, with a smattering of latecomers. Maître d' Ben Chekroun staggers the reservations so that the entire room doesn't sit down or leave at the same time and so that no table feels rushed.

Because many of the floor staff have been at the restaurant for years, the minutiae of service are second nature, a learning process catalyzed by the presence of Miss Le Coze, as she's referred to by everyone except Ripert. As she walks through the dining room, waiters go into high-performance mode. Her standards are incredibly high, but they yield results.

"We have to perform to give you an illusion of effortless perfection. For you to have the right food in front of you at the right time, excellent and at the right temperature, and obviously having clean china—all those little details you'd never think of are vital."

—Eric Ripert

The Players

MAÎTRE D': Maître d' Ben Chekroun oversees the entire dining room: working with reservationists, fielding VIP requests, deciding who sits where; hiring, training, and supervising dining room staff; greeting and seating guests.

WINE DIRECTOR: Aldo Sohm is responsible for the restaurant's entire wine program, what goes on the wine list, and what gets paired with the tasting menu.

SOMMELIERS: Four sommeliers help diners make their wine choices, share glass-refilling duties with front waiters, and decant old Bordeaux. They are also responsible for restocking the wine cooler behind the bar with bottles from the upstairs wine-storage room after dinner service.

CAPTAIN TOURNANT: A free-floating captain who works the entire dining room, making sure that all of the tables are being served properly and the bus stations are running efficiently.

CAPTAIN: The six captains have the main staff interaction with guests. Each is responsible for seven to eight tables, making sure they are appropriately served and maintained by the front and back waiters and busboys. They explain the menu, take orders, and handle special requests.

FRONT WAITER: The restaurant's six front waiters are responsible for setting the tables, serving the food from one of the four bus stations to the tables, explaining the dishes to guests, pouring the appropriate sauces, refilling wine and mineral water glasses, and clearing the table after each course.

BACK WAITER: The six back waiters are the backbone of service, according to Ripert. As the liaison between the dining room and the kitchen, they're responsible for placing the orders that their captains give them; maintaining and monitoring the orders' progress on the kitchen's dry-erase board; and telling the chef de cuisine when the table is ready for the next course to be prepared. They also carry the trays of food from the kitchen to the designated bus station and return trays of dirty dishes to the dishwasher whenever they see them, regardless of which station they're on. They're responsible for making sure their station is supplied with napkins, silverware, plates, and glasses. Between lunch and dinner service, they dry wine glasses and fold napkins.

BARTENDER: In addition to serving those who drink and/or dine at the bar, the bartender (one at lunch, two at dinner) supplies all cocktails, soft drinks, bottles of wine and water, and additional glassware requested by the front waiters and sommeliers.

BUSBOY: There are six busboys on the floor at any time, responsible for refilling tap water glasses, offering bread, crumbing the table, and resetting between seatings. Another busboy mans the coffee station in the kitchen.

HOSTESSES: Two women open the door for arriving guests and take their coats, reversing the process as they leave.

The Hub

The gueridon is the hub of service. There are four in the dining room, two on each side. Each holds a supply of plates, silverware, napkins, glasses, and check holders so that tables can be serviced as quickly as possible, whether it's replacing a dropped knife or bringing an extra plate for a shared dish. It is where the food is first brought from the kitchen, to be served by the front waiters, and where dirty plates are returned before being taken to the dishwasher. At two of the stations hidden from view in little niches, front waiters use computers to order drinks and wine, print checks, and run credit cards.

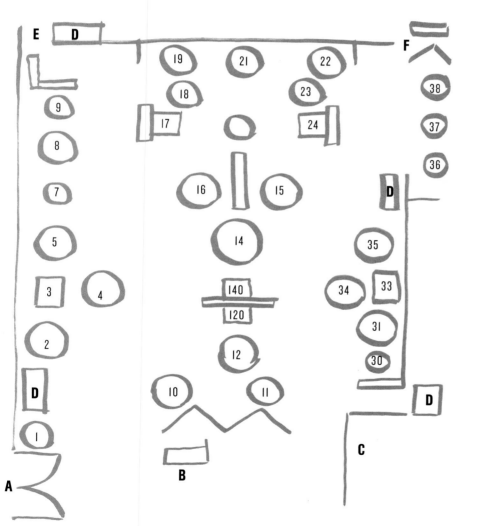

THE DINING ROOM AT A GLANCE

A. Front door
B. Host stand
C. Bar
D. Bus stations (gueridons)
E. Door to restrooms and Les Salons
F. Door to kitchen
1–38, 120, 140. Tables

THE OLD ORDER: COMPUTERS NEED NOT APPLY

While most restaurants today have touch-screen computers that feed orders to the kitchen, the system at Le Bernardin consists of a dry-erase board and dupes (slips of paper from the waiter's pad). Each row of boxes on the board in the kitchen represents one table in the dining room at any given time; each box represents a course. (Boxes are added for the tasting menu.) The names of any VIPs or regulars are written on the side of the box, to the right of the table number, along with any dietary restrictions, and before service, the maître d'

will repeat this information to the chef. As soon as a table comes in, that table gets circled on the board and canapés are sent out. As soon as they order, the back waiter, who's responsible for placing orders and taking out food, marks the first box. That means the order is in and the kitchen has started cooking it. As soon as that course leaves the kitchen, the back waiter crosses off the box, and the expediter—the person who's standing at the pass and calling out the orders—marks the time on the ticket. The waiters will not instruct the kitchen to fire the table until the previous

course has been cleared. The chef de cuisine is monitoring the table, checking to make sure too much time hasn't elapsed since the previous course went out, and that nothing is wrong.

The relationship between the back waiters, the chef de cuisine, and the front waiters, who serve the food once it's brought out, is based on timing. "Most restaurants have computers," says sous-chef Adam Plitt, "but I find this system so much better. You can see everything that's going on in front of you."

A. Number of people at the table

B. Table number

C. Time, marked by chef at the pass, telling when each course goes out (23 means 23 minutes after the hour, and so on)

D. Position number of guests at the table

E. Indicates that course was sent out

F. Table number and number of covers repeated

G. Indicates special guest

H. Name of guest

I. Top, white copy is for the chef at the pass

J. For the person at the fish pass

K. Stays with the captain

L. For the back waiters at the pass

M. Goes to the cashier

The Elements of Service

HIRING

Maître d' Ben Chekroun and general manager David Mancini look for candidates with a two- or three-star background, four whenever possible. But the number of high-end restaurants opening in New York means that it's not always easy to find people with the appropriate experience. As a result, says Mancini, "We'll go with our gut and hire the people we like. We'll train people and give them the experience they need. We've hired people from McDonald's; they may not have had the experience, but they had the demeanor and the willingness to please, and it came through." The real question is whether they're confident enough to handle the pressure. "By the end of their first week, I know if they'll make it," says Chekroun.

French waiters were once the norm, but today there is just one French captain and two Americans; the others are from Spain, Morocco, Ecuador, Cameroon, and Guatemala. And while men still dominate, there is now one woman captain, and three of the four sommeliers are women. The restaurant doesn't hire captains; it promotes front waiters.

TRAINING

Maguy Le Coze and Eric Ripert set the standard of perseverance and constant training, which Chekroun continues with his staff. For him, it's important that each hire knows what goes into every other job on the floor. For example, before they begin working in the restaurant, front waiters spend a week observing all the other positions, first in the kitchen, then in the dining room, where they follow a back waiter, "so they can respect that position and see how hard it is," says Chekroun. Next, they trail a front waiter for a few days to watch how he acts, how he talks to the guests, how he serves, clears, and so on. Finally, they sit down with a captain and go over all the points related to the dining room. "A lot of information is thrown at them," says Chekroun. "And it doesn't stop.

"People stay with us a long time, and the work becomes natural to them. Any back waiter can set and clear a table and describe a dish as well as a front waiter. Any busboy can do a back waiter's job. With time and experience, there's almost a cross-training going on. So whenever possible, we promote someone from within."

MISS LE COZE: AN EYE FOR PERFECTION

When Maguy Le Coze is on the floor, the staff are at full attention. They stand straighter. They focus more intently. That's because she can notice mistakes from tables away.

"It's hard: She sees everything," says captain Mark Kopera, who has worked with her since the restaurant opened. "The standard isn't just for one night or one table, it's for every table every service. And that's the only way to do it in this business."

"What makes Maguy angry?" asks Ben Chekroun with a smile. "Not focusing. Not paying attention to a table. Not implementing the basics of service. Not being courteous. This is a luxury business. As a waiter, you are here to please and accommodate. 'No' is not something that should be in our vocabulary."

"It's subtle," says Le Coze. "There aren't huge mistakes, but there are always little things. It's good when I've been away for a few days, because I return with a fresh eye. If there's someone new on the floor, I can tell if he hasn't finished his training. I make sure that it's not me who tells him. I tell Ben Chekroun, who talks to the captain, who then brings it up at the evening meeting. That way everyone can learn from it."

KNOWLEDGE

"Things may change from one restaurant to another—we might serve from the left and clear from the right; maybe at Jean Georges they clear from the left and serve from the right," says Chekroun. "But the most important thing is the level of service. It's Le Bernardin: If somebody wants something, they get it right away." The staff must constantly watch their guests and stations: "You have to read and anticipate. You have to know what's going to happen in your station in two, three, four, five, six minutes—that if the food for table thirty-eight will be coming out, you have to make sure that table is ready to receive it. You have to know the menu by heart, know your station, where the silverware goes on the table, where the plates and glasses are set, exactly where the napkin is—the whole technical side."

ATTITUDE

"In the beginning, we were much more formal than today. For male guests, you wouldn't dream of not wearing a tie!" says Le Coze. "Later, with Eric, we really set about loosening it up. We said to the waitstaff, 'Imagine you're walking into an Italian trattoria. You see the people smiling, that certain way of doing things. Now think three steps away from that. . . .' That's the atmosphere Eric wanted. He'd stand in the kitchen door, and each time he saw a busboy who wasn't smiling, *oof!*"

Today, new customers are often surprised by how friendly the waiters are. (One woman, mortified that her husband had ordered a Diet Coke with his meal, was put at ease by the French captain, who responded, "Would you prefer Diet Pepsi, for ze new generation?")

"It sounds cheesy and naïve, maybe, but we want people to leave happy with a smile," says Ripert. "We don't want you to come and have an educational program awaiting you. It doesn't matter which agenda you have—to celebrate, to eat, to do business, to entertain the family, to seduce—we have to provide what you expect, but without compromising our soul."

THE SIXTH SENSE

The ability to read a guest is key to providing four-star service, according to Chekroun. For example, he says, "You can tell when somebody's used to going to four-star restaurants or if it's their first time. I can see when they walk through the door if they're comfortable, or if they don't know where to walk, what to do. They might be nervous. It's our job to put them at ease."

Intuition is even more important on the floor. "When a conversation stops between two people—not a lull but tension at the table—you know the service has to pick up," David Mancini explains. "Or if a person starts glancing around the restaurant, more than people usually do to say, 'Oh, look at the painting'—

before the person gets bored and says, 'Where's my waiter?'—you must be there before they do that."

TEAMWORK

Chekroun sees service as a chain: "I really believe that if you remove one link, it will break. Anybody on the chain, from when you make a reservation to the moment you leave, can ruin your experience."

"It's teamwork. There's no other word for it," says captain Edgar Aguilar. "Even though the service is broken into sections, that's merely strategic. When we grab a busboy from another station, there's no such thing as, 'It's not my station.' We all put in the same work."

PRESENTATION

In 2002, Ripert decided that the food should be sauced tableside, adding another dimension to service. "We learned that if we put the sauce on the plate in the kitchen, by the time it arrives at the table, it doesn't look so great anymore," he explains. "So we put the sauce on at the table, which serves several purposes: warmer service, better flavors, and presentation."

Adds captain Mark Kopera, "Now it's a lot more visual. When you sauce the dish at the table, the dish opens up. It's a little like a dance, when you have two sauces and one person does the broth and another finishes with an emulsion or oil."

BREAKING WITH TRADITION: WOMEN AT LE BERNARDIN

Until 1998, the only women that could be found at Le Bernardin were either opening doors and hanging coats or working in the office. "It's not that we weren't hiring women," says Le Coze. "They weren't applying." Michelle Lindsay, who came from the Culinary Institute that year and, after finishing her trail at the end of her first day, was hired as a cook, became the kitchen's first female sous-chef in 2000. Because of her ability to create new dishes for the restaurant, in 2005 Ripert moved her to Ripert Consulting, where she works closely with clients like the Ritz-Carlton, developing recipes, selecting tableware, doing cost analysis and so on.

In recent years, she has been followed up the ranks by other women, to the point that David Mancini had to expand the women's locker room in 2007. As of this writing, the restaurant employs one female sous-chef and two female line cooks, with just one woman in pastry (which is where women in restaurants tend to work). In the dining room, three of the four sommeliers are women, and there is one female captain, who at the age of twenty-two became the first in the restaurant's history.

The women in the dining room say that they've encountered nothing but praise from diners—though the sommeliers are occasionally challenged on their knowledge. "They seem really surprised, and really excited," says captain Angela Paxton. "A lot of VIPs

who have been coming for twenty years say, 'It's so great to see you here,' and a lot of people I used to wait on at Per Se come here, too, so it's like family, I guess."

In the kitchen, it can be more stressful. Sous-chef Jennifer Carroll says, "A lot of girls aren't used to all the sarcasm. You just have to remember that nothing's personal. If you take it personally, as a woman, with all our emotions, you'll never survive."

Soa Davies was the chef de cuisine at Splendido in Vail, Colorado, before she arrived at Le Bernardin, where kitchen policy dictated that she start at the beginning, on garde-manger. After making her way up to saucier, she decided that she had had enough of the long, intense kitchen hours and wanted to develop her creativity. She moved to the office and helps to create new dishes. Being a woman in the Le Bernardin kitchen, she says, is a blessing and a curse. "Obviously we're a minority, and I'm not going to lie and say we don't get better treatment, because we do—Chris [Muller] is more apt to let the women do less arduous tasks. But that means we have to work harder to overcome the stereotype that we're weaker." Davies says this shared experience on the line tends to create strong bonds between the women: "It's really nice having someone who completely understands. Sometimes you become so much one of the boys, you forget you're a girl."

THE MAÎTRE D'

Two titans of industry with an unwavering preference for the same table have reservations for the same time. A giant branch of cherry blossoms from one of the towering floral arrangements has toppled onto a guest's head. A man who just might be from the Michelin Guide has arrived. And the air-conditioning is too arctic for half of the diners. For maître d' Ben Chekroun, it's another easily managed lunch service.

Since 1993, the Moroccan native, who started as a captain tournant, has welcomed diners with a warm smile and discreet manner. But podium-conducting represents only a fraction of his duties. He is responsible for the entire front of house, as well as for who staffs it. Somehow he stays both cool and humble, a rare combination in the industry.

His day begins at 10 A.M. He checks the reservations for the day and tries to accommodate last-minute requests; prints out a reservation report for the day for the kitchen and floor staff, which notes special occasions; guests' dietary requests and food preferences; and notes seating and waiter preferences of regular customers, which he then has the captains enter into the computer system. Before lunch service begins, he and general manager David Mancini

check the dining room to see if anything requires attention, whether it's wilted flowers in the summer (the building turns off the air-conditioning at night) or unpressed tablecloth edges. "It's been years, so I can read the room right away," he says.

Once the guests arrive, he starts assessing the mood in the dining room in a variety of ways: "I think in the U.S., people like a buzz, even in a four-star. But we want to keep the pace under control; we want to have a staff that's busy but not hectic." At night, he adds, "We like to have maybe a little sexiness in the mood. We have candles, we dim the lights, we have music."

Through his hiring and training practices, Chekroun has helped set the dining room of Le Bernardin apart from other top restaurants in New York. "I like it to be a very professional experience,

but a little bit on the friendly side," he says. "Friendly-elegant. Not too much fanfare or ceremony. I want the staff—captains and front waiters especially—to learn how to read the guests, if they want to chitchat a little bit or be left alone. Guests should have amazing service, without noticing the waiters as they serve and clear. And ideally guests get the feeling that the staff is there to please you and are friendly from the heart, not because that's what they have to do."

Although he's still young, Chekroun is one of the city's few remaining career maître d's. "Every year there's a new project," he says. "It could be the aesthetic, a change in the room, opening the Salon upstairs; it could be a change in the way we serve. That keeps you motivated. The restaurant keeps evolving, and that's why I—and most of the staff—stay."

HOW TO FOLD A MADELEINE NAPKIN

Delicious little cookies are served warm in these.

1. Fold a square napkin at the four corners to meet in the center. Repeat.

2. Flip over the napkin and fold in the four corners to meet in the center. Repeat.

3. Holding the center on top, pull up the four bottom points. Spread and fill.

Invisible Perfection: What the Diner (Hopefully) Doesn't Notice

A meal at Le Bernardin is usually so relaxed and gracious, it's hard to imagine the military precision with which the dining room is run. Every morning and between meals, the area is prepared according to maître d' Ben Chekroun's extensive checklist. During meals, every staff member adheres to strict training guidelines so that diners can focus on enjoying the food.

"For you to have the right food in front of you at the right time, excellent and at the right temperature, served on clean china, without a dead flower in front of you, a light blinding you, a candle smelling too strong." says Ripert. "We have one hundred thirty-eight people who are promoting that experience. When we succeed, it looks effortless, but it's not. It's all codified into different organizations. It's totally controlled—and you should have no idea."

Who knew, for example, that the florist comes in daily to change the blooms on every table and pumps out the water in the vases around the room, replenishing it with clean water? Or that the restaurant keeps its 4500 pieces of silver and flatware sparkling by cleaning it weekly in a burnishing machine in the basement? Or that it owns 5000 pieces of china and spends $120,000 a year just replacing chipped and broken items?

As for setting up the room for service, "*Mise en place* is ninety percent. I'm sure everyone here will tell you that—out here or in the kitchen," says captain Mark Kopera. Before guests arrive, he scans the room, ticking off an internalized checklist: "Make sure everything is on the table, the napkins are straight, and the tablecloths are centered. Make sure the chair is just kissing the cloth—not too far forward, not too far back. Make sure the silver is clean and wiped, no water spots. Make sure the glasses are lined up properly. Candle, flowers, water level . . ." After a while, he says, "You learn how to take a picture—your station, the room. It hurts your eye when it's not that way.

"The most important invisible detail is just the benefit of it feeling fresh after twenty-one years. Too often a lot of the high-end restaurants that have been able to survive at least ten years get lazy. And that's the kiss of death."

PURE DECADENCE

- For several months, one customer came in four nights a week with ten friends and requested a fourteen-course tasting menu, demanding that no dishes be repeated. "It got to the point where we'd take a piece of snapper and a piece of mint and put them on a plate," recalls Muller.
- For his sixtieth birthday, a longtime diner rented out the restaurant for 150 famous friends. The entire dining room was redesigned to fit a stage, where Bruce Springsteen and Bette Midler played. The finale? A trapeze artist.
- When Le Bernardin received a four-star review from *The New York Times*, the restaurant's impromptu celebration included three kilograms of Iranian osetra caviar, along with "all the foie gras we could eat, and bottles and bottles of Champagne and Bordeaux," recalls Ripert.

THE NUMBERS

Tablecloths ordered weekly	800
Napkins ordered weekly	4500
Monthly flower bill	$12,000
Price of charger plate from JL Coquet	$160
Price of silver wine bucket	$295
Types of glasses stocked behind the bar	24
Glasses hand-washed per day	1300
Waitstaff who are actors	0
Captains who are French	1
Captains who are American	2
Captains who started as busboys or dishwashers	2

CARDINAL SINS

When a new employee starts working at the restaurant, maître d' Ben Chekroun gives him a list of 129 details ("Monumentally Magnificent Trivialities") to keep in mind at all times—details that he and Le Coze can tell are off seconds after entering the room. It's a constant battle to keep everything consistent and up to the established standards.

1. Not acknowledging guests with eye contact and a smile within 30 seconds. First impressions count!

2. Not thanking the guests as they leave. Last impression!

3. Not remembering the guests' likes and dislikes!

4. Not opening the front door for guests.

5. Silverware set askew on the tables.

6. Tabletop that isn't picture perfect.

7. Forks with bent tines.

8. Unevenly folded napkins.

9. Chipped glassware.

10. Tables not completely set when guests are being seated.

11. Dead or wilted flowers on the tables.

12. Tables that are not leveled.

13. Salt and pepper shakers that are half empty.

14. Salt or sugar crusted inside the shakers.

15. Carelessly placed items on the tables.

16. Table linen with small holes, rips, or burns.

17. Clutter or junk. Watch the trays, gueridons, etc.

18. Pictures on walls not leveled.

19. Tables not properly cleared.

20. Burned-out lightbulbs.

21. Clattering dishes. Be quiet!

22. Dropping china, silverware, or glassware.

23. Murky or smelly water in flower vases.

24. Wobbly tables or chairs.

25. Broken chairs.

26. Needing to be center of attention. Give the ego a break!

27. An "I'm doing you a favor" attitude.

28. Socializing with certain guests while ignoring others!!!!!!!!!!!!!!!!!!!

29. Being too familiar or excessively chatty.

30. Having a visible reaction to the amount of the tip.

31. Ignoring obvious attempts to get attention.

32. Making light of a guest's complaint.

33. No sense of humor.

34. Orders that arrive incomplete.

35. Not acknowledging guests as soon as they're seated.

36. Not providing service to tables in order of their arrival.

37. Wrong pacing: meal service too fast or too slow.

38. Not providing a place for meal debris—e.g., shells!

39. Food sitting visible on gueridon.

40. Necessary condiments that don't arrive with food.

41. Lack of eye contact.

42. Talking to the order pad.

43. Not repeating each item as the guest orders.

44. Not naming each item as you serve.

45. Addressing the woman as "the lady." (Times are changing!)

46. Thumbs on the plate during service.

47. Stacking or scraping dishes in front of guests.

48. Approaching a table with another table's dirty dishes.

49. Entering the guests' conversation without invitation.

50. Interrupting or asking questions while a guest's mouth is full.

51. Handling silverware by the eating surfaces.

52. Holding glasses by the bowl or rim.

53. Language that is too formal or casual.

54. Asking men for their orders before asking women.

55. Not having total focus when at the table.

56. Giving guests the feeling of being "processed."

57. Not really listening when spoken to.

58. Being too hurried to be attentive.

59. Not establishing rapport with the guests.

60. Appearing stressed or out of control.

61. Not bringing something the guest requests.

62. Providing inconsistent service. (Dig down, you can do it.)

63. Not bringing a replacement (sugar, butter, etc.) before taking the empty one away.

64. Not removing extra place settings.

65. Inability to answer basic menu questions.

66. Not knowing what brands are carried at the bar.

67. Placing a cocktail napkin askew or upside down.

68. Not warning about hot plates or beverages.

69. Dropping plates instead of presenting them.

70. Not bringing all the serviceware needed for the menu item.

71. Serving with an elbow in the guest's face.

72. Inconsistent service methods.

73. Not refilling water or coffee.

74. Not moving with the "speed of the room."

75. Not checking back within a few minutes of serving the course.

76. Not visually checking on each table regularly.

77. Not clearing one course completely before serving the next (e.g., toast, finger bowls).

78. Removing plates before all guests are finished.

79. Clearing plates without permission.

80. Not clearing plates promptly.

81. Vanishing waiters.

82. Not continuing to service the table once you have presented the check.

83. Watching while the guest completes the credit card slip.

84. Dribbling wine on the table while pouring.

85. Resting the wine bottle on the rim of the glass.

86. Spilling food or beverage.

87. Wet, stained, or incorrectly added checks.

88. Poor personal sanitation practices (touching, scratching, etc.).

89. Standing around doing nothing.

90. Using poor grammar when addressing a guest.

91. Pointing in the dining room.

92. Rattling pocket change.

93. Walking past items dropped on the floor!!!!!!!!!!!!!!

94. Answering a question with a question.

95. Soiled or ill-fitting uniforms.

96. Filthy footwear.

97. Slouching or poor posture.

98. Distracting accessories.

99. Obvious hangovers.

100. Bandages on hand.

101. Smelling like cigarettes.

102. Excuses for anything—anytime.

103. Personal conversations loud enough for guests to hear.

104. Whining or complaining.

105. Arguments or displayed anger.

106. Flirting with guests.

107. Speaking in incomplete sentences.

108. Not serving hot food hot.

109. Cold bread or rolls stale around the edges.

110. Incomplete orders.

111. Improperly chilled wine or beer.

112. Drinks without a stirrer or straw.

113. Improper glassware.

114. Dried-out or slimy fruit garnish.

115. Lukewarm coffee.

116. Overly strong or weak iced tea.

117. No fresh glass with a fresh drink.

118. Water, iced tea, or coffee not promptly refilled.

119. Coffee in the saucer!!!!!!!!!!!!!!!!!!

120. Pouring anything from a stained container.

121. Awkward, improper, or inept wine service.

122. Popping a Champagne cork.

123. Pouring regular coffee into a cup instead of decaf.

124. Not getting the order right the first time.

125. Serving the wrong drink.

126. Not serving wine promptly.

127. Dirty or spotted flatware.

128. Crumbs on chairs.

129. To be continued . . .

THE KEY TO THE CELLAR
THE WINE DIRECTOR

Even if you don't know that much about wine, a walk through Le Bernardin's cellar is awfully seductive. In the narrow, chilly storage area located next to the bus station upstairs in the Salon is a floor-to-ceiling row of Domaine de la Romanée-Conti, including a few magnums; a cubby filled with '82 Cheval Blanc; rare boutique chardonnays from California; an $8000 bottle of Pétrus.

THE NUMBERS

Bottles in the restaurant cellar	14,000
Bottles in storage in New Jersey	6630
Wine list selections	900
Percent of customers who order red wine	30
Percent of customers who order California chardonnay	40
Bottles of Domaine de la Romanée-Conti sold annually	200
Bottles of Domaine de la Romanée-Conti allotted the restaurant annually	300–400

(additional bottles are acquired through auctions and other distributors)

Sommeliers	4
Women sommeliers	3

The room, with its basic plywood shelving stretching twelve feet high and twenty feet long, is unremarkable, but you can get drunk on power just standing there.

Le Bernardin has a new wine director. By the age of thirty-three, the Austrian sommelier Aldo Sohm had made a name for himself in New York after holding the position at Wallsé restaurant in 2004. He has since won sommelier competitions, including the 2008 prize from the Worldwide Sommelier Association. And now, at thirty-six, he's in charge of one of New York's most prestigious wine lists.

Because the restaurant attracts wine lovers who are willing to pay for the best, "everyone wants to be on Le Bernardin's list," Sohm says. "It's very, very helpful, but it can also be a headache, because you have to filter." Still, the restaurant gets the biggest allocation of Romanée-Conti and Domaine Leflaive in the United States and has first pick of cult California chardonnays such as Kistler cabernet and Peter Michael, Sea Smoke pinot noir, and Araujo—"my headache wines," as he calls them, because they're so popular yet so hard to get.

Since he began in May 2007, Sohm has set about tasting every dish and sauce on the menu to determine which wines pair best. He's also been rethinking the wine list. "As a wine director, you see the first results after half a year; after a year you see it completely," he explains. "My first signature is to bring in more grower Champagnes—even American sparklings. Then I want to bring the wines back to Burgundy, which match incredibly well with our food. And then wines with less oak, more minerality—a big step in these oaky times." He is also restructuring the restaurant's German and Austrian selection. "I was very careful, because in the media it was expected that I would go very heavy on Germany and Austria. But I didn't. I saw the German part of the wine list was a little old-fashioned. I tried to put it in a new-fashioned way, which means away from the sweetness, focusing on extreme minerality and on dry-style wines, which are trendy and which matter to our food."

Matching wines to the spice-infused sauces can be tricky; it can also pose problems for sommeliers, who are understandably eager to serve their best

THE RAREST BOTTLES
IN THE CELLAR

La Tâche Grand Cru—Domaine de la Romanée-Conti 1990	$5000
Romanée Conti—Domaine de la Romanée-Conti 1996	3550
Vosne-Romanée 1er Cru Cros Parantoux—Domaine Méo-Camuzet 1996	1300
Château Pétrus, Pomerol 1982	8000
Château Lafite Rothschild 1961	5000
Château Margaux 1990 (Magnum)	5000
Château Cheval Blanc 1982	3300
Meursault 1er Cru "Rougeots"—Domaine J-F Coche-Dury 1989	3000
Paul Jaboulet Aîné Hermitage "La Chapelle" 1983	1170
Château de Beaucastle 1989	2600

THE BEST REDS
TO DRINK WITH FISH

Wine director Aldo Sohm's top choices, in order of his preference

Vosne-Romanée 1er Cru "Les Beaux Monts"—Domaine Daniel Rion '01	$130
Morey-Saint-Denis 1er Cru "Les Chauffots"—Domaine Hubert Lignier '01	195
Chambolle Musigny Vieilles Vignes Domaine Comte de Vogue 1999	430
Domaine des Lambrays Clos des Lambrays 1998	320
Château Pichon de Longueville Baron 1999	250
Château Trotanoy Pomerol 1998	600
Giuseppe Quintarelli Valpolicella Superiore 1998	165
Barbaresco Costa Russi Gaja 1990	820
Flowers Pinot Noir "Andreen-Gale Cuvée" Sonoma Coast 2004	140
Cabernet Sauvignon Robert Stemmler Sonoma 1991	100

wines, but who may conquer the food in the process. "For instance, with some big chardonnays and California reds, the food doesn't stand a chance," Sohm says. He and the four sommeliers he oversees meet frequently to review the menu and discuss suitable wine pairings. "We taste a lot, especially the sauces. Whenever I have time, I sit down with a dish and six glasses of different styles of wines—oaked and non-oaked chardonnay; non-oaked, like a sauvignon blanc; an aromatic variety, like a Riesling or a Condrieu, even different styles of reds. We sip and see what matches and what doesn't, to get what kind of direction we should move with this dish."

Some diners are surprised to find such an extensive offering of red wines in a fish restaurant, but they're even more surprised to learn that the white-wine myth doesn't hold. "There are naturally more tannins in red wines than in whites, especially in cabernet sauvignon and syrah, which can make them seem bitter when they're drunk with fish," says Sohm. "So I try to find wines with less astringency and more smoothness, and a little bit of acidity to balance the food. Since the movie *Sideways*, everything changed anyway to pinot noir! We're still very strong on Burgundies, but we're running into conflict a little bit with Chef because he prefers to drink Bordeaux. We found a way to make him happy: You just have to get a really ripe Bordeaux. Not just top ones; you can even serve him a ripe second growth from 2001 all the way down to 1997, in which the fruit is more delicate and refined; the tannins are more on the velvety side, complementing the fish."

Sohm is a compulsive organizer. ("I'm Central European! I spend a lot of time in the cellar double-checking things.") His first challenge was to completely rearrange and organize the cellar ("The entire Salon was full of bottles for two days; we had to carve out little paths") and update the computer system. Soon the wine program, like this now meticulous wine cellar, will bear his stamp.

A WINE FOR EVERY SPICE

"Pairing wines with the spices that Chef Ripert loves is the challenge in my job," says wine director Aldo Sohm. "These are my best recommendations."

Asian-inspired dishes: Certain Alsatian styles of wines—the richer Tokay Pinot Gris Schwarzber '02 from Dirler, for example, or the more delicate and refreshing Sylvaner "Z" '02 from Kubler—or modern dry-style Rieslings from Germany—the easygoing but superb Tesch '06 Riesling St. Remigiusberg Spaetlese Dry or the powerful, super-mineral Riesling "Kastanienbusch" Grosses Gewaechs '05 from Oekonomierat Rebholz—work with no problem at all; they cover the spiciness of the food with a little residual sugar. Certain Loire wines, such as Vouvrays, also work well.

Béarnaise sauce: Because of its slightly sour and fruity elements, you can go with a red, such as a California pinot noir. What's even more exciting is to go into a ripe Burgundy, 2001 vintage or even older, down to '98, '97.

Cardamom: Its acidity magnifies the acidity of the wine. Since the focus at Le Bernardin is so strong on Burgundy, I recommend a little bit of an aged style like Corton-Charlemagne that will give you richness, earthiness, even nuttiness, as well as a similar exotic spice.

Caviar: At the 2004 sommelier world championship, one of the most frequent questions was what to serve with caviar. A lot of people recommended only one thing: Australian Riesling, which I couldn't understand. Personally, I'm very traditional with caviar. I serve it with Champagne, without a doubt.

Lemongrass: It's simple for me because it has green, fresh flavors, so I choose a sauvignon-blanc-based wine, or a viognier-based wine like Condrieu, which has similar green elements and a slightly low acidity. You just have to be careful which other spices are in the sauce.

Raw fish: Here you need something lighter, more delicate, something with punchy minerality: a Chassagne-Montrachet Morgeot from Henri Germain, a wonderful premier-cru vineyard.

Surf-and-turf: I'd choose a Burgundy, a Vosne-Romanée, something richer or with more earthiness. You can even go with a ripe Bordeaux.

Tandoori: I'd choose a California wine because the wine has a pretty rich taste. Currently we serve the dish with a buttery chardonnay from Kistler, even though it's not my style at all.

Wasabi: Right now we're having trouble pairing wines with the salmon with pea-wasabi sauce. The pea has a sweet taste, and a lot of chlorophyll, too. Then comes the spicy wasabi, which is kind of hard to handle. Then on top of that comes the salmon; if you go too harsh on the minerality, such as a Meursault, the wine will seem tannic, even though it's a white. You get a velvety feeling on your palate that's almost like fur. So you need to go with something a little softer, a little more on the aged side. You could even try a California chardonnay. But the better thing to go with is an aromatic variety, such as a dry muscat with a lower acidity to soften it out. The residual sugar of a new-style Austrian Riesling, which has four grams to the typical two grams of most whites, manages to balance the spiciness from the wasabi. I like the Sylvaner "Z" '05 from Domaine Paul Kubler in Alsace.

DINING IN PRIVATE
LES SALONS

For those who wonder when Le Bernardin is going to open a second location, they already have—and it's even closer than you think. Go through the dining room and take a right. Up the stairs you might be greeted with cocktails and hors d'oeuvres, then shown into one of three private rooms.

Or perhaps the partitions will be raised to make room for ninety guests. The quality of the meal and the level of service are identical to downstairs. The only difference is that this kitchen, smaller than the one downstairs, will send out up to ninety of the same dish in rapid succession, so that guests eat almost simultaneously.

The kitchen is about one third the size of the one downstairs, which is already compact by restaurant standards. During service, one to three sous-chefs and up to six cooks from the main kitchen are dispatched to prepare the meal (or meals; there are generally three events at the same time), returning downstairs to finish the rest of their shift the moment the last entrée leaves through the sliding doors.

This three-ring four-star circus is a two-woman show. Since 2000, Karin Burroughs and an assistant, Kate Zmigrodsky, have operated the baby Bernardin out of a modest room in the basement headquarters. They serve as reservationists, event planners, food and wine advisers, florists, lighting designers, staff managers, customized menu printers, and concierges six nights a week for up to 288 parties a year serving 24,000 diners.

Cheerful, outgoing, and corporate in a way that makes them stand out when they walk through the kitchen, clipboards in hand, they're as unruffled when asked to provide an ice sculpture of a meerkat as they are when determining if the restaurant's teak ceiling can support a trapeze artist. (It can.)

During lunch, the events are mostly business get-togethers, product launches, and media events. Nearby investment banks, such as Goldman Sachs and BNP Paribas, use the space for entertaining clients, most of whom have to be back at the office in an hour. At dinner, it's corporate but more celebratory: law

firm acquisitions, financial deal closings, board meals. Weekends are for birthdays, anniversaries, and small weddings.

The Salon, as it's often referred to, is extremely important in terms of revenue, says David Mancini, general manager. "The dining room has x number of chairs; you can't put in any more seats to increase revenue. You have hours of operation that limit you. But we have a clear playing field and great revenue streams in the Salon."

Years ago, the Salon was an afterthought. If the staff didn't make it in the dining room, they were sent to the Salon. Even the uniforms were different. Today it's on equal footing in terms of service—the only difference is that business meetings can be completely private—and selection.

PART FOUR

THE BUSINESS

The first person in the office in the morning is usually one of three reservationists. She puts on her headset, logs on to a program that could probably be used to direct flights at JFK, and, before the lines even open at nine o'clock, starts returning calls. "Good morning, Le Bernardin. This is Sviatlana speaking. How may I assist you? May I please put you on hold?"

Only reservationists with "a smile in their voice" are hired. An accent doesn't hurt. Or having Balthazar on your résumé. Or patience with those who insist on an eight o'clock table for six—tonight, claiming they know Eric/Ben/Maguy/the wine critic at *The New York Times*.

"If you've been here, you're in the system," says Sylvie Ordonez, who has sat at a cubicle for three years. She clicks on a name from the evening's list and up pops the guest's number of visits (285 is the record), cancellations, and preferences noted by the maître d' and dining staff ("CEO, wants table 2, requests Mark as captain, only eats well-done Kobe beef with ketchup"). "The system doesn't lie." The lower corner of her screen shows the number of callers on hold. Because it's the first of the month—the day when tables for the following month open up—that number hovers around fifteen all morning. Since there are only thirty tables available for each service, disappointing people is part of the job. But they learn to do it gently, offering waiting lists or alternate dates. On the rare occasion, they can be swayed to bump someone up on the waiting list. (Just don't try it for Valentine's Day: Last year the list was 115 people long.)

DIRECTOR OF MOVING PARTS

At a certain point, Maguy Le Coze and Eric Ripert decided that life could be easier if they brought in someone from outside the restaurant—preferably someone with a more corporate background—to help them run it more efficiently.

But when David Mancini, then the director of restaurants and catering for the Metropolitan Museum of Art in New York, interviewed for the position in 2003, he thought he didn't stand "a snowball's chance. First of all, I'm not French," he says with a laugh. "But when Eric said to me, 'I want to run this company like an American company, not a French company,' I knew I had a better chance." In the ensuing four years, he's brought in systems of standardization (an employee handbook, a sexual-harassment policy, a 401[k] plan for all workers) and management that the restaurant had never had before. Perhaps more important, he even standardized emergencies.

"Standardization can be an ugly word, but in a time of crisis, you need to be able to do certain things quickly and efficiently," he says. "If Ben [Chekroun] calls me at eleven P.M. and says, 'David, we have no gas. What do I do?' I'm able to tell him who to call, right up to the president of the company. And we have woken presidents of companies at one, two in the morning—electric, gas, linen. I mean, the president of the linen company has been called at one-thirty in the morning, being told, we're preparing for a big day tomorrow and all our linen is horrible. I thought that was a little harsh, but all our vendors know that we are extremely particular, and they know we concentrate on the detail."

Luckily, details are Mancini's stock in trade, since, as he puts it, "there are a lot of moving parts here. I mean that figuratively and literally, because it's a twenty-two-year-old restaurant, and things happen. Parts that I haven't even thought of are starting to move." Rusty pipes break behind the bar. Grease traps crack and empty into the health club below in the middle of the day. (This has happened so many times that the restaurant sends the club complimentary dinners. "We have a great relationship with them now," notes Mancini.) Refrigerators filled with tens of thousands of dollars worth of food conk out overnight. At one point, the air pressure between the first and second floors of the twenty-story building was imbalanced, causing food odors to linger in the upstairs law firm, which almost sued. "There were some real challenges right off the bat," Mancini admits with a sheepish grin.

Having such emergency procedures in place—and there will always be an emergency—allows a restaurant to focus on more important matters, such as growth. "When Gilbert was here, the food was great and the company was maturing," says Mancini. "Since Eric took over, the food has matured. But there are other parts of the company that didn't keep up: the infrastructure of running the company, personnel files, how we hire. Nobody wrote profiles of what we're looking for in terms of a candidate; it was just, whoever walked through the door, did we like them? We now have profiles we have created for each position in the company.

"So much time was spent on the table and the dish that not enough time was spent on running the operation, and I take great pride in coming in and trying to do that. But none of it would happen if Maguy and Eric weren't so open

- Le Bernardin is a company that's in the business of being a restaurant, and there are three components for being a good company: In this case it's the cuisine, the service, and the management. And all have three common denominators: quality, consistency, and attention to detail in every aspect.
- Don't lower your quality for short-term profitability, even if you have a tight month. We're never going to stop ordering lobster and truffles.
- The service should exceed the guests' expectations. It's a cliché, but it's really hard to do. Also, service must be intuitive and anticipatory: Did conversation just stop at table thirty-four? Time to refill the wine.
- Management must define the playing field for everybody, from the kitchen to the dining room. We do this through our employee handbook and by being firm, fair, and consistent.
- Be humble and maintain a sense of balance. Remember how you got where you are. Shun celebrity status and be a celebrity within your own company.
- Keep growth under control. You can be great and not be large.
- Promote from within; we've had captains who started as dishwashers. But be sure to give the employee expectations and information about the new role to be able to succeed.
- Diversity is key. Our dining room staff comes from around the world, and we're bringing in more women.
- Build loyalty. Promoting from within is one way to do it. We also offer everyone full medical benefits after six months and a 401(k) plan after one year, and we pay a finder's fee to those who bring in good candidates.
- Praise in public and criticize in private. Easier said than done.
- Set the standard at the top. Maguy and Eric work long hours and demand a lot from themselves; everyone here follows suit.

to change. They don't mind hearing a dissenting point of view. They're confident, they understand themselves, they work within themselves, they're humble. They know they need to hire people who are decision-makers, and listen to those opinions."

Mancini and Maguy Le Coze are in constant contact, no matter where Le Coze is in the world. Every week he writes a recap for her, and together they regularly go over the profit-and-loss statement. "For someone untrained in accounting, she does better than anybody I know," he says. "She's ruthless about the numbers. And she should be." (During their weekly P&L meetings with their accountant, Frédérique Reginensi, Le Coze literally goes down the small-type list with a ruler, questioning expenses from food costs to credit-card fees and a company called Fix My Gasket ["They only fix the refrigerator gaskets!" she said with only-in-New-York delight].)

"Everybody has said the biggest change has been her," says Mancini. "Everybody told me when I got here: 'Be careful. She's really tough to work for.' That hasn't changed. She's tough. But she and Eric listen a lot. And great companies listen a lot."

In four short years, Mancini has had a visible impact on the company, and not just in terms of averting disasters. One of his proudest accomplishments is the hiring of many more women since he's been with the restaurant. He's also busy working with maître d' Ben Chekroun to finalize the restaurant's first training manual for waitstaff. In between, there's a new kitchen to install in the Salon, air-conditioning to even out, new silver to order.

For Mancini, the only kind of day is one in which nothing actually appears wrong to diners. "There is a public image and a private image, and the public image always, absolutely has to stay the same," he explains. "Sometimes you have to make it work with tape and wire, but the guests can never see us sweat. They never see a blip or a glitch. Those are the most satisfying days for me, when you can improvise and it looks flawless."

THE CHARITY CONNECTION

Mandy Oser is Ripert's director of strategic partnerships and his right hand, pretty much in charge of his life at work. She also handles all media and the legal aspect of most projects. On this particular day, she pulls a thick folder from a filing cabinet. It holds the charity requests the restaurant has said no to so far this year. It's the beginning of May.

Le Bernardin has long been active on the charity circuit, doing up to three events a month, whether it's cooking meals that are bid on at auctions or setting up a table at a benefit, cooking in someone's home, or donating tables or a private room at the restaurant. In fact, the dry-erase calendar hanging on Ripert's office wall gets only four types of events written on it: press, travel, vacation, and charity.

"Yes, it's all tax-deductible and promotional," says Ripert, "but that's not the drive. We do it because we feel for it, we have a connection, like with City Harvest." The twenty-five-year-old organization collects leftover food from restaurants every day and delivers it to area soup kitchens and others in need; Ripert is on its board. The restaurant has a dedicated refrigerator into which everything from leftover staff meals to Kobe beef and fresh pea shoots is put for the afternoon pickup. "New York has so much great food left over, so we support City Harvest. To me, there's no other way," says Ripert. "I don't feel good about succeeding, making money, while people starve. We're not talking about a third-world country, we're talking about down the block."

Ripert, a practicing Buddhist, also supports Tibet House in New York and the Tibetan Aid Society in San Francisco out of gratitude to what they've brought to his life. "I'm so thankful to those people who have shared their philosophy with me," he says. Le Coze is a passionate champion of cancer charities (her mother died of breast cancer), and the restaurant also donates to Citymeals-on-Wheels, various Hurricane Katrina recovery efforts, and the James Beard Foundation. ("Even with the scandals years ago, it's still the best nonprofit organization for chefs. They've done a tremendous job promoting the industry.")

"We're constantly giving back," Ripert says. "One year I calculated that we spent around $200,000 of our own money to help raise millions of dollars for charities. The benefit is that we feel good about it, of course, and we feel passionate about it. There's also the visibility aspect that's beneficial to the restaurant; you can't quantify it. At our level we don't treat it like a business," he says. But each event requires an increasing outlay of time, staff, and food costs. "It's becoming a bit of a burden for us," he admits. "It's hard for me to participate in a benefit and then get reimbursed for my staff or the food—I'd rather the money go to the charity—but now sometimes we have to because we're talking about cooking for six hundred people." For larger events—a request for a station and five hundred portions, for example—even pastry chef Michael Laiskonis also comes, so two chefs represent the restaurant.

In the end, says Ripert, "For Maguy and me, being able to contribute has been one of the best benefits of having a successful restaurant."

GIVING TILL IT HELPS:
HOW TO FEED 500 IN CHICAGO

Rarely does the restaurant get to cook in its own kitchen for a charity event. And rarely will the restaurant use another kitchen's ingredients. At this point, they have the packing list down pat. Here's what they send:

- 1 executive sous-chef (usually Eric Gestel)
- 1 sous-chef
- 2 cooks
- 4 knife kits, FedExed ahead to avoid airport security
- 4 bottles Sitia extra virgin olive oil
- 300 pounds fish and 2 kilograms caviar, packed in ice and sealed in Styrofoam coolers
- 1 box sea salt
- 5 coolers filled with produce, such as hard-to-find micro greens.
- 1 aerator gun with extra CO_2 cartridges, used to froth mashed potatoes, sauces, or dessert

Average Costs

Transportation and shipping	$300–500
Ingredients	$6000

Ripert Consulting

While his peers were becoming household names, or simply rich, Ripert stayed in the kitchen. It wasn't until his son was born in 2004 that he realized that making more money for his family and his staff wasn't necessarily a bad thing. The question was how to do it in a way that didn't take away from Le Bernardin. He believed it would be fatal—if not impossible—to try to replicate the restaurant. ("Our baby is very demanding and very fragile. It's not like we're dealing with a concept that's easy to manage. You have to be focused at all times. This is not a yacht, this is a cruise ship, and you don't move a cruise ship the way you move a high-speed boat.")

With Maguy's blessing, he began Ripert Consulting, an independent business that would generate the money needed to keep the key players at the restaurant loyal while freeing him from his kitchen duties to go out and make a bigger name for Le Bernardin.

That same year, he was approached by Michael Ryan of the Ritz-Carlton on Cayman Island to bring his food and name to two restaurants in its new Caribbean resort. The offer was irresistible: Ritz-Carlton would provide everything except the chef de cuisine and the menu. "Basically we take care of creativity and assisting them in evaluating the business to make sure the

standards are respected," says Ripert. "They manage the business with their own human resources department and their own philosophy. The chef comes from us, so he understands the food; the rest is Ritz-Carlton style. We now have a license for three restaurants with them: Blue in the Grand Cayman; Westend Bistro in Washington, D.C.; and 10 Arts in Philadelphia."

In addition, Ripert Consulting has advised the hotelier André Balazs on his Miami properties and has been testing the television and branding waters. Michelle Lindsay is the director of operations, in charge of translating Le Bernardin's food for all new projects.

FOOD COSTS EXPLAINED

In a perfect restaurant world, food costs should be 30 percent of sales. But a host of factors, from the weakening dollar to the spike in gas prices, has had an impact on Le Bernardin's profit. "For fifteen years, our food costs were 30 percent for the year," says Ripert. "In 2007 we started to have some problems, but we kind of maintained it. The next year it exploded. The euro is very high. We use a lot of olive oils and products from Europe.

BARGAIN OF THE CENTURY

When you consider that a three-course menu is $64 at lunch, some of the choices begin to look like steals. Here's what certain dishes cost the restaurant to make (not including labor):

Mushroom appetizer	$10.89
Codfish entrée	16.92
Monkfish entrée	14.71
Baked lobster entrée	27.58
Organic Scottish salmon	16.90
Surf-and-turf (Japanese Kobe beef and escolar) entrée	20.36

Fish costs have risen dramatically due to supply and demand and the price of gas. So we have a hard time keeping the costs where they are. Take a dish like the wild salmon at dinner. It's $22 a pound. Then you add the truffle—we don't skimp; we use the real truffle, not oil. It's a dish that costs us easily $25 to $30, depending on the size of the salmon. We're not going to make money on that diner. We have to multiply by 3.3 to get 30 percent—that's 99 bucks for one dish. Then you add the bread, the canapé, the butter, the appetizer, the second appetizer, the dessert, and the cookies. That order screws us up completely, and it's a dish we sell a lot. Eventually we make the money on the wine.

The difference between French and American restaurants is that in America it's understood and expected to spend money on wine. In France, they're willing to spend more on the food.

"The theory is that your prime cost—the food cost and wine cost together—is one of your percentages. Then you add the labor cost. That gives you about 60 percent if you manage well. Operating costs are about 30 percent in New York. So your theoretical profit is 10 percent—if it's managed properly, exactly by the books. So our profit is sliding. If we didn't have the volume we have, we'd be bankrupt. It's impossible to serve the quality we do for the price that we charge."

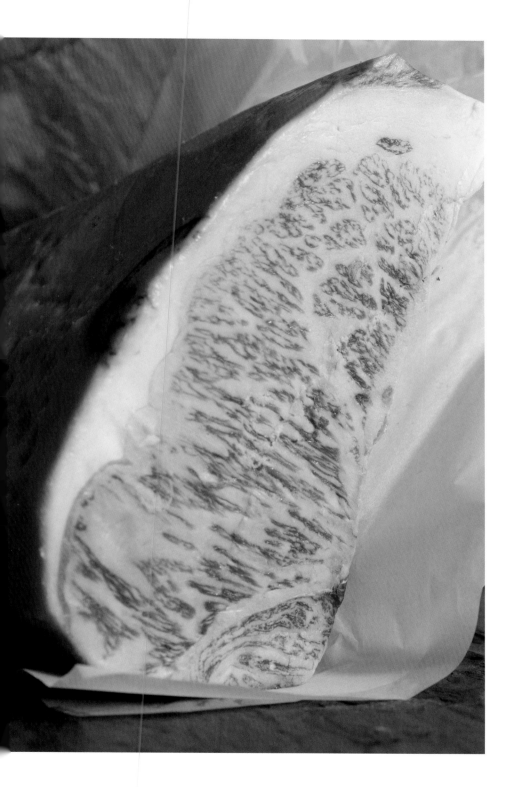

THE HIGH PRICE OF LUXURY

What are some of the more expensive ingredients?

Bonito
(from Japan): $300/package.
"Because it's double thick, double shaved, double smoked," says Muller.

Canned black truffles
(from France): $200/can.
"April through November, when we can't get them fresh, we'll buy like 400 cans. That's $80,000 right there. At any given moment, we have 15 cans sitting upstairs," says Muller.

Caviar:
$125/ounce Iranian Osetra;
$42/ounce farm-raised Italian.

Foie gras
(from New York State): $36/pound.

Fresh yuzu
(from Asia): $4/each.
"This little citrus is imported from Japan—when we can get it. We go through about twenty a week and grate them on salmon ceviche and sea urchin foam."

Kobe beef
(from Japan): $72/pound.

Langoustines
(from Iceland): $4.50/each.

Organic soy sauce:
$90/bottle.
"Charlie Trotter turned us on to this stuff about six years ago. You can't even compare it to regular soy. They bring it in through little fish bellies or something like that," jokes Muller. "We were braising pork belly in it, going through twelve bottles every two weeks."

Setia extra virgin olive oil
(from Greece): $30/750 milliliters.

Smoked salt
(from Denmark): $115/pound.
"You can get this stuff for $3 a pound, but it's not even close," says Muller.

Solera vinegar
(from Spain): $125/4-ounce bottle.
"We use a few drops on the octopus dish."

Truffle jus (from France): $60/12-ounce can.

STARSTRUCK AND BEYOND

Le Bernardin has long been at the top of critics' lists, from *The New York Times* to *New York* magazine, as well as democratic guides such as Zagat. But when it was among four New York restaurants to receive three stars in the first *Michelin Guide to New York* in October 2005, it changed the business

THE BEST WAYS TO GET A TABLE

- Call at 9 A.M. on the first business day of the month.

- Try for a reservation on off days and times: a 7:00 table is easier to come by on Mondays and Tuesdays; be willing to eat at 5:15 or 10:00 on Fridays or Saturdays.

- If you're trying for a last-minute table, call at 2 P.M., when unconfirmed tables are released for the same evening.

- Reservationists like it when callers are precise about dates and times. Have alternate dates and times ready just in case.

- Pray for bad weather, which leads to cancellations—even on Valentine's Day.

- Get to know maître d' Ben Chekroun. He's the true keeper of the tables.

in a new way. "That same day we were flooded with reservations," says Ripert. "We're still learning about its impact. It gave us a whole new clientele, mostly upscale Europeans and Japanese whom we didn't necessarily have before." The morning that the staff found out they'd won three stars, Ripert was running around the office and kitchen, spraying everyone with Champagne (he got approval from the sommelier to use Krug), and everyone was hugging. Le Coze, who was on her way back to New York from Paris, allegedly cried throughout the entire flight. That night, they threw a party in the Salon that lasted until all hours, featuring platters of barbecue from a local barbecue restaurant—without a doubt the most meat that's ever been served at Le Bernardin.

But the story doesn't end there. A Michelin inspector can come in any day; different ones are sent throughout the year, making them hard to recognize. (Sometimes the staff thinks they can spot one: "by his attitude," said one captain; "by his accent," said another; "the way he ordered," said the maître d'.) And stars from Michelin and *The New York Times* are no longer the only critical forces driving business to the restaurant. These days, says Ripert, food blogs are important, too. "In terms of younger clientele, we can't underestimate their power," he says. "Grub Street, eGullet, Eater, even Daily Candy, all influence younger diners today. You can't be insensitive to the media."

As for the future, Ripert and Le Coze take nothing for granted. They don't know whether they will be able to renegotiate the lease when it expires in 2011, but they believe they would not be able to re-create Le Bernardin in another location. And even if they can stay for another twenty-five years, says Ripert, there's no guarantee that the support from the public and the media will still be there. "After all," he says, "you're only as good as your last meal."

"Maguy and I have a lot of interaction and discussion. We have a good game: if I have an idea and I think I'm right, my job is to convince Maguy. If I can't, we kill the idea. And it's the same if she has an idea. And I think that gives us a lot of strength."

—Eric Ripert

PART FIVE

THE RECIPES

Like the restaurant itself, the food that we serve is always evolving. Inspiration for a new dish or direction can come from anywhere, whether it's a flavor I recall from a trip to Barcelona or a barbecue sauce made by a line cook for a staff meal (it was fantastic with skate). The following recipes are my favorites from recent years—the result of a lot of collaborative effort, reflecting the taste memories and creativity of so many of us here in the Le Bernardin kitchen—along with my own stories and tips, and sketches from my notebooks.

The recipes are organized by the station at which they're prepared, as described on pages 27–29. Those from the monk and sauce stations are main courses. Those from garde-manger, vegetable, and hot apps are designed as appetizers, but most can be doubled to serve the same number of people as entrées. The dessert recipes (pages 204–19) are by pastry chef Michael Laiskonis.

SALMON

WILD ALASKAN AND SMOKED SALMON WITH APPLE, CELERY, AND BABY WATERCRESS AND JALAPEÑO EMULSION

This simple appetizer epitomizes Le Bernardin's philosophy of food: the fish is the star, and every other ingredient has to highlight it. One of our cooks, Soa Davies, created it; it was so perfect that we put it on the menu without changing a thing. The texture of the rich fish and the light and delicate apple sets up a delightful contrast.

SERVES 4

PHOTOGRAPH ON
PAGE 86

THE JALAPEÑO EMULSION
½ cup minced jalapeños
   (seeds removed)
1 teaspoon minced shallot
6 tablespoons extra virgin
   olive oil
¼ cup fresh lemon juice
Fine sea salt and freshly ground
   white pepper

THE APPLE SLICES
1 large Granny Smith apple

THE SALMON
5 ounces wild Alaskan salmon
5 ounces smoked salmon
Fine sea salt and freshly ground
   black pepper
¼ cup extra virgin olive oil

THE GARNISH
½ Granny Smith apple,
   cut into ¼-inch-thick julienne
1 celery stalk, peeled and cut
   into thin half-moons
1 teaspoon celery leaf julienne
1 teaspoon Italian parsley julienne
½ petal Lemon Confit (PAGE 224),
   briefly blanched and minced
Fine sea salt and freshly ground
   black pepper
½ teaspoon extra virgin olive oil
Juice of ½ lemon
4 slices jalapeño
¼ cup micro watercress

For the jalapeño emulsion, combine the jalapeños, shallot, olive oil, and lemon juice in a blender and process until smooth and emulsified. Season to taste with salt and white pepper. Transfer to a container and refrigerate until ready to use.

For the apple slices, peel the apple and slice ¼ inch thick, using a mandoline; you need 20 slices. Trim the slices into rectangles about 2½ inches by 1 inch. Blanch the slices in boiling water for about 2 seconds, then cool in an ice bath. Drain and pat dry with a paper towel.

Slice the wild salmon into 12 rectangles, each about 2½ inches by 1 inch. Trim the edges to make even edges. Repeat with the smoked salmon.

To assemble, arrange the salmon and apple slices down the center of each plate, overlapping them slightly, in the following order: wild salmon, apple, smoked salmon, apple; repeat two more times, and finish with a slice of smoked salmon (3 slices wild salmon, 5 slices apple, and 3 slices smoked salmon per plate). Season with salt and pepper and drizzle extra virgin olive oil over and around the salmon and apples on each plate.

In a small bowl, combine the julienned apple, the celery, celery leaf, parsley, and lemon confit. Season with salt and pepper and toss with the olive oil and lemon juice. Arrange the garnish over the salmon and apples and sprinkle with the jalapeño slices and watercress. Spoon about 2 tablespoons of the jalapeño emulsion over and around each plate, and serve immediately.

Wearing plastic gloves will prevent any reaction while removing the seeds from the jalapeños

FLUKE

WHITE-SOY-YUZU-MARINATED FLUKE,
SEAWEED, AND SPICED "RICE CRISPIES"

David Kinch, the incredible chef at Manresa in
Los Gatos, California, introduced me to this white
soy sauce. It's not as pungent as soy, it doesn't stain
the food, and it has a wonderful caramely taste,
but it's too liquid to adhere to the fish. We were
looking for a way to add some body to it when we
remembered the "magic powder" (xanthan gum)
that Michael Laiskonis was using in the pastry
department. The "rice crispies" need to be started
one to two days before you plan to serve the dish.

SERVES 4

PHOTOGRAPH ON
PAGE 84

THE SPICED RICE CRISPIES
¼ cup sushi rice
¾ cup water
2 tablespoons rice wine vinegar
Fine sea salt and freshly ground
  white pepper
Espelette pepper powder
Canola oil for deep-frying

THE FLUKE
8 ounces sushi-quality fluke fillet
½ teaspoon xanthan gum
  (SEE SOURCES, PAGE 229)
¼ cup water
¼ cup white soy sauce
2 teaspoons yuzu juice
1 teaspoon fresh lemon juice
Espelette pepper powder

THE SEAWEED
2 pieces frozen aki nori, defrosted
  and torn into twenty 1-inch pieces
1 small sheet dried yaki nori,
  toasted in a hot pan for
  3 seconds on each side, then
  cut into 20 julienne strips

For the "rice crispies," soak the
rice in cold water to cover for
30 minutes.
  Preheat the oven to 375°F.
  Drain the rice and put it in a
small baking dish. Add the ¾ cup
water, the rice wine vinegar, salt,
white pepper, and Espelette pepper
to taste. Cover, transfer to the oven,
and cook, for about 25 minutes,

until the rice is tender (the rice will
not have absorbed all the water).
  Spread the rice in an even layer
on a Silpat-lined baking sheet. Dry
the rice in a 180°F oven overnight
or a very dry place for 2 days, or
until completely dry and brittle.
  To fry the rice, heat the canola
oil in a small deep pot to 400°F.
Fry small clumps of rice in batches
about 30 seconds per side, until it
puffs and turns golden brown.
Drain on a paper-towel-lined plate.
When it is cool, break up the rice
into 20 small pieces.
  Slice the fluke fillet into very thin
slices. Arrange one-quarter of the
slices in the center of each plate to
form a 3-by-6-inch rectangle.
  For the marinade, using a handheld immersion blender, blend the
xanthan gum into the water. Strain
through a fine-mesh sieve into a
bowl. Whisk in the white soy sauce.
  Just before serving, whisk
the yuzu and lemon juices into
the marinade.
  To serve, season the fluke with
Espelette pepper. Brush some of
the marinade onto each rectangle
of fluke, completely covering the
surface. Randomly arrange 5 pieces
of aki nori, 5 strips of yaki nori
julienne, and 5 rice crispies clusters
over each fluke rectangle. Serve
immediately.

TUNA

YELLOWFIN TUNA, FOIE GRAS, AND TOASTED BAGUETTE
WITH CHIVES AND EXTRA VIRGIN OLIVE OIL

Le Bernardin was the first restaurant in America to serve tuna carpaccio, and it's been a signature dish ever since. I never intended to change the original but when I was in Sweden with my friend Laurent Manrique, we had a venison carpaccio with foie gras. That's when I thought about using foie gras with tuna. Start the foie gras terrine three days ahead.

SERVES 4

PHOTOGRAPH ON
PAGES 82–83

THE FOIE GRAS TERRINE

1 whole Grade A foie gras
  (about 1½ pounds), soaked
  overnight in ice water
1 tablespoon fine sea salt
½ teaspoon freshly ground
  white pepper
¼ teaspoon sel rose (OPTIONAL)
6 cups Chicken Stock (PAGE 220)

THE TUNA

12 ounces sushi-quality
  yellowfin tuna

THE GARNISH

1 demi baguette (about 5 inches)
Fine sea salt and freshly
  ground white pepper
¼ cup extra virgin olive oil
2 teaspoons minced shallot
2 tablespoons thinly sliced chives
½ lemon

For the foie gras, drain the foie gras and pat dry. Cover with plastic wrap and let stand at room temperature for 1 hour.

Separate the 2 lobes, keeping one covered while you work on the other. From the underside of the foie gras, carefully slice through the lobe to the main vein. Split the foie gras apart and butterfly one lobe by making an outward cut at each side of the vein. Remove the primary vein and then the small veins throughout the foie gras. Repeat with the remaining lobe.

Mix the salt, white pepper, and sel rose together. Season the foie gras on all sides. Wrap tightly in plastic wrap and refrigerate for 24 hours.

Form the foie gras into a log approximately 2½ inches thick by 6 inches long on a piece of parchment paper, twisting and squeezing the ends so it is compact. Unwrap the foie gras and transfer to a piece of cheesecloth. Rolling away from you, roll the foie gras up into a tight log,

again twisting the ends to compress it. Tie each end with a piece of kitchen twine.

Bring the chicken stock to a boil in a pot large enough to hold the foie gras. Add the foie gras and cook for 2 minutes, or until it reaches an internal temperature of 90°F. Remove the foie gras from the stock and chill immediately.

Remove the cheesecloth and reshape the foie gras into a log one more time with plastic wrap. Refrigerate overnight.

To prepare the tuna, you'll need a template so all slices are the same size. You can use an 8-inch bread and butter plate, or a cardboard round cut to that size. Slice the tuna into ¼-inch-thick slices. Lay a large sheet of plastic wrap, at least 2 feet by 3 feet, on a work surface. Lay the tuna slices on the plastic, leaving an inch between them. Cover the tuna with another large sheet of plastic. Using a kitchen mallet, gently pound the tuna to a thin, even layer about ⅛ inch thick. Using the template and a sharp knife, cutting through both layers of plastic and the tuna, cut out four portions (reserve the trimmings for another use). Place the tuna on a baking sheet and refrigerate for at least 30 minutes. (The tuna can be prepared a few hours ahead of time.)

Preheat the oven to 350°F.

Cut the heels off the baguette and discard. Cut the bread into 4 very thin lengthwise slices. Arrange the slices on a parchment-paper-lined baking sheet and cover with another sheet of parchment paper and another baking sheet (so the slices stay flat). Toast the slices in the oven until they are lightly browned and crisp, 5 to 7 minutes. Allow the slices to cool to room temperature.

To serve, slice 4 long, thin slices (about ⅛ inch thick) of foie gras; the slices should be as long as the baguette toasts. Place a foie gras slice on top of each baguette toast, and place in the center of an oval plate. Peel off the top piece of plastic wrap from a portion of tuna, invert the tuna (so the plastic-wrapped side is in your hand), and lay it over a foie gras toast. Peel off the other piece of plastic wrap. Repeat with the remaining tuna. Season the tuna with salt and white pepper and brush with the extra virgin olive oil. Sprinkle the shallots and chives over the tuna. Squeeze a little lemon juice over each portion and serve immediately.

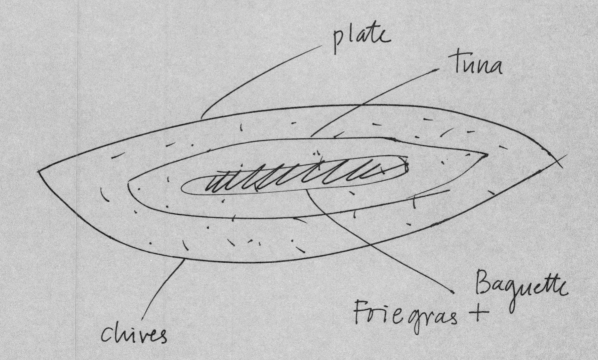

plate

tuna

chives

Foie gras +

Baguette

TUNA

SEARED AND MARINATED YELLOWFIN TUNA TARTARE
"SANDWICH" WITH GINGER OIL

I wanted to serve a tartare that wasn't just another tartare—something with some crunch. Then I had a tuna sashimi in Barcelona served with crispy flatbread and found the element I'd been looking for. We played around with the concept, but the dish felt incomplete until we added seared tuna, which brought spice and complexity.

SERVES 4

THE SEARED TUNA
8 ounces sushi-quality
  yellowfin tuna
Fine sea salt
2 teaspoons Spice Rub
  (RECIPE FOLLOWS)
2 teaspoons extra virgin olive oil
Freshly ground white pepper

THE TUNA TARTARE
8 ounces yellowfin tuna
1½ tablespoons Ginger Oil
  (PAGE 223)
1 tablespoon wasabi paste
1 tablespoon minced scallion
  (white part only)
2 teaspoons minced jalapeño
1 tablespoon cilantro julienne
1 tablespoon yuzu juice
2 tablespoons canola oil
¼ teaspoon Sriracha chile sauce
Fine sea salt and freshly ground
  white pepper

THE SAUCE
¼ cup crème fraîche
1½ teaspoons yuzu juice
¼ teaspoon wasabi paste
¼ teaspoon Dijon mustard
Fine sea salt and freshly ground
  white pepper
Espelette pepper powder

THE GARNISH
4 Flatbread Crackers
  (RECIPE FOLLOWS)
½ lemon
12 micro cilantro sprouts

For the seared tuna, trim any blood line or dark spots from the tuna. Lightly season on both sides with salt and the spice rub and drizzle the olive oil over each side. Heat a large nonstick pan over high heat. Sear the tuna in the hot pan turning once, until browned on both sides but still raw in the center. Set aside.

For the tuna tartare, cut the tuna into ¼-inch dice. Refrigerate.

For the sauce, whisk the crème fraîche, yuzu juice, wasabi paste, and mustard together in a small bowl. Season with salt, white pepper, and Espelette pepper powder. Thin with water as needed; the consistency should be just pourable.

When ready to serve, slice the seared tuna steak into very thin slices; you need 24 slices total. Lightly season the slices with salt and pepper and brush with extra virgin olive oil.

Combine the diced tuna, ginger oil, wasabi, scallion, jalapeño, cilantro, yuzu juice, canola oil, and chile sauce in a stainless steel bowl. Gently mix and season with salt and white pepper.

To serve, place one-quarter of the tuna tartare in the center of each plate, lightly packing it into the shape of a flatbread cracker. Lay the crackers on top of the tartare. Drape the tuna slices over the crackers (6 slices per serving). Spoon some sauce around each plate. Squeeze lemon juice over the tuna, and garnish with the micro cilantro sprouts. Serve immediately.

1½ teaspoons ground ginger
1 teaspoon ground coriander
½ teaspoon fine sea salt
¼ teaspoon cayenne pepper
¼ teaspoon Espelette
    pepper powder
⅛ teaspoon freshly
    ground white pepper

Combine all the ingredients and mix well. Store in a tightly sealed container for up to 1 week.

FLATBREAD CRACKERS

MAKES ABOUT 4 DOZEN

These crackers are also great with cheese.

1½ cups all-purpose flour
1 teaspoon fine sea salt
½ cup water
2 teaspoons extra virgin
    olive oil

Combine the flour and salt in small bowl. Whisk together the water and extra virgin olive oil, add to the flour, and mix until smooth. Cover the dough and refrigerate for 1 hour.

Preheat the oven to 300°F. On a lightly floured surface, roll out the dough very thin, using a rolling pin. Cut the dough into 1 ⅜-by-4¾-inch rectangles. Place the rectangles on a Silpat-lined baking sheet. Bake the crackers until golden brown, about 10 to 15 minutes. Cool on a rack. Store in a tightly sealed container for up to 1 week.

KANPACHI

KANPACHI TARTARE WITH WASABI TOBIKO AND GINGER-CORIANDER EMULSION

This dish has the essence of a glass of Champagne: the fish is like the liquid, and the flying fish roe, combined with the bite from the wasabi, are like the bubbles on top. Kanpachi is a rich, slightly buttery young hamachi—you can use the latter as an alternative.

SERVES 4

PHOTOGRAPH ON
PAGE 87

THE GINGER-CORIANDER EMULSION
2 teaspoons wasabi paste
3 tablespoons fresh lime juice
1 tablespoon fresh lemon juice
1½ tablespoons Ginger Oil
    (PAGE 223)
¼ cup canola oil
¼ teaspoon sugar
Fine sea salt and freshly ground
    white pepper

THE KANPACHI TARTARE
8 ounces sushi-quality kanpachi,
    cut into ¼-inch dice
2 teaspoons wasabi paste
1 teaspoon Ginger Oil (PAGE 223)
1 teaspoon canola oil
1 teaspoon fresh lime juice
1 teaspoon fresh lemon juice
4 teaspoons cilantro julienne
Fine sea salt and freshly ground
    white pepper
2 teaspoons wasabi tobiko

THE GARNISH
4 teaspoons wasabi tobiko
8 micro cilantro sprouts

For the ginger-coriander emulsion, combine the wasabi, lime juice, and lemon juice in a blender and blend well. With the blender running, slowly add the ginger oil and then the canola oil, blending until emulsified and smooth. Add the sugar and season to taste with salt and white pepper. Set aside.

For the tartare, combine the kanpachi, wasabi paste, ginger oil, canola oil, lime juice, lemon juice, cilantro, and salt and pepper to taste in a bowl, mixing gently. Adjust the seasoning if necessary. Gently fold in the wasabi tobiko.

To serve, place a 3-inch ring mold on a serving plate and add one-quarter of the tartare in an even layer. Spread 1 teaspoon of the wasabi tobiko on top of the tartare. Lift off the mold, and repeat to make 3 more servings. Garnish the top of each tartare with 2 micro cilantro sprouts. Spoon the emulsion over and around the tartare, and serve immediately.

FLUKE

PROGRESSIVE TASTING OF MARINATED FLUKE:
FOUR DIFFERENT CEVICHES, FROM SIMPLE TO COMPLEX

This dish was inspired by my trip to Peru in 1998. It starts with a basic dish, then adds one element in each subsequent variation, building in flavors and richness. With so many components, it naturally requires a lot of work. But it's a great crowd pleaser and stayed on the menu for nine years—our clients wouldn't let me change it!

SERVES 4

PHOTOGRAPH ON
PAGE 85

THE FLUKE JUICE
6 ounces fluke fillet, diced
¾ cup fresh lemon juice
¾ cup fresh lime juice
1 tablespoon sugar
1 tablespoon fine sea salt
½ small red onion, sliced

THE FLUKE
8 ounces sushi-quality fluke fillet
Fine sea salt and freshly ground
   white pepper
Espelette pepper powder

THE FIRST MARINADE
6 tablespoons Fluke Juice
2 tablespoons cilantro julienne
2 tablespoons red onion julienne
1 teaspoon hot sauce

THE SECOND MARINADE
6 tablespoons Fluke Juice
2 tablespoons cilantro julienne
2 tablespoons red onion julienne
1 teaspoon hot sauce
1 tablespoon finely diced tomato
1 teaspoon minced jalapeño
2 teaspoons mint julienne
2 teaspoons basil julienne
4 teaspoons extra virgin olive oil
2 teaspoons lemon oil
   (SEE SOURCES, PAGE 229)

THE THIRD MARINADE
¼ cup Fluke Juice
¾ teaspoon hot sauce
1 tablespoon finely
   diced tomato
1 tablespoon Ponzu (PAGE 225)
⅜ teaspoon wasabi paste
¾ teaspoon Ginger Oil (PAGE 223)
1½ teaspoons thinly sliced
   scallion (white part only)
¾ teaspoon finely grated
   orange zest
1½ tablespoons soy sauce

THE FOURTH MARINADE
¼ cup Fluke Juice
¾ teaspoon hot sauce
1½ teaspoons Ponzu (PAGE 225)
⅜ teaspoon wasabi paste
¾ teaspoon Ginger Oil (PAGE 223)
1½ teaspoons thinly sliced
   scallion (white part only)
¾ teaspoon finely grated orange zest
1½ tablespoons soy sauce
3 tablespoons coconut milk

THE GARNISH
Espelette pepper powder
Curry powder

For the fluke juice, combine all of the ingredients in a small stainless steel bowl. Cover and let macerate for 1 hour in the refrigerator.

For the fluke, slice the fillet on the bias into ½-inch-by-2-inch slices. You need 16 slices for each portion (64 total). Lay them in a single layer on a large plate. Cover with plastic wrap and refrigerate.

Strain the juice through a fine-mesh sieve.

For the marinades, combine all of the ingredients for each marinade together in a bowl; discard any excess juice.

Season the fluke with salt, white pepper, and Espelette pepper. Add 16 fluke slices to each marinade.

When ready to serve, divide each ceviche among four small bowls. Sprinkle a small amount of Espelette pepper over each ceviche, and sprinkle a little curry powder over the fourth ceviche. Arrange the bowls of ceviche in order on four serving plates, from simple to complex. Serve immediately.

CONCH

THINLY SLICED CONCH MARINATED PERUVIAN-STYLE, WITH DRIED SWEET CORN

Traditionally, the seafood in a ceviche is marinated in citrus for at least an hour, but I've always found this makes the fish dry and tasteless. Instead, we make our ceviches *à la minute* to maintain the identity of the fish; it's more tender and delicate this way. We serve this dish in a shell bowl at the restaurant, but you can use soup plates or small bowls.

SERVES 4

THE CONCH JUICE

3 ounces conch trimmings (from the conch used below), cut into small pieces
¼ cup fresh lemon juice
¼ cup fresh lime juice
1 tablespoon extra virgin olive oil
1 teaspoon sugar
¼ small red onion, minced
2 tablespoons chopped cilantro, including stems
Fine sea salt
Espelette pepper powder

THE CONCH

8 ounces cleaned conch (trimmings used in conch juice)
Fine sea salt and freshly ground white pepper

THE MARINADE

2 tablespoons extra virgin olive oil
2 teaspoons lemon oil
1 teaspoon hot sauce
2 tablespoons red onion julienne
1 tablespoon finely diced tomato
1 teaspoon minced jalapeño
2 tablespoons cilantro julienne
2 teaspoons mint julienne
2 teaspoons basil julienne
Fine sea salt and freshly ground white pepper to taste
Espelette pepper powder to taste

THE GARNISH

4 teaspoons fresh corn kernels
4 teaspoons freeze-dried corn kernels
12 micro cilantro sprouts
Espelette pepper powder

For the conch juice, combine all of the ingredients in a small stainless steel bowl. Cover and let macerate for 1 hour in the refrigerator.

Strain the juice through a fine-mesh sieve. Refrigerate until cold, or until ready to use.

Meanwhile, tenderize the conch by pounding it with a stainless steel mallet. Cut into 1-inch squares. Arrange the conch pieces in one layer on a plate, cover with plastic wrap, and refrigerate until ready to use.

For the marinade, combine the conch juice with all the marinade ingredients in a bowl.

When ready to serve, season the conch with salt and white pepper. Add the conch to the marinade, stirring to coat, and marinate for 2 minutes.

To serve, divide the conch among four small bowls, stacking the pieces so they have some height. Spoon 1 tablespoon of the marinade over each serving. Sprinkle the fresh corn over the ceviche, garnish with the freeze-dried corn and micro cilantro sprouts, and sprinkle with Espelette pepper. Serve immediately.

a good substitute for conch is fresh sliced red snapper

CALAMARI

SAUTÉED CALAMARI FILLED WITH SWEET PRAWNS
AND WOOD EAR MUSHROOMS, IN CALAMARI CONSOMMÉ

I love Vietnamese spring rolls and thought it would be fun to make them with calamari instead of rice paper. However, none of the calamari we experimented with were supple enough to be stuffed with filling. Finally we found an incredibly tender Spanish version, and this dish was born.

SERVES 4

THE CALAMARI CONSOMMÉ
1 teaspoon canola oil
3 garlic cloves, sliced
½ small Thai red chile pepper, stem and seeds removed
1 pound plus 2 ounces cleaned calamari (bodies and tentacles)
1½ cups Fumet (PAGE 221)
1½ cups water
Fine sea salt and freshly ground white pepper
1 egg white
½ garlic clove, minced

THE CALAMARI AND FILLING
1 ounce rice vermicelli
4 ounces prawns, peeled and minced
4 ounces peekytoe crabmeat, cleaned
¼ cup dried wood ear mushrooms, rehydrated in warm water, drained, and minced
¼ cup minced onion
¼ cup finely grated carrot
Fine sea salt and freshly ground white pepper

5 tablespoons Shrimp Stock (PAGE 221), reduced to 2½ tablespoons
4 teaspoons soy sauce
12 baby calamari, cleaned, tubes and tentacles separated
1 tablespoon canola oil, plus additional for deep-frying
Wondra flour

THE GARNISH
½ cup Mushroom Stock (PAGE 220)
8 pieces dried wood ear mushrooms
12 baby arugula leaves

For the calamari broth, heat the canola oil in a small pot over medium heat. Add the sliced garlic and red chile pepper and sweat until softened but not browned, about 1½ minutes. Add 1 pound of the calamari and cook for 2 to 3 minutes, stirring frequently; do not let it color. Add the fumet and water and bring to a boil, then reduce the heat and simmer for 40 minutes.

Season the broth to taste with salt and white pepper and remove from the heat. Strain through a fine-mesh sieve, cool, and chill.

To clarify the broth, cut the remaining 2 ounces calamari into small pieces. Whisk the egg white until frothy, then stir in the calamari and minced garlic. Pour the cold broth into a pot and whisk in the egg white mixture. Slowly bring to a simmer, stirring constantly with a wooden spoon so the egg white doesn't stick to the bottom of the pot. Stop stirring once the "raft" comes together, and simmer gently for 10 minutes. Carefully ladle the consommé through a sieve lined with a coffee filter into a pot, being careful not to break up the raft too much. Set aside. (The consommé can be made up to 2 days ahead and kept refrigerated.)

For the calamari filling, soak the vermicelli, drain, and chop.

Preheat the oven to 375°F.

Combine the shrimp, crab, mushrooms, onion, carrot, and vermicelli in a bowl, mixing thoroughly. Season to taste with salt and white pepper. Spread the filling out in a baking dish or pan and bake until the shrimp is just barely cooked, 3 to 5 minutes. Let cool.

Stir the filling with a fork to break apart the bigger pieces. Mix in the shrimp stock and soy sauce, and season to taste. Stuff each baby calamari tube three-quarters full with filling. Secure the open ends with a toothpick. (This can be made earler in the day and kept refrigerated.) Refrigerate until ready to cook. (Reserve the tentacles in the refrigerator.)

Heat some canola oil in a deep pot to 400°F. Warm the mushroom stock in a small saucepan, add the dried wood ear mushrooms, and let soften. Bring the consommé to a boil; keep warm.

To cook the stuffed calamari, heat the remaining 1 tablespoon canola oil in two nonstick sauté pans over medium-high heat. Season the calamari with salt and white pepper. Sear very quickly on both sides. Transfer to a plate.

Meanwhile, dust the tentacles with Wondra flour and fry in the hot oil until they are golden brown in color and crispy. Transfer to a paper-towel-lined plate to drain and season with salt and white pepper.

To serve, place 2 pieces of wood ear mushroom in the center of each shallow bowl. Remove the toothpicks from the calamari and arrange on top of the mushrooms, like the petals of a flower. Place the arugula leaves between the calamari. Place the fried tentacles in the center of the stuffed calamari in each bowl. Pour the consommé around, and serve immediately.

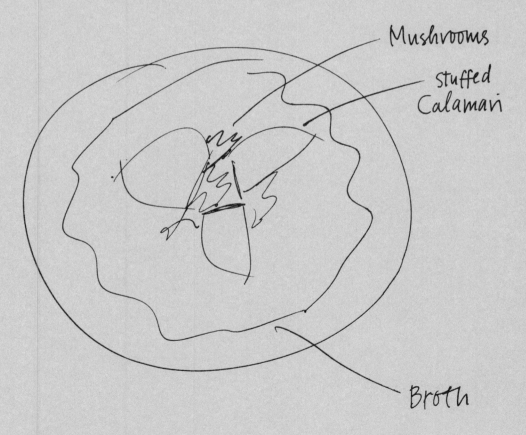

Mushrooms

stuffed Calamari

Broth

CRAB

INSPIRED BY PERUVIAN CAUSA: LAYERED CRAB, AVOCADO, AND POTATOES SPICED WITH YELLOW AJÍ PEPPER SAUCE

After my 1998 trip to Peru, I tried to make a traditional *causa*—a kind of cold potato salad—but ran into trouble because American potatoes are too starchy. After a few years of experimentation, I finally figured out the right ratio to enhance the crab. The resulting flavors are silky yet powerful, thanks to the spicy condiments. In addition, the richness of the avocado complements the texture of the crab.

SERVES 4

THE ONION RELISH
2 tablespoons finely diced red onion
2 tablespoons red wine vinegar
2 tablespoons finely diced ají Amarillo pepper
2 tablespoons finely sliced chives
½ teaspoon fresh lime juice
1½ teaspoons extra virgin olive oil
Fine sea salt and freshly ground white pepper

THE POTATOES
2 Yukon gold potatoes
4 teaspoons canola oil
1 teaspoon ají Amarillo pepper puree (SEE SOURCES, PAGE 229)
1 teaspoon fresh lime juice
Fine sea salt and freshly ground white pepper

THE GARNISH
2 quail eggs
1 avocado, peeled, pitted, quartered, and sliced crosswise ¼ inch thick
4 micro cilantro sprigs or 4 whole cilantro leaves

THE PEPPER SAUCE
¼ cup mayonnaise
1½ teaspoons ají Amarillo pepper puree (SEE SOURCES, PAGE 229)
1 tablespoon warm water
Juice of ½ lemon
Fine sea salt and freshly ground white pepper
Espelette pepper powder

THE CRAB
3 tablespoons mayonnaise
6 ounces peekytoe crabmeat, cleaned
1 tablespoon fresh lemon juice
Fine sea salt and freshly ground white pepper

For the relish, combine the onion and red wine vinegar in a small cup and allow the onion to macerate for 2 hours.

Add the potatoes to a pot of cold salted water and bring to a boil. Reduce the heat slightly and cook until they are tender, 20 to 25 minutes, before finishing the relish.

Meanwhile, put the quail eggs in a small saucepan, cover with water, and bring to a simmer over medium heat. Simmer for 4 minutes, then drain the eggs, and rinse them under cold water. When they are cold, peel and quarter the eggs. Set aside.

When the potatoes are done, drain, peel, and immediately rice them into a bowl. Add the canola oil, ají pepper puree, and lime juice, and mix well. Season with salt and white pepper. Roll out the potato mixture between two sheets of parchment paper until it is ⅛ inch thick. Refrigerate until ready to use.

If you find the rolled potatoes hard to cut, place the sheet in the freezer for about 10 minutes

For the pepper sauce, combine the mayonnaise, ají pepper puree, water, and lemon juice in a small bowl. Season to taste with salt, white pepper, and Espelette pepper. Refrigerate.

For the crab, fold the mayonnaise into the crabmeat. Add the lemon juice and season to taste with salt and white pepper. Refrigerate.

Drain the macerated red onions and transfer them to a small bowl. Add the diced ají pepper, chives, lime juice, and extra virgin olive oil.

Mix well, and season to taste with salt and white pepper. Refrigerate until ready to use.

To assemble the layers, place four 1½-inch ring molds on a baking sheet lined with parchment paper. (If you don't have four molds, assemble one or two causas at a time.) Fill each mold with 1 tablespoon of the crab mix. Cut eight 1½-inch circles out of the rolled potato mixture and place one potato circle on top of the crab in each mold. Arrange a layer of the avocado on top of the potato in

each mold (you may have some left over). Top with another tablespoon of the crab mix. Place another potato circle on top of the crab mix in each mold and finish each mold with 1 tablespoon of the relish, spreading it into an even layer.

Using a metal spatula, transfer each mold to a small bowl. Carefully remove the ring mold. Garnish the top of each causa with 2 quail egg quarters and a micro cilantro sprig. Spoon the sauce around, and serve immediately.

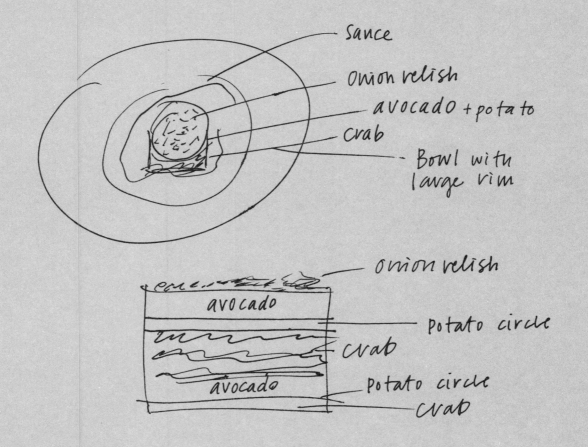

ESCOLAR

ESCOLAR POACHED IN EXTRA VIRGIN OLIVE OIL WITH SEA BEANS,
POTATO CRISPS, AND LIGHT RED WINE BÉARNAISE

At the restaurant one day, we got the idea for the red
wine in this sauce while making brown butter. Since
it doesn't use any eggs, it's much lighter than a true
béarnaise, but the wine gives the illusion of lightness
to the rich fish.

SERVES 4

PHOTOGRAPH ON
PAGES 88–89

THE POTATO CRISPS
Canola oil for deep-frying
1 Yukon Gold potato, scrubbed
Fine sea salt

THE RED WINE BÉARNAISE
½ cup dry red wine
½ cup red wine vinegar
1 tablespoon black peppercorns
1 teaspoon minced shallot
3 tarragon sprigs
1 thyme sprig
3 tablespoons Brown Butter
   Sauce (PAGE 223)
4 tablespoons unsalted butter
Fine sea salt and freshly ground
   white pepper

THE TUNA
1 cup extra virgin olive oil
Four 4-ounce white tuna
   (escolar) steaks
Fine sea salt and freshly ground
   white pepper

THE GARNISH
½ teaspoon thinly sliced
   tarragon leaves
1½ teaspoons minced shallot
1 teaspoon coarsely ground
   black pepper
4 to 5 sea beans, broken into
   2-inch pieces

For the potato crisps, heat the
canola oil in a small deep pot to
300°F. Using a Japanese mandoline,
slice the potato into very thin slices
(about ¹⁄₁₆ inch thick). Using a 1-inch
round cutter, cut circles from the
slices; you need 20 slices total. Fry
the potato circles in the hot oil
until golden brown and crisp. Drain
on a paper-towel-lined plate and
season with salt.

For the red wine béarnaise, combine the wine, vinegar, peppercorns,
shallot, tarragon, and thyme in a
saucepan, bring to a boil, and reduce
the liquid to 2 tablespoons.

Add the brown butter sauce to
the reduced wine. Then gradually
whisk in the butter. Strain through
a fine-mesh sieve into a small saucepan and season with salt and white
pepper. Set aside.

For the tuna, heat the oil to 160°F
in a large sauté pan over very low
heat. Season the tuna on both sides
with salt and white pepper, place it
in the pan, and cook for 5 to 6 minutes, turning once, until medium-
rare to medium. Test for doneness
by inserting a metal skewer into the
center of the fish; when left in for
5 seconds, it should feel just warm
when touched to your lip. Transfer
the fish to a paper-towel-lined plate
and allow it to rest for a few minutes
before slicing.

While the tuna is cooking, mix
the tarragon, shallot, and black pepper in a small bowl. Gently warm
the red wine béarnaise.

To serve, slice the tuna into
¼-inch-thick slices and arrange
down the center of each plate.
Sprinkle a little of the garnish over
the center of the slices of tuna and
place the potato crisps and sea
beans on top. Spoon the warm red
wine béarnaise around the plates,
and serve immediately.

use a sharp knife to prevent the tarragon from bruising while cutting

HAMACHI

RARE-SEARED YELLOWTAIL HAMACHI MARINATED
IN TANDOORI SPICES WITH PICKLED CUCUMBER
AND MANGO SALAD

I first encountered tandoori powder in California and
instantly knew I wanted to cook with its sweet, exotic
flavor. I thought hamachi would be a good match
for it, because its texture and density are similar to
chicken. While we were marinating the fish in olive
oil, lemon juice, and tandoori powder, we realized we
already had a great sauce, rich in spice and acidity.
The cucumber adds a hint of freshness to the dish.

SERVES 4

PHOTOGRAPH ON
PAGE 90

THE PICKLED CUCUMBER
AND MANGO SALAD

2 tablespoons rice wine vinegar

1 teaspoon sugar

2 tablespoons extra virgin olive oil

1 tablespoon Indian pickled mangos,
pureed

2 Japanese cucumbers, quartered
lengthwise, seeded, and cut into
¼-inch slices

Fine sea salt and freshly ground
white pepper

1 teaspoon cilantro julienne

THE HAMACHI

Four 3-ounce sushi-quality
yellowtail hamachi fillets, skin
removed, trimmed to even
rectangles

Fine sea salt and freshly ground
white pepper

2 garlic cloves, minced

2 teaspoons dried thyme

4 teaspoons tandoori powder

¼ cup extra virgin olive oil

1 lemon, halved

THE GARNISH

¼ cup micro greens

Fine sea salt and freshly ground
white pepper

½ teaspoon Sherry Vinaigrette
(PAGE 224)

For the cucumber and mango salad,
combine the vinegar and sugar in
a sauté pan over low heat and heat,
stirring, until the sugar dissolves.
Add the olive oil and pickled mango
puree and bring to a simmer. Add
the cucumbers and cook for 1 to
2 minutes. Season with salt and
white pepper and remove from the
heat. Strain and refrigerate until
chilled. Just before serving, add the
cilantro julienne.

For the fish, season both sides
of the hamachi with salt and white
pepper. Combine the garlic, thyme,
and tandoori powder in a small bowl,
then rub the fillets with the mixture.
Put the fish in a shallow dish, and
drizzle the fillets with the extra
virgin olive oil, turning once, and let
marinate for 5 minutes.

Preheat a sauté pan over medium-
high heat. Remove the hamachi
fillets from the marinade (reserve
the marinade) and sear for 1 to 2
minutes per side; the fish should be
very rare but not cold in the middle.

To serve, place a 1½-inch ring
mold on one side of a serving plate.
Pack one-quarter of the cucumber salad into the mold. Carefully
remove the mold and repeat with
the remaining three plates. Slice the
hamachi into ¼-inch-thick slices and
shingle the slices on the other side
of the plates. Squeeze some lemon
juice over the hamachi and then add
lemon juice to taste to the reserved
marinade. Lightly season the micro
greens with salt and white pepper,
and gently toss with the sherry vinaigrette. Top the cucumber salads
with the micro greens, drizzle the
marinade around the hamachi, and
serve immediately.

PORK BELLY–CALAMARI

CRISPY BRAISED PORK BELLY AND BABY CALAMARI BASQUAISE

One night in France, chef Michael Sarran served me a dish of squab with a squid-ink sauce, which sparked this dish. It's full of very complex flavors: the sweet pepper compote, the smoky squid ink (we get our calamari from Spain), and dried bonito flakes. It's a healthy, satisfying, makes-you-happy-when-you-eat-it dish. I love it. (You have to start the pork belly portion of the dish the day before you intend to serve it.)

SERVES 4

THE PORK BELLY
1½ pounds pork belly
1½ teaspoons canola oil
½ head garlic, cloves separated and peeled
2 shallots, split in half
½ cup dry white wine
¼ cup rice wine vinegar
½ cup soy sauce
4 pieces (about ½ ounce) dried bonito flakes
5 cups Chicken Stock (PAGE 220)
Fine sea salt and freshly ground white pepper

THE SAUCE
2 teaspoons canola oil
¼ cup thinly sliced pork belly trimmings (from the pork belly)
½ garlic clove, thinly sliced
½ shallot, thinly sliced
3 tablespoons rice wine vinegar
1 cup reserved braising liquid (from the pork belly)
1 piece dried bonito flakes
½ teaspoon squid ink

THE BASQUAISE
2 tablespoons olive oil
½ cup small dice onion
1 tablespoon minced garlic
½ cup small dice red bell pepper
½ cup small dice yellow bell pepper,
1 cup small dice tomato
1 slice prosciutto
Fine sea salt and freshly ground white pepper
Espelette pepper powder

THE BABY CALAMARI
1 teaspoon canola oil
2 ounces cleaned baby calamari
1 teaspoon Garlic Butter (PAGE 222)
Fine sea salt and freshly ground pepper

THE GARNISH
1 teaspoon Italian parsley julienne

To make the pork belly, preheat the oven to 275°F.

Put the pork belly in a large pot, add enough cold water to cover, and bring to a boil. Remove the pot from the heat, remove the pork belly, and set aside.

Heat the canola oil in a medium casserole over medium heat. Add the garlic and shallots and sauté until they are caramelized, about 5 minutes. Deglaze the pot with the white wine, stirring up any brown bits, and reduce the wine by half.

Add the rice wine vinegar, soy sauce, bonito flakes, and 3 cups of the chicken stock. Season the pork belly with salt and white pepper, and add to the pot. Bring to a boil, cover the pot, transfer to the oven, and braise for about 3 to 3½ hours, until the pork belly is very tender; add up to 2 more cups chicken stock as needed to keep the pork covered. Cool the pork belly to room temperature in the braising liquid.

Transfer the pork belly to a shallow baking pan lined with parchment paper. Lay a piece of parchment on top, place another pan on top of it, and weight the pork belly with a few cans or other weights, distributing them evenly. Refrigerate the pork belly overnight (any remaining liquid will be pressed out and the pork belly will be evenly compacted into a thinner block). Strain the braising liquid and refrigerate it.

The next day, remove the pressed pork belly from the refrigerator and cut four 1¾-inch squares out of it; reserve the trimmings for the sauce. Refrigerate the pork belly until ready to use.

For the sauce, heat the canola oil in a sauté pan over medium-high heat. Add the pork belly trimmings and lightly brown them, stirring frequently. Add the garlic and shallot and cook until tender. Add the rice wine vinegar, bring to a boil, and reduce by half. Add the reserved braising liquid and bring to a boil. Add the dried bonito flakes, reduce

the heat to a simmer, and cook for about 20 minutes, until reduced by one-quarter. Stir in the squid ink, then strain the sauce into a saucepan and set aside.

For the basquaise, heat the olive oil in a heavy casserole. Add the onion and sweat over medium-low heat until tender. Add the garlic and bell peppers and cook until the peppers are soft. Add the tomatoes and prosciutto and simmer, stirring often, for 30 to 40 minutes, until most of the liquid has reduced. Season to taste with salt, white pepper, and Espelette pepper powder. Set aside.

When ready to serve, preheat the oven to 350°F.

Heat a small nonstick sauté pan until hot. Put the pork belly squares

in the pan, skin side down, transfer the pan to the oven, and cook until the pork belly is warmed all the way through and the skin is crispy.

While the pork belly is cooking, cook the calamari: Heat the canola oil in a sauté pan until very hot. Add the calamari and garlic butter, season to taste with salt and white pepper, and sauté for 1 to 2 minutes, until tender.

Meanwhile, reheat the basquaise and sauce.

To plate, spoon one-quarter of the basquaise in the middle of a small bowl. Place a crispy pork belly on top. Spoon some baby calamari around the pork belly, garnish with the parsley, and pour 3 tablespoons of sauce around. Repeat with the other three bowls.

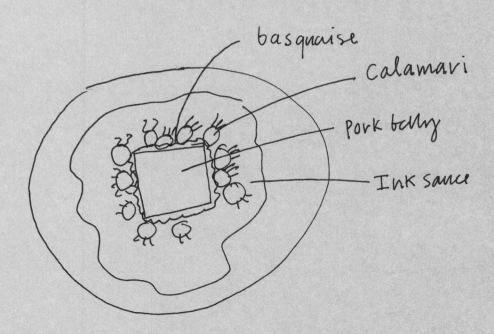

OYSTERS

BAKED KUMAMOTO OYSTERS WITH FRESH THYME AND SWEET GARLIC BUTTER

We always offer a variety of oysters from both coasts. Some of my favorites are Belon, Beau Soleil, Peconic Bay, and the Kumamoto oysters from Washington State, which have a firm texture and creamy flavor with a mildly fruity finish. If Kumamoto oysters are unavailable, any plump, medium-size oyster will work. Don't overcook them; they'll lose their flavor and dry out.

SERVES 4

PHOTOGRAPH ON
PAGE 91

3 cups kosher salt
28 Kumamoto oysters, shucked
½ cup Garlic Butter (PAGE 222), softened
12 sprigs fresh thyme
½ lemon

Preheat the oven to 400°F.

Mix 1 cup of the kosher salt with just enough water to make it the consistency of wet sand. Place 7 small mounds of the salt on each of four serving plates to hold the baked oysters. Set aside.

Spread the remaining 2 cups salt on a baking sheet. Place about a teaspoon of the garlic butter on each oyster and nestle the oysters in the salt. Scatter the thyme over the oysters.

Bake for about 5 minutes, or until the butter is bubbling and lightly browned.

To serve, place each oyster on a mound of salt on the serving plates. Drizzle with lemon juice, and serve immediately.

This recipe works well for clams also

CRAB

WARM PEEKYTOE–MARYLAND LUMP "CRAB CAKES" WITH
SHAVED CAULIFLOWER AND DIJON MUSTARD EMULSION

This great crab dish has the lightness of a snowball.
The spiciness and acidity of the mustard sauce
season the crab, and the cauliflower adds texture and
crispness. The restaurant goes through cases and
cases of cauliflower to get the perfect thin slices. Use
a Benriner or Japanese mandoline to make yours very
thin.

SERVES 4

THE DIJON MUSTARD EMULSION
¼ cup crème fraîche
1 tablespoon Dijon mustard
Fine sea salt and freshly
 ground white pepper
1½ teaspoons thinly sliced chives

THE GARNISH
¼ head cauliflower
6 chives, cut in half
Maldon sea salt

THE "CRAB CAKES"
2 tablespoons water
6 tablespoons unsalted butter,
 cut into ½-inch cubes
5 ounces Maryland lump
 crabmeat, cleaned
3 ounces peekytoe crabmeat,
 cleaned
Fine sea salt and freshly
 ground white pepper
Espelette pepper powder
1 tablespoon thinly sliced chives
Fresh lemon juice to taste

For the Dijon mustard emulsion, gently heat the crème fraîche in a small saucepan. Whisk in the Dijon mustard and season with salt and white pepper. Set aside.

For the cauliflower, separate the florets, trying to keep them as large as possible. Slice the florets very thin on a Japanese mandoline; you will need 20 slices.

For the "crab cakes," make a beurre monté by bringing the water to a boil and gradually whisking in the butter. Add 2 tablespoons of the Dijon mustard emulsion and the lump crabmeat. Gently heat for 2 minutes, then add the peekytoe crabmeat, and cook for another 2 to 3 minutes. Season with salt, white pepper, and Espelette pepper. Add the chives and lemon juice. Reheat the mustard emulsion.

To serve, place the crab in the center of each of four small bowls, with the peekytoe on the bottom and the lump on top. Stir the chives into the mustard. Garnish each "crab cake" with 5 cauliflower slices, arranging them around and on top of the crab. Place 3 chive halves on top of each mound, and sprinkle with a little Maldon sea salt. Spoon the Dijon emulsion over and around the "crab cakes." Serve immediately.

CAVIAR–PASTA
IRANIAN OSETRA CAVIAR IN A NEST OF TAGLIOLINI
WITH QUAIL EGGS AND BACON CARBONARA SAUCE

On a trip to Italy, I was savoring a great bottle of Brunello in Montalcino when I had the idea that it would be nice to do a luxurious carbonara. The trick was balancing the flavors of three such salty ingredients—bacon, caviar, and Parmesan. The solution was the cream and eggs.

SERVES 4

PHOTOGRAPH ON
PAGE 93

THE CARBONARA SAUCE
6 ounces applewood smoked bacon,
    2 ounces cut into large pieces,
    4 ounces cut into ¼-inch dice
1½ teaspoons cracked black
    pepper, plus more to taste
1 cup crème fraîche
1 large egg yolk
3½ tablespoons freshly
    grated Parmesan
Fine sea salt
2 teaspoons thinly sliced chives

THE PASTA
4 ounces dried tagliolini

THE GARNISH
4 quail egg yolks
4 generous teaspoons Iranian
    osetra caviar

For the sauce, sauté the 2 ounces bacon in a large sauté pan until crisp. Add the black pepper and cook for 30 seconds. Stir in the crème fraîche and bring to a simmer. Off the heat, whisk in the egg yolks, then add 1 tablespoon of the Parmesan cheese. Strain the sauce and season with salt. Set aside.

Sauté the remaining 4 ounces bacon until it is crisp. Set aside.

When ready to serve, cook the pasta in a large pot of boiling salted water until al dente; drain.

Meanwhile, rewarm the sauce in a small pot. Combine the bacon, chives, and cracked black pepper to taste in a medium bowl. Add the warmed sauce and the remaining 2½ tablespoons Parmesan cheese to the bowl, mixing well. Adjust the seasoning.

Add the pasta to the sauce, tossing to coat, and let sit for 1 minute so it absorbs some of the sauce.

To serve, use a meat fork to twirl one-quarter of the pasta in the center of each of four small bowls, creating a nest in the middle of the pasta. Place a quail egg yolk in each nest and top with 1 teaspoon of the caviar. Spoon some of the sauce around and serve immediately.

If the osetra caviar is unavailable substitute a good-quality American sturgeon roe

LOBSTER

CELERIAC SOUP WITH LOBSTER FOAM AND PÉRIGORD TRUFFLES

The first time I heard of a savory cappuccino was in the early 1990s, when Guy Savoy was doing a mushroom version in his restaurant in Paris. I came up with this dish in the winter, during truffle season; for me, only Périgord truffles, with their incredibly refined, earthy, soul-of-the-woods flavor and smell, would do. They're always so wonderful with lobster, and I knew they would work well with the celeriac.

SERVES 4

PHOTOGRAPH ON
PAGE 96

THE CELERIAC SOUP
2 cups 1-inch dice celeriac
1½ cups water
2 tablespoons unsalted butter
Fine sea salt and freshly
    ground white pepper

THE LOBSTER FOAM
1 tablespoon extra virgin olive oil
12 ounces lobster shells
1 tablespoon tomato paste
2 tablespoons brandy
1 cup heavy cream
1 tablespoon lobster roe

THE GARNISH
1 teaspoon unsalted butter
4 ounces cooked lobster meat,
    cut into ¼-inch dice
Fine sea salt and freshly
    ground white pepper
½ ounce black truffle

For the soup, combine the celeriac with the water, butter, and salt and white pepper to taste in a small pot and bring to a simmer. Simmer until the celeriac is tender.

Drain the celeriac, reserving the cooking liquid, and transfer to a blender. Puree until smooth, adding the cooking liquid as needed to thin to the consistency of a thick soup (you'll need about half the liquid). Set aside.

For the lobster foam, heat the oil in a casserole over medium-high heat. Sear the lobster shells, turning occasionally, for 2 minutes, or until they turn bright red. Add the tomato paste and cook, stirring, for 2 minutes. Add the brandy, bring to a boil, and reduce slightly, until the pan is almost dry. Add the cream, bring to a simmer, and simmer for about 15 minutes, until reduced by one-quarter.

Strain the cream through a fine-mesh sieve. Using a handheld immersion blender, temper in the lobster roe. Set aside.

For the garnishes, melt the butter with 1 tablespoon water in a small pan. Add the lobster, season with salt and white pepper, and heat through. Meanwhile, bring the soup to a boil, thinning it with more of the reserved cooking liquid if necessary.

Bring the lobster cream to a boil. Remove from the heat and blend with the handheld immersion blender until very frothy.

To serve, divide the lobster meat among four coffee cups or small bowls and pour the soup over the lobster. Spoon the lobster foam over the soup and grate the truffle over the foam. Serve immediately.

OCTOPUS

WARM SPICY OCTOPUS WITH BLACK OLIVE AND PRESERVED LEMON,
SHERRY VINEGAR GELÉE, AND EXTRA VIRGIN OLIVE OIL

As a teenager, I would spend weekends in Barcelona, where one of the hot spots was the trendy Casa Tejada. This restaurant had an amazing ambience, served the best Serrano ham, and was famous for its warm octopus with paprika. This dish is based on that memory. The octopus is both firm and tender, and the fact that it's cooked in a broth made with prosciutto gives it a kind of odd meatiness.

SERVES 4

PHOTOGRAPH ON PAGE 97

THE OCTOPUS
½ small onion, quartered
6 cloves garlic, cut in half
½ celery stalk, thinly sliced
    on the bias
½ small carrot, peeled and
    thinly sliced on the bias
2 Italian parsley sprigs
One ½-inch thick slice prosciutto
    (about 3 ounces)
½ teaspoon cayenne pepper
Fine sea salt
2 pounds octopus, tentacles only
Freshly ground white pepper
¼ teaspoon spicy pimentón

THE GARNISH
½ petal Lemon Confit (PAGE 224),
    briefly blanched and minced
2 teaspoons minced Niçoise olives
1 tablespoon Garlic Oil
    (RECIPE FOLLOWS)
1 tablespoon extra virgin olive oil
1 tablespoon thinly sliced chives
Sherry Gelée (PAGE 225)

For the octopus, combine the onion, garlic, celery, carrot, parsley, prosciutto, and cayenne in a pot and add enough water to cover the octopus. Season the water with enough salt so it tastes like the ocean. Bring to a boil and infuse for 5 minutes.

Add the octopus and bring to a simmer, then reduce the heat and cook at a low simmer for about 1 hour, or until the octopus is tender when pierced with a knife. Cool the octopus in the braising liquid to room temperature.

Drain the octopus and cut into ½-inch-thick slices. Arrange on four appetizer plates. (This can be done ahead of time; cover and refrigerate.)

When ready to serve, preheat the oven to 300°F.

Put the plates in the oven for about 30 seconds to warm the octopus. Season with salt, white pepper, and pimentón.

To serve, garnish the octopus with the lemon confit and Niçoise olives, spoon the garlic oil and extra virgin olive oil over the octopus, and sprinkle with the chives. Spoon a small amount of the sherry gelée over the octopus. Serve immediately.

GARLIC OIL
MAKES ¼ CUP

¼ cup extra virgin olive oil
1 garlic clove, thinly sliced

Combine the oil and the garlic in a small pan and bring to a boil over medium heat. Turn off the heat and let the garlic infuse for 25 minutes.

Strain the oil and refrigerate for up to 1 week. Bring back to room temperature before using.

ask your fishmonger for tentacles ONLY

SCALLOPS

ULTRARARE CHARRED SEA SCALLOPS
WITH SMOKED SEA SALT

There's nothing better than scallops right out of the shell—barely cooked or even raw. This is my version of scallop sashimi; the sea salt, from Denmark, is an amazing ingredient that's responsible for the dish's smoky, charred flavor.

SERVES 4

THE GARNISH
8 Niçoise olives
1 teaspoon smoked viking salt
    (SEE SOURCES, PAGE 229)
Freshly ground black pepper
3 to 4 tablespoons extra virgin
    olive oil
4 micro chives

THE SCALLOPS
8 large sea scallops (about
    12 ounces)
2 teaspoons olive oil
Fine sea salt and freshly ground
    white pepper

For the olives, preheat the oven to 180°F.

Cut the olives in half and remove the pits. Spread the olives on a parchment-lined baking sheet and bake until dry, 1 to 1½ hours. Remove from the oven and allow to cool.

Roughly chop the olives. Set aside.

For the scallops, pull off the muscles and discard. Rub the scallops with the olive oil and season with salt and white pepper.

Heat a cast-iron griddle over medium-high heat. Put the scallops on their sides on the griddle and sear just the edges, turning them as necessary. The scallops should still be rare.

To serve, slice the scallops in half crosswise and place 4 halves on each plate, cut side up. Garnish each half with the dried olives, smoked salt, and black pepper. Drizzle the extra virgin olive oil over the scallops and garnish each plate with a chive. Serve immediately.

BACALAO

GRILLED SALTED COD SALAD WITH AVOCADO, ROMAINE,
AGED SHERRY VINEGAR, AND EXTRA VIRGIN OLIVE OIL

Every recipe is a collaboration. This was originally inspired by the Catalonian salt-cod salad *escaixada*, which I tasted on a trip to Spain. Our executive sous chef, Eric Gestel, came up with the idea of grilling the cod, and Leo Marino, a former sous chef and now chef in our restaurant in Washington, D.C., added smoked salt for heightened depth. It's a great example of ingredients from different cultures coming together in one dish.

SERVES 4

PHOTOGRAPH ON
PAGE 94

THE SALTED COD SALAD
Two 6-ounce codfish fillets
1 teaspoon smoked viking salt
   (SEE SOURCES, PAGE 229), plus
   additional as needed
2 tablespoons plus ½ teaspoon
   extra virgin olive oil
Freshly ground white pepper
2 teaspoons thinly sliced chives
2 teaspoons minced red onion
2 teaspoons sherry vinegar

THE GARNISH
1 sweet potato
12 romaine heart leaves
   (very small inner leaves)
Fine sea salt and freshly
   ground white pepper
2 teaspoons Sherry Vinaigrette
   (PAGE 224)
20 micro arugula leaves
4 teaspoons micro greens
4 pieces Tomato Confit
   (PAGE 224), quartered
¼ cup Guacamole (RECIPE FOLLOWS)
2 teaspoons extra virgin olive oil
1 teaspoon Tomato Water
   (RECIPE FOLLOWS)
½ teaspoon Sherry Gelée (PAGE 225)

do not be afraid to use extra olive oil if the salt cod seems dry

For the salted cod, season both sides of the cod with 1 teaspoon smoked salt. Place on a towel-lined plate, cover, and refrigerate for 24 hours.

The next day, preheat the oven to 400°F.

Wash the sweet potato and pierce the skin in a few places with a paring knife. Wrap in aluminum foil and bake directly on an oven rack until tender, about 40 minutes. Let cool completely.

Peel the sweet potato and cut into ¼-inch slices. Cut 1 or 2 slices into ¼-inch dice. You need 16 pieces for this recipe. Cover and set aside. Reserve the remaining sweet potato for another use.

Preheat a grill. Rinse the cod and dry it well. Marinate the cod with ½ teaspoon of the olive oil and white pepper.

Grill the cod, turning once, until marked on each side and just cooked to medium-rare; take care not to overcook it. Then put the fish in the refrigerator to prevent it from overcooking.

When the fish is cool, gently flake it into a bowl. Add the remaining 2 tablespoons olive oil, the chives, red onion, and sherry vinegar. Gently mix together, trying not to break up the fish. Season to taste with white pepper and smoked salt.

When ready to serve, season the romaine leaves with sea salt and white pepper and toss with 1 teaspoon of the sherry vinaigrette. Season the arugula and micro greens with salt and pepper and toss with the remaining 1 teaspoon sherry vinaigrette. Place a 3½-inch ring mold in the center of one appetizer plate and spoon one-quarter of the cod

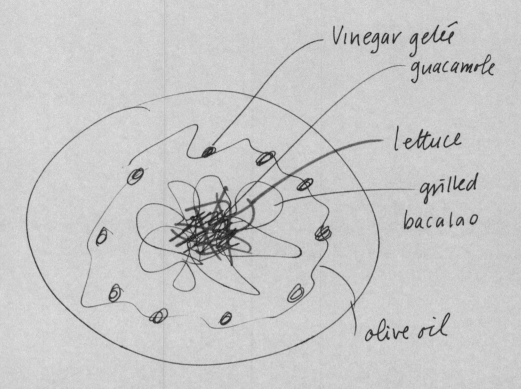

Vinegar gelée
guacamole

lettuce

grilled
bacalao

olive oil

GUACAMOLE
MAKES ABOUT 1 CUP

1 Hass avocado
1 tablespoon minced
  red onion
1 tablespoon lime juice
¼ teaspoon sherry vinegar
Fine sea salt and freshly
  ground white pepper

Cut the avocado in half and
remove the pit. With a large
spoon, scoop the flesh into a
stainless steel bowl. Add the
red onion, lime, and sherry
vinegar and gently mash with
a fork. Season with salt and
white pepper.

TOMATO WATER

1 large tomato, cored and cut
  into quarters
2 slices of small red onion
1 small clove sliced garlic
1 cilantro sprig
1 basil sprig
½ teaspoon minced jalapeño
2 tablespoons extra virgin
  olive oil
1 tablespoon sherry vinegar
Fine sea salt and freshly
  ground white pepper

Combine all of the ingredients
in a small bowl. Cover and
refrigerate overnight.
  Remove the cilantro and
basil stems and discard.
Transfer the tomatoes and
liquid to a food processor and
pulse lightly. Strain through
a fine-mesh sieve, gently
pressing on the tomatoes to
release all the juices. The result
will look like a loose coulis.

salad into the mold. Lay 4 tomato
pieces on top of the cod salad, and
place 2 sweet potato dice between
the tomato pieces. Put 1 tablespoon
of the guacamole in the center of
the salad. Arrange one-quarter of
the romaine on top of the guacamole, and top with one-quarter
of the arugula and micro greens.
Remove the ring mold and repeat to
make 3 more salads.
  Drizzle ½ teaspoon extra virgin
olive oil around each plate. Drizzle
5 dots of tomato water into the
olive oil on each plate and spoon
5 small dots of sherry gelée in
between the dots of tomato water.
Serve immediately.

NOTE

Both the cod and the tomato
water have to be started one
day in advance

LANGOUSTINES

SPICY LANGOUSTINE SAMBAL WITH CHAYOTE AND PEAR BÂTONNETS

This dish is at once delicate and powerful; the spices in the Indonesian-inspired sauce tease the taste buds—it's almost *too* spicy, but you still want more. Positively addictive.

SERVES 4

PHOTOGRAPH ON
PAGE 95

THE SPICY LANGOUSTINE SAMBAL
4 tablespoons plus 1 teaspoon
  canola oil
½ garlic clove, thinly sliced
½ shallot, thinly sliced
A ½-inch piece of ginger, peeled
  and thinly sliced
1½ teaspoons Thai red curry paste
1½ cups Shrimp Stock (PAGE 221),
  reduced to ¾ cup
Fine sea salt and freshly ground
  white pepper
1 lime, cut in half

THE PUREE AND GARNISH
1 chayote squash
½ Bartlett pear
Fine sea salt and freshly ground
  white pepper
1 teaspoon unsalted butter
2 tablespoons micro celery leaves

THE LANGOUSTINES
2 tablespoons canola oil
8 langoustines, shelled
Fine sea salt and freshly ground
  white pepper
Espelette pepper powder

For the sambal, heat 1 teaspoon of the canola oil in a small sauté pan over medium-high heat. Add the garlic, shallot, ginger, and curry paste and cook until tender. Add the shrimp stock and bring to a boil. Reduce to a simmer and cook for 15 minutes.

Strain the sauce into another pan and reduce by half. Strain again. Set aside.

Cut 6 thin lengthwise slices from the chayote. Cut 2 of the slices into bâtonnets for garnish. Put in a bowl of ice water and set aside. Blanch the remaining 4 slices in boiling salted water until they are tender; chill in an ice bath, drain, and set aside. Coarsely chop enough of the remaining chayote to make ½ cup. Set aside.

Cut 2 thin slices from the pear and cut into bâtonnets for garnish. Put in a bowl of ice water and set aside. Coarsely chop enough of the remaining pear to make ¼ cup.

For the puree, cook the chopped pear and chopped chayote in boiling lightly salted water until very

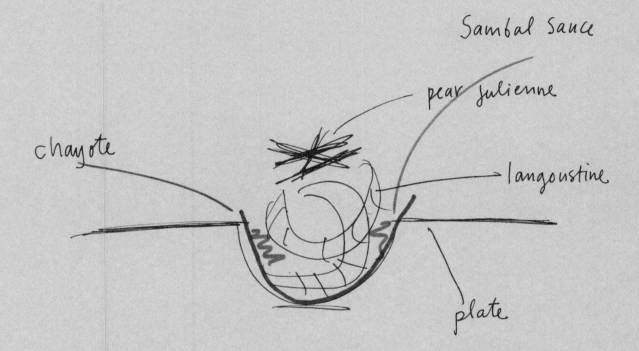

chayote

Sambal Sauce

pear Julienne

langoustine

plate

soft. Drain, reserving the water. Puree the pear and chayote in a blender, adding the cooking water as needed to make a smooth puree. Season the puree with salt and white pepper, and keep warm.

For the langoustines, heat the 2 tablespoons canola oil in a non-stick sauté pan over medium-high heat. Season the langoustines with salt, white pepper, and Espelette pepper. Add the langoustines to the pan and sauté 1 to 2 minutes on each side, until seared and just cooked through.

Stir the butter into the pear and chayote puree and season it. Bring the sambal to a boil, then remove from the heat and, using a hand-held immersion blender, mix in the remaining 4 tablespoons canola oil and season to taste.

To serve, spoon 1 tablespoon of the puree into the center of each of 4 small bowls. Stack 2 langoustines on top of the puree. Place a chayote slice to the side of the langoustines. Drain the pear and chayote bâtonnets and arrange a

small mound on top of each stack of langoustines. Garnish with the micro celery.

Finish the sauce with a squeeze of lime juice. Spoon the sauce around the langoustines. Serve immediately.

LOBSTER

WARM LOBSTER TIMBALE IN A CHAMPAGNE-CHIVE NAGE

This was inspired by a dish Gilbert Le Coze had on the menu when I started at Le Bernardin: sliced raw scallops finished by pouring a hot poaching liquid over them. I thought adding vibrant Champagne at the last minute would be the perfect way to finish the lobster. I first served it this way at a Champagne dinner for Alain Ducasse.

SERVES 4

THE NAGE
3 quarts cold water
1 cup champagne vinegar
3 cups dry Champagne
1 tablespoon fine sea salt
1 teaspoon white peppercorns
8 garlic cloves, peeled
2 large onions, cut in half
1 tomato, cored
2 medium fennel bulbs, trimmed and cut in half
2 medium carrots, peeled and cut in half
4 celery stalks, cut into quarters
2 medium leeks (white part only), cleaned and cut into 4 pieces each
4 cilantro sprigs
4 basil sprigs
4 parsley sprigs

THE LOBSTER TIMBALE
½ cup ⅛-inch-thick slices onion
½ cup peeled carrot, cut in half and sliced thin on the bias
½ cup thinly sliced fennel
½ cup peeled celery, sliced thin on the bias
Two 1¾-pound lobsters
1 tablespoon minced shallot
1 teaspoon minced tarragon
Fine sea salt and freshly ground white pepper
5 tablespoons unsalted butter, softened

TO FINISH
8 tablespoons (1 stick) unsalted butter, softened
2 tablespoons dry Champagne
2 tablespoons thinly sliced chives
Fine sea salt and freshly ground white pepper

For the nage, combine all of the ingredients except the herbs in a large pot. Bring to a boil, then lower to a simmer and cook for 2½ hours. Take the nage off the heat, add the herbs, and let infuse for 10 minutes.

Strain the nage (discard the vegetables); there should be about 3 quarts of nage. Reserve 1 cup of the nage for the sauce; set the rest aside for cooking the lobsters.

For the lobster timbale, blanch the onion, carrot, fennel, and celery separately in boiling salted water and chill in ice water; drain and set aside.

Dilute the remaining nage with an equal amount of water and bring to a boil in a large pot, then lower to a simmer. Kill each lobster by plunging a chef's knife into the shell between the eyes and bringing the knife down through the head to cut

cut the herbs right before serving to get the most flavor

it in half. Add the lobsters to the simmering nage and cook for 12 minutes. Remove the lobsters from the nage and let them rest for 5 minutes.

Carefully pull off the tail from each lobster. (Reserve the claws for another use.) Crack the shell of each tail, being careful to leave the meat intact. Pull the tail meat out of the shell and remove the intestinal tract. Slice the tails into ⅛-inch-thick slices. Lay the slices on a parchment-paper-lined baking sheet and sprinkle with the shallot, tarragon, salt, and white pepper. Dot with 1 tablespoon softened butter.

Preheat the oven to 350°F.

To finish the sauce, bring the reserved 1 cup nage to a boil in a saucepan. Gradually whisk in the butter, then add the Champagne and chives. Season to taste with salt and white pepper. Keep warm.

Reheat the lobster in the oven for 2 to 3 minutes, until it is just warm to the touch. Meanwhile, gently reheat the vegetables in the remaining 4 tablespoons butter and season to taste.

To serve, place a 2-inch ring mold in the center of a soup plate and arrange one-quarter of the warm lobster slices in the mold, overlapping them slightly. Arrange one-quarter of the vegetables on top of the lobster. Lift off the ring mold, and repeat to make 3 more timbales. Transfer the sauce to a sauceboat, and pour the sauce around the timbales just before serving.

Champagne Nage

Vegetable garnish

Sliced lobster

CAVIAR–SEA URCHIN

IRANIAN OSETRA CAVIAR NESTLED IN LINGUINE WITH WARM SEA URCHIN SAUCE

There's a lovely harmony between the sweet, briny sea urchin and the salty caviar. At the same time, the pasta adds structure and texture. We serve this appetizer only in winter, when the sea urchins are best.

SERVES 4

PHOTOGRAPH ON PAGE 92

THE SEA URCHIN SAUCE
½ cup sea urchin roe
8 tablespoons (1 stick) unsalted
    butter, softened
1 tablespoon water
Fine sea salt
Espelette pepper powder

THE PASTA
2 ounces dried linguine

TO FINISH
1½ teaspoons thinly sliced chives
1 tablespoon freshly grated
    Parmesan cheese
Fine sea salt and freshly ground
    white pepper
½ lemon

THE GARNISH
1 ounce Iranian osetra caviar

For the sea urchin sauce, puree the sea urchin roe in a blender. Pass it through a fine-mesh sieve, and return to the blender. Blend the puree with the softened butter.

To finish the sauce, bring the water to a boil in a small saucepan. Gradually whisk in the sea urchin butter, about 1 tablespoon at a time. Season with salt and Espelette pepper and keep warm.

When ready to serve, cook the pasta in a large pot of boiling salted water until al dente; drain.

Put the chives in a medium stainless steel bowl, add the warmed sauce and Parmesan cheese, and mix well. Season with salt and white pepper if necessary. Gently toss the pasta with the sauce.

To serve, use a meat fork to twirl one-quarter of the pasta and mound it in the center of a small bowl. Repeat three times. Drizzle 1 tablespoon of the sauce remaining in the stainless steel bowl around each mound. Squeeze the lemon juice over the pasta and place 1½ teaspoons of the caviar on top of each mound of pasta. Serve immediately.

If you cannot find Sea urchin ask a dependable sushi restaurant for a source

OCTOPUS

BRAISED BABY OCTOPUS WITH BLACK TRUMPET–TRUFFLE
PUREE AND HERB-INFUSED RED WINE–SQUID INK SAUCE

The acidity of the red wine and the earthiness of the
truffle—it's a slightly weird combination of earth and
sea, but it completely elevates the octopus to another
level. Very rich, very satisfying.

SERVES 4

THE OCTOPUS
1 tablespoon canola oil
4 baby octopus, cleaned and rinsed
1½ tablespoons thinly sliced shallots
1 tablespoon thinly sliced garlic
1 ounce Spanish chorizo
  (preferably Palacios), thinly sliced
1 tablespoon tomato paste
1 tablespoon all-purpose flour
3 cups Chicken Stock (PAGE 220)
¼ cup red wine vinegar
1 tablespoon herbes de Provence,
  tied up in a square of cheesecloth
½ cup dry red wine, reduced to
  2 tablespoons
1 teaspoon squid ink
  (SEE SOURCES, PAGE 229)
Fine sea salt to taste

THE BLACK
TRUMPET–TRUFFLE PUREE
1 large Yukon Gold potato
8 ounces trimmed black
  trumpet mushrooms
2 tablespoons unsalted butter,
  cut into small pieces
¾ cup whole milk, warmed
1 tablespoon truffle puree
Fine sea salt and freshly
  ground white pepper

THE GARNISH
Aged Solera sherry vinegar
  (SEE SOURCES, PAGE 229)

For the octopus, heat the canola oil
in a large sauté pan over high heat.
Add the octopus and cook about
2 minutes, just until it changes
from purple to red. Transfer to a
plate. Add the shallots, garlic, and
chorizo to the pan and cook until
the shallots are softened. Add the
tomato paste and cook for 1 minute,
then stir in the flour. Cook for 2 to
3 minutes to make a roux. Add the
octopus, chicken stock, red wine vinegar, and herb sachet and bring to
a boil. Reduce the heat and simmer
for 45 minutes, or until the octopus
is tender.

Meanwhile, for the black trumpet-
truffle puree, put the potato in a
saucepan of cold salted water and
bring to a boil. Reduce the heat
slightly and cook 20 to 25 minutes,
until tender.

While the potato cooks, blanch
the black trumpet mushrooms in a
pot of boiling salted water for 2 to 3
minutes, until tender. Transfer to a
blender and puree.

Drain the potato, peel, and
immediately rice it into a bowl.
Stir in the butter and warm milk,
and pass through a fine-mesh sieve
into a bowl. Stir in the truffle and
black trumpet purees and season
to taste with salt and white pepper.
Keep warm.

When the octopus is tender, stir
in the reduced red wine and the
squid ink. Season to taste with salt.
Transfer the octopus to a bowl and
strain the sauce, then return the
octopus to the sauce.

To serve, spoon 2 tablespoons of
the black trumpet–truffle puree into
the center of each plate and spread
into a circle. Place the octopus in
the center of the puree, tentacle
side up, drizzle 5 drops of sherry vinegar around each plate, and spoon
a ring of sauce around the octopus.
Serve immediately.

MONKFISH

PAN-ROASTED MONKFISH WITH TRUFFLED POTATO FOAM
AND RED WINE–BRANDY SAUCE

At Le Bernardin, we've been hesitant to use foams, gelatins, and other modern techniques because they're more about the technique than the ingredients, and we really believe the star of the plate is the fish. But some of the recipes do get small doses; in this case it's the potato foam, because the dish felt too heavy with traditional potatoes. The sauce needs to be started a day in advance.

SERVES 4

PHOTOGRAPH ON
PAGE 100

THE RED WINE–BRANDY SAUCE
¼ cup diced celery
¼ cup diced carrot
¼ cup diced onion
1 garlic clove, peeled and cut in half
3 button mushrooms, diced
1 thyme sprig
2 Italian parsley sprigs
One 750-ml bottle dry red wine
1½ pounds chicken parts, bones in
Fine sea salt and freshly ground
    black pepper
All-purpose flour for dusting
¼ cup canola oil
½ slice smoked bacon
½ cup brandy
½ cup Chicken Stock (PAGE 220)

THE POTATO FOAM
1 Yukon Gold potato
½ cup whole milk, warmed
2 tablespoons unsalted butter
¼ cup Truffle Butter Sauce
    (PAGE 223), warmed
3 tablespoons truffle juice
Fine sea salt and freshly ground
    white pepper

THE VEGETABLES
¼ cup 1-inch pieces baby
    green beans
¼ cup peeled fava beans
¼ cup 1-inch pieces wax beans
8 Brussels sprouts leaves
1 baby carrot, peeled and quartered
1 baby turnip, peeled and quartered

2 ounces black trumpet mushrooms,
    lightly sautéed
1 tablespoon foie gras fat or
    unsalted butter
Fine sea salt and freshly ground
    white pepper

THE MONKFISH
1 tablespoon canola oil
Four 6-ounce monkfish loins
Fine sea salt and freshly ground
    white pepper
Wondra flour

For the red wine–brandy sauce, combine the celery, carrot, onion, garlic, mushrooms, herbs, and red wine in a bowl. Put the chicken in a baking dish or bowl and pour the marinade over it. Cover and refrigerate for 24 hours.

Remove the chicken from the marinade and lay on a baking pan. Strain the marinade; reserve both the vegetables and liquid. Season the chicken with salt and black pepper and dust lightly with flour. Heat the canola oil in a heavy pot over medium heat. Add the chicken and cook, turning occasionally, until golden brown on all sides. Transfer the chicken to a plate and discard all but 1 tablespoon of the fat from the pot.

Add the bacon to the pot and cook until crisp. Add the reserved vegetables and cook until lightly caramelized. Deglaze the pot with the brandy, scraping up the browned bits. Add the chicken, reserved marinade liquid, and the chicken stock and bring to a boil. Reduce the heat and simmer very gently for about 3

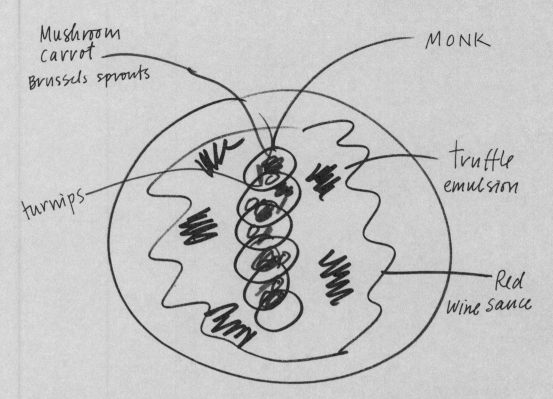

Mushroom
carrot
Brussels sprouts

MONK

truffle
emulsion

turnips

Red
wine sauce

hours, skimming occasionally, until the chicken is falling off the bone. Strain the sauce through a fine-mesh sieve into a saucepan. Over medium heat, reduce the sauce to 1 cup. Season with salt and white pepper, and set aside.

For the potato foam, fill a saucepan with cold salted water, add the potato, and bring to a boil. Reduce the heat slightly and cook until the potato is tender, 20 to 25 minutes. Drain, peel, and rice the potato, then pass through a fine-mesh strainer or drum sieve.

Transfer the warm potato to a pan and stir in the milk, butter, truffle butter sauce, and truffle juice. Season to taste with salt and white pepper. Keep warm.

For the vegetables (except the mushrooms), bring a large saucepan of salted water to a boil. Blanch

each type of vegetable separately until crisp-tender—about 3 minutes for the beans, 2 minutes for the Brussels sprouts, and 4 minutes for the carrot and turnip. When each vegetable is done, drain and immediately plunge into an ice water bath to cool. Drain and set aside.

Preheat the oven to 400°F. Bring a pot of salted water to a boil.

For the monkfish, divide the canola oil between two ovenproof sauté pans and heat until very hot but not smoking. Season the monkfish on both sides with salt and white pepper and lightly dust with Wondra flour. Add the monkfish to the pans and cook until golden brown, about 3 minutes. Transfer the pans to the oven and cook the fish for 3 to 4 minutes, or until a metal skewer can be easily inserted into the fish and, if left in for 5 sec-

onds, feels just warm when touched to your lip. Remove the monkfish from the pans and allow the fish to rest for a minute.

Meanwhile, transfer the truffled potato base to a whipped cream dispenser (see Sources, page 229); set aside. Bring the sauce to a simmer. Reheat the vegetables in the boiling salted water, then drain, transfer to a small mixing bowl, and toss with the foie gras fat or butter. Season to taste with salt and white pepper.

To serve, slice each monkfish loin into five to seven ⅜-inch-thick pieces (depending on the size) and arrange down the center of each plate. Arrange the vegetables on top of the fish and spoon 3 tablespoons of the sauce around each. Dispense the foam into a cup and spoon 2 tablespoons on top of the fish and red wine sauce.

HALIBUT

POACHED HALIBUT WITH MARINATED GRAPES AND CHERRY TOMATOES,
PICKLED SHALLOTS, AND VERJUS-LEMONGRASS INFUSION

Verjus—literally, "green juice"—is the unfermented juice of wine grapes.
We've found that it goes very well with fish. We use two different brands,
one for its mild sweetness and the other for its acidity.

SERVES 4

THE VERJUS-LEMONGRASS INFUSION

1½ cups white verjus
½ cup Fumet (PAGE 221)
¼ teaspoon coriander seeds
¼ teaspoon fennel seeds
¼ teaspoon black peppercorns
1 star anise
1 lemongrass stalk, pounded and thinly sliced
1 teaspoon fresh lime juice
A 2-inch piece of ginger, peeled and sliced
1 small hot red pepper
4 tablespoons (½ stick) unsalted butter, cut into ¼-inch cubes
Fine sea salt and freshly ground white pepper

THE HALIBUT

Poaching Liquid (PAGE 180)
Four 6-ounce halibut fillets
Fine sea salt and freshly ground white pepper

THE GARNISH

4 small cherry tomatoes, peeled and cut in half
4 green grapes, peeled and sliced ¼ inch thick
1 tablespoon Pickled Shallots (PAGE 225)
1 baby fennel bulb, trimmed and thinly sliced
2 radishes, trimmed and quartered
12 sea beans (1½-inch pieces)
½ small Japanese cucumber, sliced ¼ inch thick and then julienned
1 teaspoon extra virgin olive oil
Fine sea salt and freshly ground white pepper
4 chives

For the verjus-lemongrass infusion, combine the verjus and fumet in a stainless steel saucepan and bring to a boil. Add coriander and fennel seeds, the peppercorns, star anise, lemongrass, lime juice, ginger, and red pepper. Let steep off the heat for 15 minutes. Strain the liquid into a saucepan and set aside.

For the halibut, heat the poaching liquid, if necessary, to 180°F, so it is just under a simmer. Season the halibut fillets on both sides with salt and white pepper. Place them in the poaching liquid and poach 5 to 6 minutes, until a metal skewer can be easily inserted into the fish and, if left in for 5 seconds, feels just warm when touched to your lip.

While the halibut is cooking, toss the tomatoes, grapes, pickled shallots, fennel, radishes, sea beans, and cucumber together with the extra virgin olive oil and salt and white pepper to taste. Set aside.

Heat the verjus-lemongrass infusion until hot and whisk in the butter. Season to taste with salt and white pepper.

To serve, remove the halibut from the poaching liquid and drain on a towel. Place a fillet in each of four deep bowls or soup plates. Arrange the vegetables on the halibut, and garnish with the chives. Spoon the verjus-lemongrass infusion around the fish, and serve immediately.

if you cannot find Japanese cucumber, you can use English instead

HALIBUT

BRAISED HALIBUT WITH ASPARAGUS AND WILD MUSHROOMS

This is the perfect one-pot meal, refined but hearty. The broth and the mushrooms give the halibut a deep, meaty flavor. When I entertain at home, I love the drama of setting the steaming casserole in the middle of the table.

SERVES 4

THE BRAISED HALIBUT

½ bunch asparagus, trimmed
1 slice of bacon, cut into ¼-inch-
    wide strips
1 tablespoon unsalted butter
8 pearl onions
4 ounces cèpes (porcini)
4 ounces chanterelles
4 ounces oyster mushrooms
4 ounces morels
2 tablespoons Garlic Butter
    (PAGE 222)
Fine sea salt and freshly ground
    white pepper
Four 6-ounce halibut fillets
2 cups Veal Jus (PAGE 222)
8 pieces Tomato Confit (PAGE 224)

THE GARNISH

1 tablespoon sliced chives

Bring a pot of salted water to a boil. Add the asparagus and cook 3 to 4 minutes, until just barely tender. Drain and immediately plunge into an ice water bath to cool; drain and set aside.

In a large casserole, cook bacon over medium heat until it has rendered its fat and is crisp. Drain on a paper towel.

Pour off all the bacon fat from the casserole; melt the butter. Add the pearl onions and 1 tablespoon water and cook until tender.

When the onions are tender, add all the mushrooms and the garlic butter, season with salt and white pepper, and cook until the mushrooms are softened, about 5 minutes.

Meanwhile, season the halibut on both sides with salt and white pepper. Add the veal jus to the pot and bring to a boil. Add the halibut, cover, and cook for 2 minutes.

Add the asparagus, tomatoes, and bacon to the casserole. Bring back to a simmer and cook for another 2 to 4 minutes, until a metal skewer can be easily inserted into the fish and, when left in for 5 seconds, feels just warm when touched to your lip.

Garnish the fish with sliced chives and serve at the table from the casserole.

HALIBUT

Start citrus-coriander oil one day in advance

POACHED HALIBUT, SWEET-AND-SOUR GOLDEN
AND RED BEETS, AND CITRUS-CORIANDER OIL EMULSION

I picked up this poaching technique from my
friend Laurent Gras, who learned it from a Chinese
chef. Cooking a delicate fish like halibut in a thick
velouté lets the fish retain its moistness and gives it a
wonderful glossiness.

SERVES 4

PHOTOGRAPH ON
PAGE 101

THE SWEET-AND-SOUR BEETS
2 cups red wine vinegar
1 cup sherry vinegar
4 cups water
½ cup kosher salt
2 medium golden beets
2 medium red beets
Fine sea salt and freshly
    ground white pepper
2 tablespoons Infused
    Citrus-Coriander Oil
    (RECIPE FOLLOWS)

**THE CITRUS-CORIANDER
OIL EMULSION**
¾ cup fresh orange juice
2 tablespoons fresh lemon juice
2 tablespoons Ponzu (PAGE 225)
2 teaspoons minced shallot
½ cup Infused Citrus-Coriander Oil
    (RECIPE FOLLOWS)
Fine sea salt and freshly ground
    white pepper
Espelette pepper powder

THE POACHING LIQUID
4 tablespoons unsalted butter
¾ cup all-purpose flour
7 cups water

½ cup fresh orange juice
½ cup fresh lemon juice
1 tablespoon vermouth
Fine sea salt

THE HALIBUT
Four 6-ounce halibut fillets
Fine sea salt and freshly
    ground white pepper

GARNISH
1 tablespoon basil julienne
1 tablespoon opal basil julienne

For the beets, divide the vinegars,
water, and kosher salt between two
medium saucepans. Add the golden
beets to one pan and the red beets
to the other. Bring to a boil, then
reduce the heat slightly and cook
the beets until tender, 45 to 60 minutes. Drain the beets and let cool.

Peel the beets and cut them into
⅛-inch-thick slices. You need 16 yellow beet slices and 12 red beet slices.
Using a 1½-inch round cutter, trim
each slice into a neat circle. Lay the
beet circles on a parchment-lined

baking sheet. (The beets can be
cooked and sliced ahead of time and
kept refrigerated until ready to use.)

For the citrus-coriander oil emulsion, combine the orange juice,
lemon juice, ponzu, and shallot in
a small stainless steel saucepan and
bring to a simmer. Whisking constantly, drizzle in the oil in a steady
stream. Season to taste with salt,
white pepper, and Espelette pepper.
Keep warm.

For the poaching liquid, melt the
butter in a small pot over medium
heat. Add the flour and stir with a
wooden spoon until the mixture
is smooth. Cook the roux, stirring
constantly, until it is a golden straw
color and has a slightly nutty aroma,
about 5 minutes. Remove from the
heat and let cool, to prevent lumps
when you add the roux to the hot
liquid.

Bring the water to a boil in a
medium pot. Add the orange juice,
lemon juice, and vermouth and
bring back to a boil. Whisking constantly, add half of the roux. Add the
rest of the roux and bring to a boil
(the mixture will look like a thick
soup). Season with salt and simmer
until all the raw flour taste has
cooked out, about 15 minutes.

Reduce the heat and let the
poaching liquid cool to 180°F, just
under a simmer. Simmer for a few
more minutes to cook the acidity
out, whisking the liquid occasionally
to prevent a skin from forming.

Preheat the oven to 350°F.

For the halibut, transfer the liquid
to a shallow pan. Season the fillets
on both sides with salt and pepper.
Place them in the poaching liquid

and poach for 5 to 6 minutes, turning once, until a metal skewer can be easily inserted into the fish and, if left in for 5 seconds, feels just warm when touched to your lip.

While the fish is poaching, season the beets with salt and white pepper and drizzle the citrus-coriander oil over them. Heat the beets in the oven until they are warm, about 2 minutes.

To serve, remove the halibut from the poaching liquid and drain on a towel. Arrange 4 golden beet slices and 3 red beet slices in a circle in the center of each plate, alternating red and yellow slices. Place the halibut on top of the beets and garnish with the basil julienne. Spoon the citrus emulsion over and around the halibut, and serve immediately.

INFUSED CITRUS-CORIANDER OIL

Grated zest of 1 orange
Grated zest of 1 lemon
2 tablespoons fennel seeds
2 tablespoons coriander seeds
½ star anise
3 basil sprigs
2 cilantro sprigs
1 tomato, cored and chopped
1 cup olive oil
½ cup extra virgin olive oil
¼ cup lemon oil
Fine sea salt

Crush the orange zest, lemon zest, fennel seeds, coriander seeds, star anise, basil, cilantro, and tomato together in a bowl. Add the 3 oils and season well with salt. Cover with plastic wrap and refrigerate for 24 hours or up to 10 days.

To use, gently warm the oil and strain it through a fine-mesh sieve; discard the aromatics.

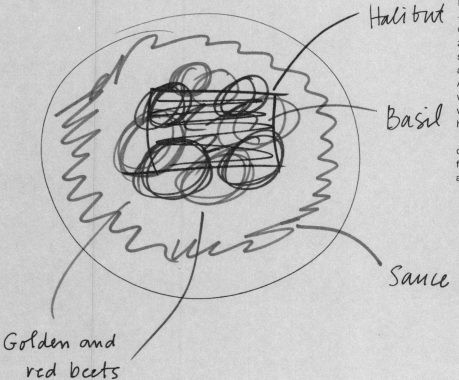

Halibut

Basil

Sauce

Golden and red beets

MONKFISH

A TRIBUTE TO GAUDÍ: PAN-ROASTED MONKFISH, CONFIT PEPPERS,
AND FIERY *PATATAS BRAVAS* WITH CHORIZO-ALBARIÑO EMULSION

After visiting the Sagrada Familia church in Barcelona, I decided to pay tribute to Antonio Gaudí, the avant-garde Catalonian architect, with this dish, which combines the strong, pungent flavors of the region. The pimentón (paprika), an essential ingredient in this cuisine, comes spicy, sweet, smoked, or as a combination; we use the spicy version. Ask your fishmonger for monkfish bones.

SERVES 4

THE RED SAUCE
1 cup ¼-inch-dice red bell pepper
½ teaspoon minced seeded
    Scotch bonnet pepper
1½ teaspoons spicy paprika
Fine sea salt
1½ teaspoons Espelette
    pepper powder

THE WHITE SAUCE
2 tablespoons mayonnaise
2 tablespoons crème fraîche
1 teaspoon fresh lemon juice
Fine sea salt and freshly ground
    white pepper

THE PATATAS BRAVAS
2 to 3 Yukon Gold potatoes
Canola oil for deep-frying
Fine sea salt

THE CONFIT PEPPERS
1 small zucchini
1 cup extra virgin olive oil
1 cup olive oil
4 garlic cloves
4 thyme sprigs
½ cup julienned red bell pepper

½ cup julienned yellow bell pepper
½ cup julienned red onion
Fine sea salt and freshly ground
    white pepper

**THE CHORIZO-
ALBARIÑO EMULSION**
Bones from 1 monkfish, chopped
    into 2-inch pieces
¼ cup extra virgin olive oil
4½ ounces Spanish chorizo,
    thinly sliced
3 tablespoons sliced shallots
1 tablespoon sliced garlic
2½ cups Albariño or other dry
    white wine
½ cup Chicken Jus (PAGE 220)
Fine sea salt and freshly ground
    white pepper

THE MONKFISH
2 tablespoons canola oil
Four 7-ounce monkfish loins
Fine sea salt and freshly ground
    white pepper
Wondra flour

THE GARNISH
Micro parsley sprigs

For the red sauce, combine the peppers, paprika, salt, and Espelette pepper in a saucepan and add just enough water to barely cover the peppers. Bring the water to a boil, then reduce to a simmer and cook until the peppers are very soft and the liquid is thick. Remove from heat and allow to cool slightly.

Puree the sauce in a blender until very smooth. Set aside.

For the white sauce, mix the mayonnaise, crème fraîche, and lemon juice together in a small bowl. Season with salt and white pepper. Refrigerate until ready to serve.

For the potatoes, cut each potato into 8 long wedges, about ¾ inch wide (without peeling them). Lay each wedge on its side and cut out the center portion with a 3-inch round cutter; discard the trimmings. Cook the potatoes in boiling salted water until they are tender, 12 to 15 minutes. Drain the potatoes and cool them on a towel-lined baking sheet, then cover with another towel and set aside.

While the potatoes are cooking, prepare the confit peppers: Slice off the skin of the zucchini and julienne the green parts. To cook the vegetables, combine ¼ cup of the extra virgin olive oil and ¼ cup of the regular olive oil in each of four small pans. (You can use one larger pan for both kinds of peppers, if you wish, combining ½ cup of each oil.) Add 1 garlic clove and 1 thyme sprig to each pan and heat over very low heat. Add one type of vegetable to each pan and cook over very low heat until tender (for the zucchini, this should be 3 to 4 minutes; for the peppers, 10 to 12 minutes; for the onion, 12 to 15 minutes). Drain the vegetables and combine them in a small pot. Season to taste with salt and white pepper.

Preheat the oven to 400°F.

For the chorizo-Albariño emulsion, put the monkfish bones in a small roasting pan and roast for 5 minutes.

Meanwhile, heat the extra virgin olive oil in a medium saucepan. Add the chorizo and cook over low heat until it has rendered its fat, about 10 minutes. Add the shallots, garlic, and fish bones to the chorizo and cook until the shallots and garlic are soft. Add the white wine, bring to a boil, and reduce by a little more than half. Add the chicken jus and simmer until lightly thickened, about 10 minutes.

Strain through a fine-mesh sieve into a bowl and season with salt and white pepper. Emulsify the sauce with a handheld immersion blender.

Heat the canola oil for the potatoes in a deep pot until it registers 400°F.

Fry the potatoes for 5 to 7 minutes, until golden brown. Drain on paper towels, and season with salt.

Meanwhile, to cook the monkfish, divide the canola oil between two large ovenproof sauté pans and heat until the oil is very hot but not smoking. Season the monkfish on both sides with salt and white pepper and lightly dust with Wondra flour. Add the monkfish to the pans and cook until the fish is golden brown. Transfer the pans to the oven and cook the fish for 3 to 4 minutes, or until a metal skewer can be easily inserted into the fish and, if left in for 5 seconds, feels just warm when touched to your lip. Turn the monkfish onto the unseared side briefly before removing from the pans. Allow the fish to rest for a minute before slicing.

While the monkfish is cooking, briefly warm the pepper confit; keep warm.

To serve, arrange 4 potato wedges in a fan on one side of each serving plate. Drizzle them with the red sauce and then the white sauce. Slice each monkfish into 5 to 7 pieces (depending on the size), and arrange the slices on the opposite side of each plate. Spoon some warm pepper confit on top of the monkfish and garnish with the micro parsley. Spoon or pour the emulsion over and around the fish, and serve immediately.

SKATE

GRILLED SKATE WITH MANGO-JALAPEÑO SALAD
IN LIME AND GUAJILLO PEPPER BROTH

Skate is a delicate fish, which can make it difficult to prepare, especially since it needs to be cooked off the bone. There's also a very small window of time in which it can be used: just out of the water, its flesh is tough, and after a couple of days, it develops a strong aroma. But it's great at carrying a lot of complex flavors, and this dish is a prime example.

SERVES 4

THE LIME AND GUAJILLO PEPPER BROTH
1 teaspoon canola oil
2 tablespoons thinly sliced shallots
1 teaspoon thinly sliced garlic
1 tablespoon thinly sliced ginger
¼ cup chopped red bell pepper
1 star anise
2 cups Pot-au-Feu Broth (PAGE 221), reduced to 1 cup
1 teaspoon Guajillo Pepper Sauce (RECIPE FOLLOWS)
Fine sea salt and freshly ground white pepper

THE SKATE
Four 6-ounce boneless, skinless skate wings
Fine sea salt and freshly ground white pepper
1 lime, cut in half
4 teaspoons Brown Butter Sauce (PAGE 223)
4 teaspoons Guajillo Pepper Sauce (RECIPE FOLLOWS)

THE MANGO-JALAPEÑO SALAD
½ mango, peeled and thinly sliced
1 jalapeño, seeded and julienned
½ teaspoon Guajillo Pepper Sauce (RECIPE FOLLOWS)
½ teaspoon Brown Butter Sauce (PAGE 223)
1 lime, cut in half
Fine sea salt and freshly ground white pepper

THE GARNISH
1 teaspoon cilantro julienne
2 teaspoons Basil Oil (PAGE 225)

Can also use a grill pan on the stovetop

For the guajillo pepper broth, heat the canola oil in a small pot. Add the shallots, garlic, ginger, and red bell pepper and cook until they start to soften but do not color, 2 to 3 minutes. Add the star anise and pot-au-feu, bring to a simmer, and cook for 10 to 15 minutes, until the flavors of the spices come out.

Add the pepper sauce to the broth and season to taste with salt and white pepper. Strain through a fine-mesh sieve into a saucepan and set aside.

For the skate, preheat a grill until it is very hot. Preheat the oven to 350°F.

Lightly oil the grill with canola oil. Season the skate wings with salt and white pepper. Place on the grill and grill on one side only.

Transfer the skate to a baking sheet, grilled side up. Drizzle a generous squeeze of lime juice over the skate and then brush each piece with 1 teaspoon of the brown butter sauce, followed by 1 teaspoon of the pepper sauce. Transfer to the oven and cook for 3 to 4 minutes.

Meanwhile, bring the broth to a boil; lower the heat to keep warm.

For the salad, combine the mango and jalapeño and toss with the pepper sauce, brown butter sauce, and lime juice to taste. Season to taste with salt and white pepper.

To serve, place a skate wing in the center of each plate. Arrange one-quarter of the salad on top of each portion. Scatter the cilantro julienne over the top. Pour the broth around the skate and spoon drops of the basil oil onto the broth. Serve immediately.

GUAJILLO PEPPER SAUCE
MAKES ¼ CUP

½ cup bourbon
2 tablespoons guajillo pepper paste
⅛ teaspoon Worcestershire sauce
⅛ teaspoon white vinegar
3 tablespoons muscovado sugar
½ teaspoon Chinese 5-spice powder
1 teaspoon chile powder
½ teaspoon garlic powder

Heat the bourbon in a small saucepan, and reduce by half. Remove from the heat and whisk in the rest of the ingredients.

Transfer to a container and refrigerate until ready to use; keeps for up to 1 week.

STRIPED BASS

BAKED LANGOUSTINES AND STRIPED BASS, CONFIT TOMATO AGNOLOTTI,
BOUILLABAISSE CONSOMMÉ, AND CURRY EMULSION

For this dish, we wanted the flavors of a bouillabaisse, but lighter and more delicate. So we clarified the bouillabaisse stock to get a more elegant consommé. At the same time, we were playing around with a garlic curry butter that became our "rouille." Ask your fishmonger for lobster bodies.

SERVES 4

PHOTOGRAPH ON
PAGES 98–99

THE TOMATO AGNOLOTTI
2 tablespoons Garlic Butter
  (PAGE 222)
1 cup chopped Tomato Confit,
  (PAGE 224)
Fine sea salt and freshly
  ground white pepper
Pasta Dough (RECIPE FOLLOWS)
Wondra flour
1 egg, whisked with 1 teaspoon
  water for egg wash
20 micro chives

THE BOUILLABAISSE BROTH
1 tablespoon canola oil
4 lobster bodies, torn in half,
  cut up
1 small fennel bulb, trimmed
  and thinly sliced
½ cup thinly sliced shallots
¼ cup thinly sliced garlic
Fine sea salt and freshly
  ground white pepper
1 tablespoon tomato paste
1 tomato, cored and chopped
½ teaspoon saffron threads

½ star anise
1 tablespoon fennel seeds
6 cups Shrimp Stock (PAGE 221)
8 ounces nonoily white fish fillets
  (such as red snapper or bass),
  cut into 2-inch pieces
2 egg whites
Roe from 2 lobsters

THE CURRY EMULSION
8 tablespoons (1 stick)
  unsalted butter, softened
2 tablespoons minced
  peeled ginger
1 tablespoon minced garlic
1 teaspoon Dijon mustard
2 tablespoons fresh lime juice
½ teaspoon Sriracha hot
  chile sauce
1 teaspoon Espelette
  pepper powder
1 teaspoon ground turmeric
¼ cup dry white wine
Fine sea salt and freshly
  ground white pepper

THE ONION AND
FENNEL COMPOTE
½ small onion, thinly sliced
½ small fennel bulb, trimmed
  and thinly sliced
Pinch of saffron threads
1 star anise
1 tablespoon unsalted butter
Fine sea salt and freshly
  ground white pepper

THE LANGOUSTINES AND
STRIPED BASS
4 tablespoons unsalted
  butter, softened
Four 5-ounce striped bass fillets,
  skin removed
Fine sea salt and freshly
  ground white pepper
4 langoustines, heads removed
  and shelled
Espelette pepper powder
1 teaspoon canola oil

For the agnolotti, melt the garlic butter in a small saucepan and cook until the shallots and garlic in it are softened. Add the tomato confit and cook until all of the confit liquid is reduced. Remove from the heat, season with salt and white pepper, and let cool completely.

To roll out the pasta dough, set the rollers of a pasta machine at the widest setting. Run the dough through the machine, fold in half, and run it through again. Repeat 3 times. The dough should be very smooth and elastic. Reduce the setting by one notch and run the pasta through; do not fold. Roll through the next-thinnest setting, and continue the process through the next-to-last setting—the dough should be very thin and the pasta sheet at least 3 inches wide.

Lay the dough sheet on a work surface dusted with Wondra flour with a long side toward you, and trim it to 30 inches long. Lightly brush the bottom half of the dough with egg wash. Starting 1 inch from the end of the sheet, place 20 mounds, about 1 teaspoon each, of the cooled tomato confit 1½ inches apart on the egg-washed dough. Fold the top half of the dough over the filling. Dust the dough with Wondra, and mold it over to seal. Cut out the agnolotti with a 1-inch round cutter. Dust a parchment-paper-lined baking sheet with Wondra and place the agnolotti on it. Dust the top of the agnolotti with more flour. (The agnolotti can be made up to a week ahead and frozen.)

For the bouillabaisse broth, heat the canola oil in a heavy stockpot.

Add the lobster bodies and sear until they turn red. Add the fennel, shallots, and garlic, and cook the vegetables until softened, 2 to 3 minutes. Season lightly with salt and white pepper. Add the tomato paste, tomato, saffron, star anise, and fennel seeds and cook for another few minutes, until all the flavors have come together. Cover with the shrimp stock, bring to a simmer, and simmer for 20 to 30 minutes, until reduced by one-third.

Add the fish and cook for 10 minutes. Season to taste with salt and white pepper, and strain the broth through a fine-mesh sieve. Cool, then chill.

To clarify the broth, whisk the egg whites and lobster roe in a bowl until frothy. Pour the cold broth into a pot, stir in the egg whites, and slowly bring to a simmer, stirring constantly so the egg whites do not stick to the bottom of the pot. Stop stirring once the "raft" comes together, and simmer gently for 10 minutes. Carefully ladle the consommé through a sieve lined with a coffee filter into a pot, being careful not to break up the raft too much. Set aside.

For the curry emulsion, combine the butter, ginger, garlic, Dijon mustard, lime juice, chile sauce, Espelette pepper, and turmeric in a food processor. Process until smooth and well blended. Transfer to a container and chill.

For the onion and fennel compote, combine all of the ingredients except the salt and pepper in a small saucepan. Bring to a simmer and cook until the onion and fennel are

PASTA DOUGH
MAKES ABOUT 1/2 POUND

4 large egg yolks
1½ teaspoons water
½ cup plus 1 tablespoon all-purpose flour, or as needed
½ teaspoon fine sea salt

Combine all the ingredients in the bowl of a stand mixer fitted with the dough hook. Mix on low speed for a few minutes, until the dough starts to pull away from the sides of the bowl and becomes smooth and elastic; add a little extra flour if needed. Form the dough into a flat rectangle and wrap tightly in plastic wrap.

Place in the refrigerator and let rest for at least 20 minutes before using.

very soft. Season with salt and white pepper. Set aside.

Preheat the oven to 375°F. Bring a large pot of water to a boil.

To finish the curry emulsion, bring the white wine to a boil in a small saucepan. Whisk in the curry butter in small increments until it is thoroughly incorporated. Pass through a fine-mesh sieve into a pan and season with salt and white pepper. Keep warm.

For the fish, brush some butter over the bottom of a baking dish large enough to hold the fillets comfortably. Season the striped bass on both sides with salt and white pepper and lay the fish in the baking dish. Brush the top of the bass with more butter and add ½ cup water to the baking dish. Put the baking dish in the oven and cook the fish 6 to 8 minutes, until a metal skewer can be easily inserted into a fillet and, if left in for 5 seconds, feels just warm when touched to your lip.

While the fish is cooking, bring the bouillabaisse broth to a boil; reduce the heat and keep warm.

Season the langoustines with salt, white pepper, and Espelette pepper. Heat the canola oil in a nonstick pan and sauté the langoustines for 1 to 2 minutes, until they just start to turn opaque.

Add the agnolotti to the boiling salted water (if frozen, they do not have to be thawed), and cook until they just start to float, 30 seconds to 1 minute. Remove with a skimmer and drain on a towel.

To serve, reheat the compote. Put a striped bass fillet in the center of each plate. Spoon 1 teaspoon of the onion and fennel compote over each fish, and top with a langoustine. Place 5 agnolotti around each fish, and spoon the bouillabaisse broth around the fish. Drizzle 1 tablespoon of the curry emulsion over the bouillabaisse on each plate. Place a micro chive on each agnolotti and serve immediately.

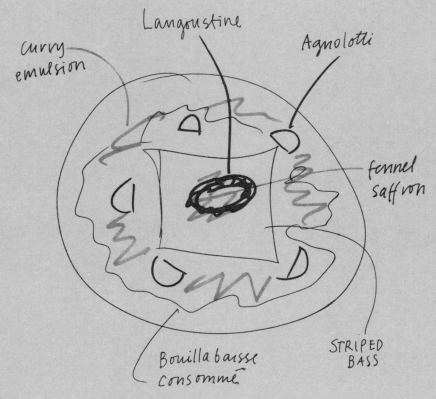

Langoustine

curry emulsion

Agnolotti

fennel saffron

Bouillabaisse consommé

STRIPED BASS

STRIPED BASS

STRIPED BASS WITH SWEET CORN PUREE,
GRILLED SHISHITO PEPPERS, SHAVED SMOKED BONITO,
AND MOLE SAUCE

Sweet, spicy, and smoky, the mole sauce in this
dish is well worth the time and effort. Its richness is
balanced and heightened by both the striped bass
and the velvety corn puree.

SERVES 4

THE SWEET CORN PUREE
2 cups fresh corn kernels
1 tablespoon unsalted butter
Fine sea salt and freshly ground
  white pepper

THE SHISHITO PEPPERS
8 shishito peppers (SEE SOURCES,
  PAGE 229)
1 tablespoon olive oil
Fine sea salt and freshly ground
  white pepper

THE MOLE SAUCE
1 tablespoon canola oil
1 teaspoon thinly sliced garlic
1 tablespoon thinly sliced shallot
1½ cups Veal Jus (PAGE 222),
  reduced to ¾ cup
½ cup red wine, reduced to
  2 tablespoons
5 ounces Shrimp Stock (PAGE 221),
  reduced to 5 tablespoons
1½ teaspoons guajillo chile puree
  (SEE SOURCES, PAGE 229)
1 teaspoon ancho chile puree
  (SEE SOURCES, PAGE 229)
1 teaspoon melted dark chocolate
1 teaspoon almond flour

THE STRIPED BASS
Canola oil
Four 6-ounce striped bass fillets
Fine sea salt and freshly ground
  white pepper
Wondra four

THE GARNISH
1 tablespoon smoked bonito flakes
  (SEE SOURCES, PAGE 229)
½ teaspoon Maldon sea salt

For the corn puree, put the kernels
in a blender and puree until smooth.
Strain the puree through a fine-
mesh sieve into a saucepan; discard
the solids. Bring to a boil, stirring
frequently and cook, stirring, until
thickened. Stir in the butter and
season with salt and white pepper.
Strain through a fine-mesh sieve,
and set aside.

For the peppers, place them on
a hot grill or under a preheated
broiler, turning occasionally, until
the skin is blistered and charred.
Transfer to a bowl, cover with plastic
wrap, and let steam for 10 minutes.
Wearing gloves, peel the blackened
skin with your fingertips and remove

the stems and seeds. Toss with the
olive oil and season with salt and
white pepper. Set aside.

Preheat the oven to 400°F.

For the mole sauce, heat the
canola oil in a medium saucepan
over medium heat. Add the garlic
and shallot and cook until softened.
Add the reduced veal jus, bring
to a simmer, and simmer for 5
minutes to infuse the flavors. Add
the reduced red wine and shrimp
stock and simmer for 5 minutes. Stir
in the guajillo and ancho purees.
Remove from the heat and set aside.

For the fish, divide the canola oil
between two ovenproof sauté pans
and heat until the oil is very hot but
not smoking. Season the striped bass
on both sides with salt and white
pepper and dust with Wondra flour.
Put the striped bass in the pans and
sear on the stovetop over medium
heat until golden brown on the
bottom, about 3 minutes. Turn the
fish over, put the pans in the oven,
and cook for another 2 to 3 minutes,
until a metal skewer can be easily
inserted into the center of a fillet
and, if left in for 5 seconds, feels just
warm when touched to your lip.

Meanwhile, reheat the sauce.
Add the melted chocolate and
almond flour and let stand for 2
minutes, then strain through a
fine-mesh sieve.

To serve, reheat the corn puree
and spoon 1 tablespoon into the
center of each plate. Arrange a
fillet on the middle of the puree
and spoon some of the mole sauce
around the fish. Garnish with 2
peppers each and sprinkle with the
bonito flakes and Maldon sea salt.

LOBSTER
ROASTED LOBSTER WITH WILTED ROMAINE, BUTTERNUT SQUASH,
CANDIED GINGER, AND PORT AND TAMARIND REDUCTION

This dish started its life as lobster and port sauce, but it eventually turned into this sweet and spicy tropical dish, with a hit of acidity from the wilted romaine.

We're very picky about our lobsters at Le Bernardin. We get them live every morning and always order females, recognizable by their hairy legs (which let them carry their eggs). They also contain the coral that we use in other dishes such as lobster cappuccino and bouillabaisse consommé. When choosing live lobsters, make sure that their shells are very hard and they have long antennae (if left in a tank too long, they tend to eat one another's antennae). And check the underside: it should be nice and plump.

SERVES 4

THE PORT AND TAMARIND REDUCTION
1 tablespoon unsalted butter
2 tablespoons thinly sliced shallots
2 tablespoons thinly sliced peeled ginger
1 slice jalapeño
1 cup port
1 cup dry red wine
2 cups Shrimp Stock (PAGE 221), reduced to 1 cup
1 cup Veal Jus (PAGE 222), reduced to ½ cup
1½ tablespoons natural tamarind concentrate (SEE SOURCES, PAGE 229)
Fine sea salt and freshly ground white pepper

THE BUTTERNUT SQUASH
1 butternut squash, at least 4 inches in diameter
1 tablespoon unsalted butter
Fine sea salt and freshly ground white pepper

THE GARNISH
2 large pieces candied ginger

THE LOBSTER
Four 1½-pound lobsters
¼ cup water
4 tablespoons unsalted butter, softened
Fine sea salt and freshly ground white pepper

THE ROMAINE
2 tablespoons unsalted butter
20 tender inner romaine leaves (from 2 heads), trimmed to 3½ inches
Fine sea salt and freshly ground black pepper
1 lemon, cut in half

For the port and tamarind reduction, melt the butter in a medium saucepan. Add the shallots, ginger, and jalapeño and cook until softened, about 5 minutes. Add the port and red wine, bring to a boil, and reduce to ½ cup. Add the shrimp stock and veal jus and bring to a boil, then reduce the heat to low and simmer for 15 minutes, or until the sauce coats the back of a spoon.

Stir in the tamarind concentrate and season to taste with salt and white pepper. Strain through a fine-mesh sieve into a saucepan and set aside.

For the butternut squash, cut four ¼-inch-thick slices from the neck of the squash; reserve the remaining squash for another use. Using a 2½-inch round cutter, cut each slice into a neat round. Bring the butter and 1 cup water to a boil in a small saucepan. Add the squash rounds, season with salt and white pepper, and cook at a simmer until the squash is tender, about 6 to 8 minutes. Let the squash cool in the liquid.

For the candied ginger, bring a small pot of water to a boil. Rinse the ginger. Remove the pot from the stove, add the ginger, and allow to soak for 5 minutes, in order to soften. Drain the ginger, pat dry, and cut into julienne. Set aside.

Preheat the oven to 350°F.

To kill the lobsters, plunge a heavy knife through the head of each one above the eyes, making sure the knife goes all the way through the head, then pull the knife in a downward motion through the eyes. Twist off the claws and reserve. Twist off the tails. Place each tail on a cutting board, press to flatten it, and, using a sharp knife, split it from end to end. Remove the vein that runs down the center of each tail. (Reserve the bodies for another use, such as lobster stock, if desired.) Refrigerate the tails until ready to cook.

For the claws, bring a large pot of salted water to a boil. Add the claws and cook for 5 minutes. Drain the claws and set aside until cool enough to handle.

Separate the knuckles from the claws. Using a pair of kitchen scissors, cut through the knuckles, and remove the meat. Crack the claws with the back of a knife and twist to open. Extract the claw meat and reserve along with the knuckles. Refrigerate until ready to cook.

To make a beurre monté for the lobster, bring the ¼ cup water to a boil in a small saucepan. Gradually whisk in the butter, about a tablespoon at a time, until fully incorporated. Season to taste with salt and white pepper and keep warm.

Season the lobster tails with salt and white pepper. Put them in a baking pan and brush them with beurre monté. Place them in the oven and bake until they just turn opaque, about 3 to 5 minutes.

Meanwhile, gently heat the lobster claws and knuckles in the remaining beurre monté. Reheat the butternut squash in its liquid; keep warm. Heat the tamarind reduction.

For the romaine leaves, melt the butter in a sauté pan. When the butter just starts to brown lightly, add the romaine leaves, season with salt, white pepper, and lemon juice, and toss.

To serve, place a slice of butternut squash in the center of each plate. Fan 5 romaine leaves around each slice. Take the lobster tails out of their shells and arrange 2 lobster tail halves, cut side up, on top of each slice of squash; place a lobster claw and knuckle on top of the lobster tails. Drape the julienned ginger over the lobster claws. Pour the tamarind reduction around the plates, and serve immediately.

SNAPPER

BAKED SNAPPER IN A SPICY-SOUR PUERTO RICAN SANCOCHO BROTH,
WITH SWEET POTATO, PLANTAIN, AND AVOCADO

For more than twenty years, Puerto Rico has been a big influence in my life. This has largely been thanks to my friendship with chef Alfredo Ayala, who has an incredible knowledge of his home island and has mastered its cuisine. He was the inspiration for this dish. The meaty broth is a perfect match for the delicacy of the fish while the avocado introduces an element of freshness.

SERVES 4

THE SANCOCHO BROTH
1 teaspoon unsalted butter
3 ounces Spanish chorizo, sliced
½ small red bell pepper, sliced (about 3 tablespoons)
½ small yellow bell pepper, sliced (about 3 tablespoons)
3 tablespoons sliced onion
1½ tablespoons sliced garlic
2 teaspoons sliced seeded jalapeño
2 cups Pot-au-Feu Broth (PAGE 221)
Fine sea salt and freshly ground white pepper

THE SOFRITO BUTTER
5 tablespoons unsalted butter, softened
¼ small red bell pepper, sliced (about 1 tablespoon)
¼ small yellow bell pepper, sliced (about 1 tablespoon)
1 teaspoon sliced garlic
½ jalapeño, sliced (about 1 teaspoon)
1 tablespoon sliced onion
1 tablespoon chopped cilantro

THE SWEET POTATOES
1 sweet potato
1 white sweet potato

THE PLANTAIN PUREE
1 ripe plantain
Fine sea salt and freshly ground white pepper

THE SNAPPER
Four 7-ounce snapper fillets
Fine sea salt and freshly ground white pepper

THE GARNISH
1 avocado, peeled, pitted, quartered, and sliced crosswise
Fine sea salt and freshly ground white pepper
1 teaspoon fresh lime juice
2 teaspoons micro cilantro or cilantro julienne

For the sancocho broth, melt the butter in a sauté pan. Add the chorizo and the bell peppers, onion, garlic, and jalapeño and cook until translucent. Add the pot-au-feu broth, bring to a simmer, and simmer for 25 minutes. Season with salt and white pepper. Strain into a saucepan and set aside.

Preheat the oven to 400°F.

For the sofrito butter, melt the butter in a sauté pan. Add all the remaining ingredients except the cilantro and cook until the vegetables are soft. Transfer to a blender and puree. Pour into a bowl and let cool, then add the chopped cilantro. Set aside.

For the potatoes, place the potatoes in a baking dish and add ¼ cup water. Cover the dish with aluminum foil and bake in the oven for 25 to 30 minutes, until tender.

Meanwhile, make the plantain puree. Peel the plantain and cook in boiling salted water until very soft. Drain and puree in a blender until smooth. Transfer to a saucepan and season with salt and white pepper. Set aside.

When the potatoes are done, remove from the oven and let cool completely. Peel and slice crosswise into ½-inch-thick slices. Using a 1-inch cutter, cut out 12 disks from each slice. Lay them out on a parchment-lined baking pan. Set aside.

When ready to serve, brush a baking dish that will hold the snapper comfortably with some of the sofrito butter and add enough water to barely cover the bottom of the dish. Lightly season the snapper fillets on both sides with salt and white pepper and place them in the baking dish. Brush the top of the fillets with the sofrito butter. Bake the fish 6 to 8 minutes, until a metal skewer can be easily inserted into a fillet and, if left in for 5 seconds, feels warm when touched to your lip.

Meanwhile, bring the broth to a boil; keep warm. Reheat the plantain puree. Season the avocado with salt and white pepper and drizzle with the lime juice.

To serve, arrange the sweet potatoes, alternating the colors, in a circle toward the edges of each plate. Put some micro cilantro on top of each disk. Spoon a small amount of warm plantain puree down the middle of each plate and place a fillet on the puree. Arrange some avocado on top of the fish. Pour the broth around each plate. Serve immediately.

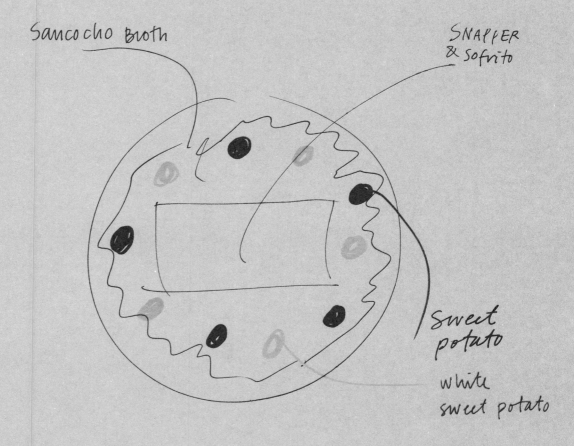

Sancocho Broth

SNAPPER & sofrito

sweet potato

white sweet potato

COD

PAN-ROASTED COD WITH SAUTÉED BABY ARTICHOKES,
PISTACHIOS, AND PARMESAN IN SAGE-AND-GARLIC BROTH

Most of the recipes of Le Bernardin are influenced by food I've eaten during my travels, in my neighborhood, or even on the street. Baraonda, an Italian restaurant in Manhattan, serves a great salad of baby artichokes and arugula. It took me years of dancing on their tables and eating that salad to come up with this dish. Codfish loves garlicky combinations, and the leanness and firmness of the artichokes gives the rich fish the illusion of lightness. The sage and garlic broth is based on my grandfather's hangover cure.

SERVES 4

THE SAGE-AND-GARLIC BROTH
1 cup Chicken Jus (PAGE 220)
½ ounce bonito flakes
A 1-ounce piece of Parmesan rind
4 sage leaves
1 tablespoon sliced garlic
Fine sea salt and freshly
    ground white pepper

THE BABY ARTICHOKES
6 baby artichokes
1 tablespoon extra virgin olive oil
2 tablespoons chopped pistachios
Fine sea salt and freshly
    ground white pepper
¼ cup dry white wine
1 teaspoon unsalted butter
¼ cup freshly grated Parmesan

THE CODFISH
4 tablespoons canola oil
Four 6-ounce codfish fillets
Fine sea salt and freshly
    ground white pepper
Wondra flour

THE GARNISH
½ cup baby arugula

Preheat the oven to 350°F.

For the sage-and-garlic broth, bring the chicken jus to a boil in a small saucepan. Remove from the heat and add the bonito, Parmesan rind, sage, and garlic. Let infuse for 10 minutes. Season the broth with salt and white pepper and strain through a fine-mesh sieve. Set aside.

To clean the artichokes, remove the tough outer leaves of the artichoke. Using a paring knife, trim the top ½ inch off of the artichoke. Store in acidulated water until ready to use.

For the codfish, divide the canola oil between two ovenproof sauté pans (or use one large pan) and heat until very hot but not smoking. Season the codfish on both sides with salt and white pepper and dust with Wondra flour. Add the codfish to the pans and sear until golden brown on the bottom, about 3 minutes. Turn the fish over, put the pans in the oven, and cook the fish for another 2 to 3 minutes, until a metal skewer can be easily inserted into the fish and, if left in for 5 seconds, feels just warm when touched to your lip.

While the fish is cooking, prepare the artichokes: Drain the artichokes, pat them dry with paper towels, and using a Japanese mandoline, thinly shave them. Heat the extra virgin olive oil in a sauté pan. Add the artichokes and pistachios and season with salt and white pepper. Add the white wine, bring to a boil, and reduce by half. Add the butter and then stir in the Parmesan. Remove from the heat.

Meanwhile, reheat the broth; keep warm.

To serve, spoon the artichokes into the center of four large bowls. Place a codfish fillet on each bed of artichokes. Scatter the baby arugula around the fish. Pour the broth into the bowls, and serve immediately.

SALMON

BARELY COOKED WILD ALASKAN SALMON, MORELS,
AND SPRING VEGETABLES IN A WILD MUSHROOM POT-AU-FEU

In this version of a pot-au-feu, the richness of the salmon is a great foundation for the truffles, which in turn heighten the vegetables and complement the morels.

SERVES 4

THE MORELS
1 teaspoon canola oil
4 ounces morels, trimmed
Fine sea salt and freshly
    ground white pepper
2 teaspoons Garlic Butter
    (PAGE 222)

THE SPRING VEGETABLES
½ bunch pencil asparagus,
    tips trimmed to 1½ inches,
    stalks reserved for another use
¼ cup green peas
¼ cup peeled fava beans
16 pieces baby leeks (white part
    only), trimmed to 1½ inches
½ cup Truffle Butter Sauce
    (PAGE 223)
Fine sea salt and freshly
    ground white pepper

**THE WILD MUSHROOM
POT-AU-FEU**
1 cup Mushroom Stock (PAGE 220)
2 dried cèpes (porcini)
1 cup Pot-au-Feu Broth (PAGE 221)
Fine sea salt and freshly
    ground white pepper
1 teaspoon truffle juice

THE SALMON
Eight 3-ounce wild Alaskan salmon
    fillets, skin removed
Fine sea salt and freshly ground
    white pepper

For the morels, heat the canola oil in a sauté pan. Add the mushrooms and sauté for 4 minutes, until tender. Season with salt and white pepper. Set aside.

For the vegetables, bring a small pot of salted water to a boil. Cook the asparagus, peas, fava beans, and leeks in the boiling water until tender, 3 to 4 minutes. Drain and immediately plunge into an ice bath to cool, then drain and set aside.

For the mushroom pot-au-feu, bring the mushroom stock to a boil in a saucepan and reduce by half. Add the dried cèpes and let infuse for 5 minutes.

Meanwhile, bring the pot-au-feu broth to a boil in another saucepan and reduce by half. Season lightly with salt and white pepper and remove from the heat.

Strain the reduced mushroom stock and add to the reduced pot-au-feu broth. Add the truffle juice, season if necessary. Set aside.

For the salmon, pour enough water to cover the bottom into a casserole that will hold the salmon comfortably. Season with salt and place the pot over medium heat. Season the salmon on both sides with salt and white pepper, place the salmon fillets in the pot, and cook at a simmer until the top of the fish is just warm to the touch, about 3 minutes.

While the salmon is cooking, bring the pot-au-feu to a boil.

Melt the garlic butter in a medium sauté pan. Add the morels and sauté briefly, about 2 minutes, until warmed through. Add the leeks, asparagus, peas, and fava beans. Add the truffle butter sauce and stir. Season with salt and white pepper.

Remove the salmon from the casserole and drain on a towel. Place one salmon fillet at the top of each serving plate, toward the right. Place a second salmon fillet at the bottom of the plate, toward the left. Pour the mushroom pot-au-feu around each plate. Spoon the vegetables and sauce over the salmon, and serve immediately.

RED SNAPPER

PAN-ROASTED RED SNAPPER WITH SAUTÉED PEA SHOOTS
AND GINGER-LEMON-SCALLION BROTH

I had terrific pea shoots at a restaurant in Hong Kong, but when we tried to get them in New York, we found them tough and stringy. Then we asked Blue Moon, an organic farm in Pennsylvania, to grow some for us. We now go through sixty pounds a week. They're a sweet, neutral green with an interesting texture—half silky, half al dente—and the ability to take on whatever flavors you put them with.

SERVES 4

THE GINGER-LEMON-SCALLION BROTH
1 tablespoon canola oil
One 2-inch piece thinly sliced peeled ginger
1 clove thinly sliced garlic
1 small thinly sliced shallot
¼ cup sliced shiitake mushroom caps
1½ cups Chicken Stock (PAGE 220)
1 ounce foie gras
Fine sea salt and freshly ground white pepper
2 scallions, green part only, thinly sliced
1 petal Lemon Confit (PAGE 224), briefly blanched and minced

THE RED SNAPPER
2 tablespoons canola oil
Four 7-ounce red snapper fillets, skin on
Fine sea salt and freshly ground white pepper
Wondra flour

THE PEA SHOOTS
1 tablespoon unsalted butter
1 garlic clove, minced
1½ teaspoons minced peeled ginger
8 cups baby pea shoots (if not available, substitute mature pea shoot tops)
¼ cup blanched green peas
1 tablespoon soy sauce
Fine sea salt and freshly ground white pepper

For the broth, heat the canola oil in medium saucepan. Add the ginger, garlic, shallots, and shiitake mushrooms and cook for 5 minutes, or until softened; do not allow them to color. Add the chicken stock and foie grac, bring to a simmer, and simmer for 20 to 30 minutes, until all of the flavors come together. Season to taste with salt and white pepper and strain through a fine-mesh sieve. Set aside.

Preheat the oven to 350°F.

For the fish, divide the canola oil between two ovenproof sauté pans and heat until very hot but not smoking. Season the red snapper on both sides with salt and white

baby spinach will also work

pepper and lightly dust with Wondra flour. Add the red snapper to the pans skin side down, briefly pressing down on each fillet with a metal spatula as you add it to prevent the skin from shrinking. Sauté the fish until the skin side is golden brown and crisp (but not burned), 3 to 5 minutes. Turn the fish over, put the pans in the oven, and cook the fish for 3 to 5 minutes longer, until a metal skewer can be easily inserted into the fish and, if left in for 5 seconds, feels just warm when touched to your lip.

While the fish is cooking, sauté the pea shoots. Melt the butter in a large sauté pan. Add the garlic and ginger and cook over medium heat for 2 minutes, or until tender. Add the pea shoots and peas and cook, stirring just until the pea shoots are wilted. Add the soy sauce and toss well. Season to taste with salt and white pepper, and remove from the heat.

Meanwhile, bring the broth to a boil. Add the scallion greens and lemon confit.

To serve, divide the pea shoots among four bowls. Place the red snapper on top of the pea shoots and pour the broth around the fish.

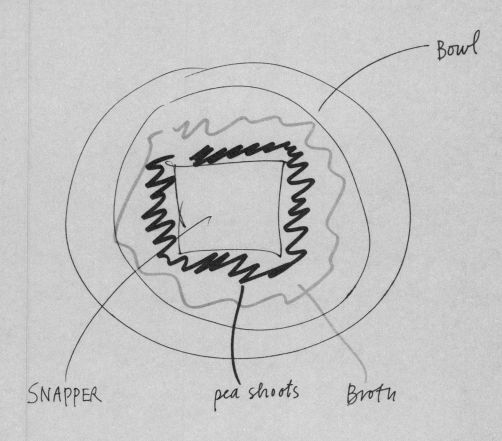

Bowl

SNAPPER   pea shoots   Broth

SURF-AND-TURF

ESCOLAR AND SEARED JAPANESE KOBE BEEF "KOREAN BBQ STYLE,"
WITH FRESH KIMCHI AND YUZU–BROWN BUTTER EMULSION

Le Bernardin has always been a fish restaurant, but for a period we had a surf-and-turf tasting, every course of which had a meat component. It broadened not only our menu, but also our expectations of fish. The combination of the very rich Kobe beef and the silky escolar in this dish is hard to beat. If you can't find Kobe at your butcher or through mail order, a well-marbled, dry-aged steak will work. Sriracha chile sauce can be substituted for the Korean hot pepper paste.

SERVES 4

PHOTOGRAPH ON
PAGES 102–3

THE KIMCHI MARINADE
½ teaspoon fine sea salt
⅛ teaspoon xanthan gum
  (SEE SOURCES, PAGE 229)
½ teaspoon Espelette
  pepper powder
Pinch of sugar
¼ cup fresh lemon juice
1 teaspoon thinly sliced garlic
1 tablespoon Korean hot
  pepper paste (gochujang)
¼ cup extra virgin olive oil

THE BBQ SAUCE
1 tablespoon sliced garlic
1 teaspoon sliced peeled ginger
¼ cup grated onion (use a
  box grater)
¼ cup white miso paste
½ cup Korean hot pepper
  paste (gochujang)
¼ cup rice wine vinegar
2 tablespoons mirin
2 tablespoons soy sauce
½ teaspoon Asian sesame oil
½ cup Ginger Oil (PAGE 223)

THE KIMCHI VEGETABLES
4 napa cabbage leaves, trimmed
Eight ¼-by-1½-inches butternut
  squash bâtonnets
Twelve ¼-by-1½-inches Asian
  pear bâtonnets

THE YUZU–BROWN
BUTTER EMULSION
4 tablespoons unsalted butter
6 tablespoons Fumet (PAGE 221),
  reduced to 3 tablespoons
2 tablespoons white miso paste
Grated zest of ½ yuzu
3 tablespoons fresh yuzu juice
Fine sea salt and freshly
  ground white pepper
1 tablespoon thinly sliced chives

THE KOBE BEEF
Four 2-ounce Kobe beef fillet steaks
  (ask the butcher for 2-by-3
  by-⅜-inch rectangles)
Fine sea salt and freshly ground
  black pepper

THE TUNA
Four 2½-ounce white tuna (escolar)
  steaks
Fine sea salt and freshly
  ground white pepper

THE GARNISH
Chives

For the kimchi marinade, mix together the salt, xanthan gum, Espelette pepper, and sugar; set aside. Combine the lemon juice, garlic, and hot pepper paste in a blender. With the blender running, slowly drizzle in the extra virgin olive oil, to emulsify. Add the dry ingredients and blend well. Refrigerate until ready to use.

For the BBQ sauce, combine all of the ingredients in the blender and blend to a puree. Strain through a fine-mesh sieve. Refrigerate until ready to use.

For the kimchi vegetables, blanch the cabbage leaves in a pot of boiling salted water for 1 to 2 minutes, just until wilted. Remove from the water, immediately plunge into an ice bath, and drain. Blanch the squash bâtonnets for 4 to 5 minutes, until tender. Remove from the water, plunge into an ice bath, and drain. Refrigerate the vegetables until ready to use.

Preheat a grill to medium-high.

For the yuzu–brown butter emulsion, melt the butter in a small saucepan over medium-high heat, then cook the butter over medium heat, whisking occasionally, until all of the milk solids are very dark but not burned. Pour into a bowl and set aside.

Heat the fumet in a small saucepan until hot but not simmering. Add the miso paste, and yuzu zest and juice. Mixing with a handheld immersion blender, add the brown butter in a slow, steady stream and blend until emulsified. Season to taste with salt and white pepper. Keep warm.

Heat a large sauté pan over medium-high heat. Season the beef on both sides with salt and white pepper. Brush 1 teaspoon BBQ sauce on each fillet, coating both sides. Quickly sear the fillets, about 45 seconds on each side, until browned on both sides and cooked to medium. Keep warm.

Toss the cabbage leaves, squash bâtonnets, and Asian pear bâtonnets with a little of the kimchi marinade and lightly warm in a small pan. (The extra marinade can be reserved in the refrigerator for up to 1 week.)

For the fish, season the escolar on both sides with salt and white pepper. Grill for 1 minute, rotate the fish 90 degrees, and grill for another minute. Turn the fish over and cook for another minute, until just medium-rare in the center.

When ready to serve, lay a cabbage leaf on the top half of each plate. Brush a thin line of BBQ sauce across the bottom half of each plate. Place a beef fillet on the BBQ sauce. Place the tuna offset and slightly overlapping the Kobe fillet. Arrange 2 butternut squash bâtonnets and 3 Asian pear bâtonnets on top of each piece of tuna. Stir the sliced chives into the yuzu–brown butter emulsion and spoon over the tuna. Garnish with some chives, and serve immediately.

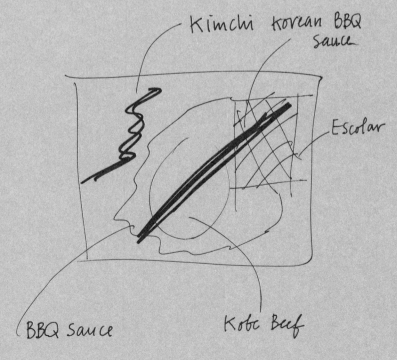

Kimchi korean BBQ
sauce

Escolar

BBQ Sauce

Kobe Beef

BLACK BASS

MASALA-SPICED CRISPY BLACK BASS WITH PEKIN DUCK–GREEN PAPAYA SALAD
IN GINGER-CARDAMOM BROTH

I was convinced that a salad of Pekin duck and green papaya would complement sautéed black bass, but Chris Muller, our chef de cuisine, made fun of me, saying it reminded him of his days cooking at Harrah's Casino in Atlantic City. So I gave him the task of coming up with a sauce for it. I must say the result—a paradox of rich versus fresh—is about as far from all-you-can-eat buffets as you can get. Ask your local Chinese restaurant for cooked Pekin duck breasts.

SERVES 4

PHOTOGRAPH ON
PAGE 105

THE GINGER-CARDAMOM BROTH

2 tablespoons canola oil
2 tablespoons sliced shallots
1 tablespoon sliced garlic
1 teaspoon sliced peeled ginger
½ cup Tomato and Cardamom Chutney (RECIPE FOLLOWS)
1 cup Chicken Jus (PAGE 220)
Fine sea salt and freshly ground white pepper
½ lime

THE BLACK BASS

2 tablespoons canola oil
Four 6-ounce black bass fillets, skin on
Fine sea salt and freshly ground white pepper
2 tablespoons Nirmala's Kitchen Guyanese garam masala (SEE SOURCES, PAGE 229)
Wondra flour

THE DUCK-PAPAYA SALAD

1 Pekin duck breast, skin removed, julienned
½ small green papaya, peeled and julienned
1 small carrot, peeled and julienned
1 tablespoon mint julienne
1 scallion, green part only, julienned
Fine sea salt and freshly ground white pepper
1½ tablespoons Ginger Vinaigrette (RECIPE FOLLOWS)
Juice of 1 lime

For the ginger-cardamom broth, heat the canola oil in medium saucepan over medium heat. Add the shallots, garlic, and ginger and cook until the vegetables start to soften. Add the chutney and cook, stirring, for 2 to 3 minutes. Add the chicken jus and bring to a boil. Reduce the heat to low and let the sauce simmer for about 5 minutes. Season to taste with salt and white pepper, and strain through a fine-mesh sieve into a saucepan. Set aside.

Preheat the oven to 350°F.

For the black bass, divide the canola oil between two ovenproof sauté pans (or use 1 large pan) and heat until very hot but not smoking. Season the black bass on both sides with salt and white pepper. Dust the skin side with the masala and then lightly dust on both sides with Wondra flour. Add the black bass to the pans, skin side down, briefly pressing down on each fillet with a metal spatula when you add it to prevent the skin from shrinking. Sauté the fish until the skin is golden brown and crisp, 3 to 5 minutes. Turn the fish over, put the pans in the oven, and cook the fish for 3 to 5 minutes longer, until a metal skewer can be easily inserted into the fish and, if left in for 5 seconds, feels just warm when touched to your lip.

While the fish cooks, prepare the duck-papaya salad: Combine the duck, papaya, carrot, mint, and scallion greens in a small bowl and season with salt and white pepper. Toss with the vinaigrette and lime juice.

Meanwhile reheat the ginger-cardamom broth; keep warm.

To serve, arrange the salad in the center of four serving plates. Place the black bass skin side up on top of the salad. Finish the broth with a squeeze of lime juice and pour around the fish. Serve immediately.

The green papaya salad is also great as a light salad

TOMATO AND CARDAMOM CHUTNEY

3 tablespoons canola oil
3 large shallots, sliced (about ½ cup)
½ head garlic, separated into cloves, peeled, and sliced (about ¼ cup)
¾ cup sliced peeled ginger (about 4 ounces)
2 teaspoons Nirmala's Kitchen Kerala green cardamom seeds (SEE SOURCES, PAGE 229)
1 star anise
2 slices jalapeño
2 tomatoes, cored and chopped
1 cup rice wine vinegar
1 tablespoon sugar
Fine sea salt and freshly ground white pepper

Heat the canola oil in a heavy saucepan over medium heat. Add the shallots, garlic, and ginger and cook until they begin to soften. Add the cardamom seeds, star anise, jalapeño, tomatoes, vinegar, and sugar and bring to a simmer, stirring. Cook the chutney, stirring occasionally, until thickened to the consistency of a jam. Season with salt as needed—the chutney should taste sweet, spicy, and sour.

Cool the chutney, transfer to a container, and refrigerate for up to 10 days.

GINGER VINAIGRETTE

1 teaspoon soy sauce
1 teaspoon hoisin sauce
1 teaspoon mirin
1 teaspoon sherry vinegar
½ teaspoon Asian sesame oil
1½ tablespoons Ginger Oil (PAGE 223)
Fine sea salt and freshly ground white pepper to taste

Combine all of the ingredients in a small bowl and mix well.

Store in a container in the refrigerator for up to 10 days. Rewhisk before using.

SALMON

BARELY COOKED WILD ALASKAN SALMON WITH DAIKON,
SNOW PEAS, ENOKI SALAD, AND SWEET PEA–WASABI SAUCE

I love this technique for cooking salmon—simmering it for just a few minutes. This simple method preserves the flavor and texture of the fish, and I have used it for many years. The salmon develops a custard-like consistency, and the sweet bite of the sauce cuts through the richness of the fish.

SERVES 4

PHOTOGRAPH ON
PAGE 104

THE SWEET PEA–WASABI SAUCE
2 cups Chicken Stock (PAGE 220)
¼ cup diced carrot
¼ cup diced onion
½ slice bacon, diced
1 garlic clove, thinly sliced
½ cup sugar snap peas, plus ¼ cup
    sliced sugar snap peas
½ cup green peas
Fine sea salt and freshly ground
    white pepper
½ cup mint leaves
1 tablespoon fresh wasabi paste
    (SEE SOURCES, PAGE 229)
1 tablespoon unsalted butter

THE WILD SALMON
Four 6-ounce salmon fillets
Fine sea salt and freshly ground
    white pepper

THE ENOKI SALAD
¼ cup small matchsticks
    daikon radish
4 snow peas, blanched briefly
    in boiling water and thinly
    sliced on the bias
1 tablespoon enoki mushroom tops
1 ounce honshimei mushrooms,
    caps only, blanched briefly in
    boiling water
Yuzu Vinaigrette (RECIPE FOLLOWS)
Fine sea salt and freshly ground
    white pepper

THE GARNISH
2 ounces baby pea shoots

For the sauce, combine the chicken stock, carrot, onion, bacon, garlic, and the ½ cup sugar snap peas in a saucepan and bring to a simmer. Cook for about 15 minutes, until the flavors come together. Strain the broth and set aside.

Blanch the green peas in boiling salted water. Drain, plunge into an ice bath, and drain again. Repeat with the remaining ¼ cup sugar snap peas. Transfer both vegetables to a blender, add 2 to 3 tablespoons water, as necessary, season with salt and white pepper, and process to a puree. Strain through a fine-mesh strainer and set aside.

Blanch the mint leaves in a pot of boiling salted water. Drain, plunge into an ice bath, and drain again. Transfer to a blender and puree, adding only as much water as needed to puree. Set aside.

For the salmon, pour enough water to cover the bottom into a casserole that will hold the salmon comfortably. Season with salt and place the pot over medium heat. Season the salmon on both sides with salt and white pepper, place the salmon fillets in the pot, and cook at a simmer until the top of the salmon is just warm to the touch, 5 to 7 minutes.

While the salmon is cooking, make the salad: Toss the daikon, snow peas, and mushrooms with the yuzu vinaigrette in a small bowl. Season to taste with salt and white pepper.

To finish the sauce, pour ½ cup of the pea broth into a small saucepan and add ¼ cup of the pea puree, the wasabi paste, 1 tablespoon of the mint puree, and the butter. Season to taste with salt and white pepper and bring the sauce to a boil. Just before serving, froth with a handheld immersion blender.

Remove the salmon from the pan and drain on a towel. Place a salmon fillet in the center of each plate. Arrange one-quarter of the daikon salad on top of each fillet and top with baby pea shoots. Spoon the pea sauce around, and serve immediately.

YUZU VINAIGRETTE
MAKES ½ CUP

1 tablespoon white miso paste
2 tablespoons fresh
   lemon juice
2 tablespoons yuzu juice
   (SEE SOURCES, PAGE 229)
2 tablespoons mirin,
   reduced to 1 tablespoon
¼ cup Ginger Oil (PAGE 223),
   strained
Fine sea salt and freshly
   ground white pepper

Whisk all the ingredients together in a bowl. Blend with an immersion blender until very smooth.

Store in a sealed container for up to 3 days.

CHESTNUT

CHESTNUT PARFAIT, *BISCUIT*, AND TUILES WITH OVEN-ROASTED BOSC PEAR AND CANDIED ORANGE PEEL

Always a staple on our winter dessert menu, the subtly sweet chestnut is expressed here in three textures—moist cake, cool parfait, and crunchy wafer—and is backed up by citrus and roasted pear. Fair warning: The candied chestnuts used as garnish are addictive. At the restaurant we prepare the pear with Minus 8 rice wine vinegar. Made from frozen grapes, it's an extraordinary product with a sweet floral flavor. We recommend you try it, but it's on the expensive side, so this recipe calls for any good rice wine vinegar. The parfait can be made ahead and kept in the freezer.

SERVES 4

THE CHESTNUT PARFAIT
- 3 tablespoons whole milk
- 2½ tablespoons sugar
- 2 large egg yolks
- 3 tablespoons sweetened chestnut puree
- 1 tablespoon plus 1 teaspoon chopped candied chestnuts
- 4 teaspoons heavy cream, whipped to soft peaks
- ½ cup cream, whipped

THE CHESTNUT *BISCUIT*
- 5 tablespoons sweetened chestnut puree
- 2½ tablespoons unsalted butter, softened
- 1 large egg, at room temperature
- 1 large egg yolk, at room temperature
- 1 tablespoon all-purpose flour
- 1 teaspoon baking powder

THE CHESTNUT TUILES
- ½ cup sweetened chestnut puree
- 3 tablespoons sugar
- 1 tablespoon unsalted butter, softened
- 1 large egg white, lightly beaten

THE BOSC PEAR
- 1 Bosc pear
- 2 tablespoons unsalted butter
- 1 teaspoon brown sugar
- ½ vanilla bean, split and scraped
- 1 teaspoon rice wine vinegar (preferably Minus 8)

TO FINISH
- ½ cup orange juice
- ¼ teaspoon vanilla extract

THE GARNISH
- 4 teaspoons chopped candied chestnuts
- 2 teaspoons minced candied orange peel
- 8 micro mint sprigs

For the chestnut parfait, combine the milk and sugar in a small saucepan and bring to a boil, stirring to dissolve the sugar. Put the egg yolks in the bowl of a stand mixer fitted with the whip attachment and begin whipping them. While whipping, carefully pour the hot milk mixture into the bowl, then continue to whip until the mixture has cooled and is light and fluffy.

Put the chestnut puree in a bowl and fold in the whipped yolk mixture. Fold in the candied chestnuts and then the whipped cream. Transfer to a pastry bag fitted with a large plain tip.

Arrange eight 1-inch-square by 1¾-inch high molds (see Sources, page 229) on a Silpat-lined baking sheet. Pipe the parfait into the molds, filling them completely, and smooth the tops. Freeze for at least 2 hours or overnight.

For the chestnut *biscuit*, preheat the oven to 300°F.

Cream the chestnut puree and butter together until smooth in the bowl of a stand mixer fitted with the paddle attachment. In a small bowl, whisk the egg and egg yolk, then slowly add to the chestnut mixture, mixing until smooth. Sift together the flour and baking powder, add to the batter, and mix until just combined.

Transfer the batter to a Silpat-lined 9-by-12-inch baking dish, and smooth and bake until the *biscuit* is golden brown and the top springs back when touched, about 15 minutes. Allow it to cool on a rack.

Carefully remove the *biscuit* from the Silpat and transfer it to a cutting board. Cut four 1½-by-3-inch rectangles out of the *biscuit*. Wrap tightly in plastic wrap and set aside.

For the chestnut tuiles, preheat the oven to 350°F.

Cream the chestnut puree and sugar together until smooth in the bowl of a stand mixer fitted with the paddle attachment. Add the butter and egg white and blend well. Using an offset spatula, thinly spread the batter, roughly into 2-inch free-form shapes onto a Silpat-lined baking sheet (make as many as the batter allows—you'll need 12, but there might be breakage).

Bake until lightly browned, 5 to 8 minutes. Allow to cool, then carefully remove the tuiles from the Silpat. Store in an airtight container until ready to use.

For the pear, preheat the oven to 350°F.

Peel the pear, cut it into quarters, and remove the core. Melt the butter in an ovenproof sauté pan over medium-high heat. Add the pear, brown sugar, and vanilla bean and cook, stirring, until the sugar has dissolved. Transfer the pear to the oven and cook until tender and lightly browned, 15 to 20 minutes.

Remove the pear from the oven and deglaze the pan with the wine vinegar, scraping up any caramelized bits. Allow the pear to cool in its liquid.

Reserve the pan juices for garnish on the plate. Cut the pear into ¼-inch dice. Set aside.

To serve, combine the orange juice and vanilla extract in a small shallow bowl. Soak each *biscuit* in the orange juice for 10 seconds, then put in the center of a serving plate. Unmold the parfaits and place 2 on each *biscuit*, leaving a small space between the parfaits. Carefully stand 3 tuiles on each *biscuit*, one between the parfaits, the others on either side. Spoon 1 tablespoon of the diced pear onto the parfaits on each plate, topped with 1 teaspoon chopped candied chestnuts and ½ teaspoon candied orange peel. Garnish each parfait with a micro mint sprig. Spoon some of the reserved pear pan juices around each dessert, and serve immediately.

CHOCOLATE–CORN

SOFT CHOCOLATE GANACHE, CORN FEUILLETINE, PRALINE CREAM, AND SWEET CORN SORBET

The combination of chocolate and corn may seem odd, but the Olmecs and Mayas were pairing them hundreds of years before Columbus arrived in the New World. Freeze-dried corn, light as a feather and deceptively crunchy, was the initial inspiration for this dessert—it tastes sweet and nutty, a bit like candied corn. The architectural presentation shows off the contrasting textures of the corn, chocolate, and hazelnut.

SERVES 4

PHOTOGRAPH ON
PAGE 111

THE CORN SORBET
1¼ cups water
¾ cup sugar
Pinch of fine sea salt
1 tablespoon light corn syrup
½ cup whole milk
1 cup fresh corn kernels

THE SOFT CHOCOLATE GANACHE
9 ounces 70% dark chocolate, finely chopped
2 cups heavy cream
¼ cup water
½ teaspoon agar-agar
1 tablespoon corn syrup
Pinch of fine sea salt
1 sheet (2 grams) gelatin, softened in ice-cold water

THE CORN FEUILLETINE
2 ounces milk chocolate, melted
½ cup hazelnut praline paste
1 tablespoon crushed caramelized hazelnuts (optional)
½ cup feuilletine (SEE SOURCES, PAGE 229)
¼ cup freeze-dried corn (SEE SOURCES, PAGE 229)
Pinch of Espelette pepper powder
Pinch of Halen Môn Welsh smoked salt (SEE SOURCES, PAGE 229)

THE PRALINE CREAM
3 tablespoons heavy cream
½ cup hazelnut praline paste

THE CORN TUILES
½ cup freeze-dried corn, finely ground (SEE SOURCES, PAGE 229)
4 teaspoons all-purpose flour
4 teaspoons confectioners' sugar
Pinch of fine sea salt
2 tablespoons skim milk
2 large egg whites

THE GARNISH
Twelve 4-by-1-inch dark chocolate plaquettes (SEE PAGE 226)

For the corn sorbet, combine the water, sugar, salt, and corn syrup in a large saucepan, bring to a boil, and boil for about 1 minute. Remove from the heat and allow syrup to cool.

Combine the milk and corn in another saucepan and bring to a boil. Transfer to a blender and puree until smooth. Pass through a fine-mesh strainer and let cool.

Combine the syrup with the corn puree and chill. Freeze in an ice cream machine according to manufacturer's instructions; pack into a container and freeze until ready to serve.

For the ganache, put the chocolate in a medium bowl and set aside. Bring the cream to a boil in a medium saucepan.

Meanwhile, combine the water, agar-agar, corn syrup, and salt in a small saucepan and gently bring to a boil, then boil gently for 2 to 3 minutes.

Remove the cream from the heat and gradually pour over the chocolate, stirring with a rubber spatula to ensure all the chocolate melts. Follow with the agar-agar mixture. Add the gelatin, stirring to dissolve. Transfer to a plastic-lined 9-by-12-inch baking pan. Allow to set on a flat surface, then freeze until firm before cutting.

With a thin warm knife (dip into hot water and wipe dry between cuts), cut the ganache into rectangles measuring 3 inches by ½ inch. Reserve in the refrigerator.

For the corn feuilletine, combine the melted chocolate and hazelnut paste in a bowl, mixing well. Stir in the remaining ingredients. Transfer to a work surface lined with a Silpat or parchment. Place a second liner or sheet of paper on top and roll to a ¼-inch thickness with a rolling pin. Chill.

Cut into rectangles measuring 3½ inches by ¾ inch and refrigerate.

For the praline cream, heat the cream just until warm in a small saucepan. Put praline paste in the bowl of a stand mixer. Using the paddle attachment, slowly incorporate the cream, mixing until emulsified. Refrigerate.

For the corn tuiles, preheat the oven to 275°F.

Combine the dry ingredients in a mixing bowl. Slowly incorporate the skim milk, followed by the egg whites. Using an offset spatula, spread ½ teaspoon of the tuile batter in a 2-inch free-form shape, on a Silpat-lined baking sheet pan. Make 8 to 10 shapes (you need only 4, but allow for breakage). Bake 5 to 8 minutes, until lightly browned.

To serve, place one rectangle of feuilletine on each plate and top each with a rectangle of ganache. Follow the ganache with a chocolate plaquette. Spread a spoonful of the praline paste onto each plate. Top with a small scoop of corn sorbet and then a corn tuile. Serve immediately.

BANANA

BANANA CRÈME BRÛLÉE, CITRUS-PISTACHIO *BISCUIT*,
AND BEURRE NOISETTE ICE CREAM WITH PEANUT CARAMEL

Improving on a classic is always a risky proposition, but one aspect of our work at Le Bernardin is to attempt exactly that. In this case, the challenge was to reinvent the traditional crème brûlée, in both flavor and presentation. We came up with this banana custard, which sits in a grid formation with a citrusy *biscuit*, crunchy caramelized banana, and nutty brown-butter ice cream. Then we transported it to an even higher dimension by adding salty peanut caramel. Try combining any leftovers in a blender with vanilla ice cream for an indulgent milk shake.

SERVES 4

THE BEURRE NOISETTE ICE CREAM
6 tablespoons unsalted butter
¼ cup nonfat dry milk
2½ cups whole milk
8 large egg yolks
2 teaspoons cornstarch
¾ cup plus 1 tablespoon sugar
2 tablespoons water

THE CITRUS-PISTACHIO *BISCUIT*
2 large eggs, separated
2½ ounces high-quality white chocolate
3½ tablespoons unsalted butter, softened
1 teaspoon Trimoline (invert sugar) (SEE SOURCES, PAGE 229)
Grated zest of ¼ orange

Grated zest of ¼ lemon
2 tablespoons sugar
3 tablespoons all-purpose flour, sifted
1 tablespoon finely chopped pistachios, preferably Sicilian

THE BANANA CRÈME BRÛLÉE
1 ripe banana
¼ cup plus 3 tablespoons heavy cream
1 large egg
1 large egg yolk
¼ cup plus 2 tablespoons sugar
1 tablespoon plus 1 teaspoon whole milk
¼ stick cinnamon
¼ vanilla bean, split

THE PEANUT CARAMEL
¼ cup Caramel Sauce (PAGE 228)
1 tablespoon whole milk
1 tablespoon chopped roasted salted peanuts

THE GARNISH
2 tablespoons plus ½ teaspoon sugar
1 banana
4 Banana Chips (RECIPE FOLLOWS)

For the beurre noisette ice cream, melt the butter in a saucepan over medium-high heat, then brown the butter over medium heat, whisking occasionally, until all of the milk solids are very dark, but not burned. Remove from the heat and set aside.

Whisk the dry milk into the whole milk in a small saucepan; set aside. Whisk together the egg yolks, cornstarch, and 1 tablespoon of the sugar in a medium pot; set aside. Combine the remaining ¾ cup sugar and the water in a small pot and cook, without stirring, over medium heat until all of the sugar has dissolved and the caramel turns a light amber color.

Meanwhile, heat the milk until hot. Remove the caramel from the heat and slowly whisk in the milk. Whisk the caramel over low heat until any lumps of caramel have dissolved. Gradually whisk the caramel into the egg yolk mixture, then whisk in the beurre noisette. Bring to a boil, stirring constantly. Transfer to a bowl and refrigerate the ice cream base for 12 hours, to give the base a better texture.

Freeze the base in an ice cream machine according to the manufacturer's instructions. Pack into a container and freeze until ready to serve.

For the citrus-pistachio *biscuit*, preheat the oven to 325°F. Gently whisk the egg yolks in a small cup; reserve three-quarters of the yolks and discard the rest. Repeat with the egg whites.

Melt the white chocolate in a small bowl over a pot of barely simmering water. Stir in the butter until incorporated. Off the heat, whisk in the egg yolks, Trimoline, and citrus zests.

Whip the egg whites and sugar together to soft peaks in a medium bowl. Fold in the flour, followed by the white chocolate mixture. Pour the batter onto a 9-by-12-inch Silpat-lined baking sheet. Sprinkle the chopped pistachios over the batter.

Bake the *biscuit* until golden brown, about 13 minutes. Allow the *biscuit* to cool on a rack, then wrap tightly in plastic wrap and refrigerate until ready to serve.

For the banana crème brûlée, preheat the oven to 350°F. Line an 8-inch square baking dish with plastic wrap, leaving an overhang.

Peel the banana and puree in a blender. Measure out ½ cup (discard any extra), return to the blender, and add 3 tablespoons of the cream. Blend until smooth; set aside.

Whisk together the egg, egg yolk, and 2 tablespoons of the sugar in a bowl; set aside. Combine the milk, the remaining ¼ cup heavy cream, and cinnamon in a small saucepan. Scrape the seeds from the vanilla bean and add the seeds and pod to the pan. Bring to a boil over medium heat. Gradually whisk the milk mixture into the eggs, then whisk in the banana puree. Strain the custard through a fine-mesh sieve.

Pour the custard into the plastic-wrap-lined baking dish. Place the baking dish in a larger baking pan and add enough hot water to the pan to come halfway up the sides of the dish. Bake until the banana crème is set and slightly firm, 15 to 20 minutes. Allow the banana crème to cool to room temperature, then cover with plastic wrap and refrigerate until ready to serve.

For the peanut caramel, gently heat the caramel sauce in a small saucepan, and whisk in the milk. Stir in the peanuts and remove from the heat. Allow the caramel to cool, then transfer to a container and cover tightly with plastic wrap. Store at room temperature if using the same day or refrigerate until ready to use.

To serve, cut eight 1½-inch squares out of the *biscuit* and eight squares out of the banana crème. Sprinkle 2 tablespoons of the sugar over the banana crème squares and caramelize the sugar with a blowtorch (or under the broiler). Arrange 2 brûlée squares and 2 *biscuit* squares to form a larger square in the center of each plate.

Peel the banana and slice it into eight ¾-inch-thick slices on the diagonal. Sprinkle the remaining ½ teaspoon sugar over the banana slices and caramelize the sugar with a blowtorch (or under the broiler). Place 3 banana slices, slightly overlapping, on one *biscuit* square on each plate, and place a small scoop of the ice cream on the other *biscuit* square. Spoon a circle of peanut caramel around each plate. Lay a banana chip diagonally across each dessert, and serve immediately.

BANANA CHIPS
MAKES ABOUT 20 CHIPS

1 ripe banana
¼ teaspoon fresh lime juice
1 teaspoon sugar
½ teaspoon egg white
  (lightly whisk to measure)

Preheat the oven to 200°F.

Peel the banana and puree in a blender. Measure out ¼ cup (discard any extra), and return to the blender. Add the remaining ingredients and process until smooth. Strain the batter through a fine-mesh sieve.

With an offset spatula, spread 2 tablespoons of the batter in a thin layer on a Silpat-lined baking sheet to make a rectangle about 4 by 6 inches. Using a cake decorator comb or the edge of a plastic dough scraper, divide the batter into long, thin strips (about ¼ inch wide). Dry the "chips" in the oven until golden brown in color but still pliable, about 1 hour.

One at a time, remove the strips from the Silpat and twist them, trying to keep them as long as possible. Allow the chips to cool completely, then store in an airtight container until ready to serve. (They can be made up to 3 days in advance.)

"EGG"

MILK CHOCOLATE POTS DE CRÈME WITH CARAMEL FOAM,
MAPLE SYRUP, AND MALDON SEA SALT

We never set out to create a "signature dish," but this tiny egg has become just that. In this complex interplay of the chocolate, caramel, and maple, the flakes of Maldon sea salt are the catalyst pushing the dish to be truly greater than the sum of its parts. It's a special pre-dessert treat we offer to VIP guests. Serving it in an egg cup makes for an elegant presentation. You'll need a fiberboard egg carton, cut to size, to make the dish.

SERVES 4

PHOTOGRAPH ON
PAGE 107

THE EGGSHELLS
(FOR THE POTS DE CRÈME)
4 large brown eggs

THE MILK CHOCOLATE
POTS DE CRÈME
1 large egg yolk (reserved from above)
1 tablespoon sugar
2½ tablespoons whole milk
2 tablespoons heavy cream
2 tablespoons finely chopped
   milk chocolate
1 tablespoon 55% finely chopped
   dark chocolate

THE CARAMEL FOAM
¼ cup sugar
1 tablespoon water
2 large egg yolks (reserved
   from above)
¾ cup heavy cream
3 tablespoons plus 1 teaspoon
   whole milk
½ sheet (2-gram sheet) gelatin,
   softened in ice-cold water

THE GARNISH
1 teaspoon Caramel Sauce (PAGE 228)
½ teaspoon maple syrup
Maldon sea salt

For the eggshells, carefully remove the tops from the eggs with an egg top cutter or a sharp paring knife. Pour out the eggs; reserve 3 of the yolks—1 for the pots de crème, 2 for the caramel foam. Rinse the shells in very hot water, carefully removing the membrane remaining inside the shells. Allow the shells to dry completely.

For the pots de crème, preheat the oven to 350°F.

Whisk the yolk and sugar together in a small bowl. Combine the milk and heavy cream in a small saucepan

EGG

Egg cup

Sea salt
Caramel
foam
Caramel
Sauce

milk chocolate
Pot de creme

and bring to a boil. Gradually whisk the milk mixture into the egg mixture. Whisk in the chocolate until it is melted and well incorporated. Strain the custard through a fine-mesh sieve into a bowl and cool it quickly over an ice bath, stirring occasionally.

Stand the eggshells in a fiber-board egg carton and put the carton in a baking dish. Divide the custard evenly among the eggshells, filling each one about halfway. Fill the baking dish with enough hot water to reach halfway up the sides of the egg carton. Cover the dish with aluminum foil and bake the pots de crème for 15 to 20 minutes, until the custard is set. Allow the pots de

crème to cool to room temperature, then refrigerate.

For the caramel foam, combine the sugar and water in a small saucepan and cook, without stirring, over medium heat until the sugar has dissolved and the caramel turns a light golden brown.

Meanwhile, whisk the egg yolks together in a bowl. Heat the heavy cream and milk together until hot. Remove the caramel from the heat and whisk in the cream mixture. Whisk the mixture over low heat until any lumps of caramel have completely dissolved and the caramel is smooth. Gradually whisk the caramel into the egg yolks, and return to the saucepan. Cook the sauce over low

heat until it reaches 183°F. Remove from the heat and add the gelatin, whisking until it dissolves. Strain through a fine-mesh sieve into a bowl and chill in an ice bath, then refrigerate until ready to use.

To serve, place the filled eggshells in four porcelain egg cups, and drizzle ¼ teaspoon of the caramel sauce over each pot de crème. Take the caramel foam out of the refrigerator and transfer it to a whipped cream dispenser. Fill the shells with caramel foam, leaving a little indentation in the center. Drizzle ⅛ teaspoon of the maple syrup into each indentation, and sprinkle each pot de crème with a few grains of Maldon sea salt. Serve immediately.

CHOCOLATE–PEANUT

DARK CHOCOLATE, PEANUT, AND CARAMEL TART
WITH CANDIED LEMON PEEL, PEANUT POWDER, AND MALTED
MILK CHOCOLATE RUM ICE CREAM

A dessert course, however refined, still appeals to the inner child in all of us, and playing off of such nostalgia is great fun. Here, the humble peanut, forever linked to chocolate, appears in a "grown-up" tart. The rich chocolate ganache gives way to a soft caramel filling hiding the crunch of salted peanuts. The peanut butter powder tastes just like peanut butter, but it's fluffy and melts instantly in the mouth.

SERVES 4

PHOTOGRAPH ON
PAGE 106

THE MALTED MILK CHOCOLATE RUM ICE CREAM
3 cups whole milk
1 cup heavy cream
2 tablespoons nonfat dry milk
1 cup plus 2 tablespoons malted milk powder
2/3 cup sugar
12 large egg yolks
3 ounces milk chocolate, finely chopped
2 ounces 64% dark chocolate, finely chopped
3 tablespoons dark rum

THE TART DOUGH
4 tablespoons unsalted butter
1/2 cup confectioners' sugar
3/4 cup all-purpose flour, sifted
3 tablespoons unsweetened cocoa powder, sifted
3 large egg yolks

THE FILLING
1/4 cup roughly chopped roasted salted peanuts
2 tablespoons Caramel Sauce (PAGE 228)
1/4 cup Chocolate Ganache (RECIPE FOLLOWS)

THE GARNISH
Candied lemon peel
1 tablespoon roughly chopped roasted salted peanuts
Peanut Butter Powder (RECIPE FOLLOWS)

For the milk chocolate ice cream, combine the milk, heavy cream, and dry milk in a pot and bring to a boil over high heat. Meanwhile, mix together the malt powder and sugar and whisk into the egg yolks in a medium bowl. Gradually add the hot cream mixture to the yolk mixture, whisking constantly. Pour back into the pot and cook over low heat, stirring constantly, for about 5 minutes, until it reaches 183°F. Remove the custard from the heat and whisk in all the chocolate, making sure it is completely melted, then stir in the rum. Transfer to a bowl and refrigerate the ice cream base for 12 hours, to give the base a better texture.

Freeze the ice cream base in an ice cream machine according to the manufacturer's instructions. Pack into a container and freeze until ready to serve.

For the tart shells, cream together the butter and sugar in the bowl of a stand mixer fitted with the paddle attachment until smooth and lightly aerated. Sift together the flour and cocoa powder, and mix into the butter. Whisk the egg yolks together and add to the bowl, mixing just until incorporated. Form the dough into a flat rectangle and wrap tightly in plastic wrap. Place in the refrigerator and let rest for at least 1 hour.

Transfer the dough to a lightly floured surface and roll out to 1/8 inch thick (you should have a square of about 12 inches). Brush away any excess flour and, using a 4 1/4-inch round cutter, cut out 4 circles. Place four 3 1/4-inch by 1/2-inch-high ring molds (or tartlet pans) on a baking sheet lined with parchment paper or Silpat. Line each ring mold with a circle, pressing the dough into the base of each ring to ensure there are no air pockets. Trim off any excess dough. Refrigerate for 30 minutes before baking.

Preheat the oven to 300°F.

Bake the tart shells on the middle rack of the oven for 7 to 8 minutes. Rotate the baking sheet and bake the shells for an additional 7 to 8 minutes, until golden brown. Remove the baking sheet from the oven and allow the tart shells to cool on a rack before unmolding them, then store in an airtight container until ready to use.

To assemble the tarts, place the baked tart shells on a clean parchment-paper-lined baking sheet. Sprinkle 1 tablespoon of the chopped peanuts over the bottom of each tart. Spoon 1½ teaspoons of the caramel sauce (gently warmed if necessary) into each shell, covering the peanuts. Place the tarts in the freezer for 15 minutes to allow the caramel to set slightly, so it can be cleanly topped with the ganache.

Remove the tarts from the freezer and spread 1 tablespoon of the chocolate ganache evenly into each one. Allow the tarts to stand at room temperature for at least 30 minutes before serving, to allow the ganache time to set. (The finished tarts can be kept at room temperature for up to 8 hours before serving.)

To serve, place a finished tart in the center of each plate. Arrange the lemon peel, the 1 tablespoon chopped peanuts, and peanut butter powder around the tart. Finish with a scoop of the malted milk chocolate rum ice cream.

CHOCOLATE GANACHE
MAKES ABOUT ½ CUP

Ganache can be made up to 1 day ahead, covered tightly, and stored at room temperature. Gently warm the ganache in the microwave or over a hot water bath if it is too firm to pour smoothly (overheating may cause the ganache to "break," or separate). It can also be used as a truffle filling or, when gently heated, as an impromptu fondue dip.

2 ounces 55% dark chocolate, finely chopped
¼ cup heavy cream
1¼ teaspoons light corn syrup
½ tablespoon unsalted butter, softened

Put the chocolate in a bowl. Combine the heavy cream and corn syrup in a small saucepan and bring to a boil. Remove from the heat and gradually pour over the chocolate, stirring with a rubber spatula to ensure all the chocolate melts. Add the butter, stirring until everything is emulsified.

PEANUT BUTTER POWDER
MAKES ABOUT ½ CUP

1½ tablespoons creamy peanut butter
1 tablespoon peanut oil
1 cup tapioca maltodextrin
(SEE SOURCES, PAGE 229)

Combine the peanut butter and peanut oil in a food processor. Add the maltodextrin in four parts, processing until fully incorporated each time. Continue to pulse until a light powder is formed.

ROSE-RASPBERRY

ALMOND TART SHELLS FILLED WITH ROSE CREAM AND RASPBERRIES,
LYCHEE GRANITÉ, AND PISTACHIO CRÈME ANGLAISE

The intriguing flavor combination of this dessert was inspired by one of the world's great pastry chefs, Pierre Hermé, whose rose macaroon made a lasting impression on our pastry chef, Michael Laiskonis. The raspberry and lychee flavors are heightened by the addition of brilliant green Sicilian pistachios. The trickiest component to prepare is the fragile sugar decoration. You can leave it out if it seems too daunting, but its delicate crunch heightens the refinement of this tart.

SERVES 4

PHOTOGRAPH ON
PAGE 110

THE TART SHELLS
2 sticks plus ½ tablespoon
    unsalted butter (about 8¾
    ounces), softened
¾ cup sugar
¾ cup plus 1½ tablespoons
    almond flour
1 large egg yolk
1 large whole egg
2¾ cups plus 3 tablespoons
    all-purpose flour
¼ teaspoon baking powder
1 tablespoon water

THE ROSE CREAM
¼ cup plus 2 tablespoons
    whole milk
1 teaspoon organic dried rosebuds
2 teaspoons sugar
1 teaspoon rose syrup
    (SEE SOURCES, PAGE 229)
1 teaspoon rose water
1 large egg yolk
⅔ sheet (2-gram sheet) gelatin,
    softened in ice-cold water
¼ cup plus 2 tablespoons heavy
    cream, whipped to soft peaks

THE RASPBERRY COULIS
⅓ cup strained raspberry puree
1 ounce fresh raspberries
    (about 15 raspberries)
½ teaspoon sugar
¼ sheet (2-gram sheet) gelatin,
    softened in ice-cold water

**THE PISTACHIO
CRÈME ANGLAISE**
2 tablespoons Crème Anglaise
    (PAGE 228)
½ teaspoon pistachio paste
    (SEE SOURCES, PAGE 229)

THE GARNISH
¼ cup lychee nectar
½ pint fresh raspberries
2 teaspoons rose syrup
4 Sugar Tuiles (RECIPE FOLLOWS)
1 teaspoon finely chopped
    pistachios, preferably Sicilian

For the tart shells, cream together the butter, sugar, and almond flour in the bowl of a stand mixer fitted with a paddle attachment, until smooth and lightly aerated.

Slowly add the eggs, scraping down the bowl as needed.

Add the all-purpose flour and baking powder, continuing to mix until everything is thoroughly incorporated. Add the water. Form the dough into a flat rectangle and wrap tightly in plastic wrap. Place in the refrigerator and let rest for at least 1 hour.

Transfer the dough to a lightly floured surface and roll out to ⅛ inch thick (you should have a square of about 12 inches). Brush away any excess flour and, using a 4¼-inch round cutter, cut out 4 circles. Place four 3¼-inch by ½-inch-high ring molds (or tartlet pans) on a baking sheet lined with parchment paper or Silpat. Line each ring mold with a circle, pressing the dough into the base of each ring to ensure there are no air pockets. Trim off any excess dough. Refrigerate for 30 minutes before baking.

Preheat the oven to 300°F.

Bake the tart shells on the middle rack of the oven for 8 to 9 minutes. Rotate the baking sheet and bake the shells for an additional 8 to 9 minutes, until they are golden brown. Remove the baking sheet from the oven and allow the tart shells to cool on a rack before unmolding them. Store in an airtight container until ready to use.

For the rose cream, combine the milk and rosebuds in a small saucepan and bring to a boil. Remove from the heat, cover, and allow the milk to infuse for 15 minutes.

Strain the milk into another small saucepan. Mix together the sugar, rose syrup, and rose water and whisk into the milk. Heat the milk mixture, stirring to dissolve the sugar. Meanwhile, whisk the egg yolk in a small bowl. Gradually add the hot milk mixture, whisking constantly. Return the cream base to the pan and cook over low heat, stirring constantly, until it thickens.

Strain the cream base into a bowl. Add the gelatin, whisking until it dissolves. Chill in an ice bath.

Place four 3-inch-diameter by 1-inch-high ring molds on a Silpat-lined baking sheet. Fold the cream base into the whipped cream and transfer to a pastry bag fitted with a large plain tip. Pipe the resulting cream into the molds. Freeze for at least 2 hours before unmolding.

For the raspberry coulis, combine the raspberry puree, fresh raspberries, and sugar in a small saucepan,

whisk together and bring to a simmer. Remove from the heat and add the gelatin, whisking until it dissolves. Allow to cool, then cover tightly with plastic wrap and refrigerate until ready to use.

For the pistachio crème anglaise, whisk the crème anglaise and pistachio paste together.

At least 2 hours before serving, assemble the tarts: Fill each baked tart shell with 1 teaspoon of the raspberry coulis (reserve the remaining coulis for another use). Unmold the rose creams and place one cream in each tart. Refrigerate the tarts until ready to serve (allow 2 hours for the cream to defrost in the refrigerator).

To make lychee granité for the garnish, place the lycheé nectar in a shallow baking pan and freeze for 1 hour, stirring every 15 minutes to break up the ice crystals.

To serve, put a tart shell on each of four dessert plates, slightly off center. Top with a rose cream. Arrange 5 or 6 raspberries in a circle on top of each cream. Spoon ½ teaspoon of the rose syrup into the middle of the raspberries on each cream, and scrape 1 tablespoon of the lychee granité onto the rose syrup. Spoon several dots of the pistachio crème anglaise in a semicircle around the cream. Top each cream with a sugar tuile, resting it on the raspberries. Sprinkle ¼ teaspoon chopped pistachios on each plate, to one side of the tart, and serve immediately.

SUGAR TUILES
MAKES 4 TUILES

Fondant and isomalt are available in baking supply stores. Be sure not to buy rolled fondant, which is used to decorate cakes and is entirely different.

---

1 tablespoon light corn syrup
1 tablespoon fondant
2 tablespoons plus 2¼ teaspoons isomalt
1 dried rosebud (SEE SOURCES, PAGE 229)
½ teaspoon finely chopped pistachios, preferably Sicilian

Combine the corn syrup and fondant in a small pot. Begin to heat the mixture, and whisk in the isomalt. Cook the mixture without stirring to 325°F. Immediately pour it onto a Silpat-lined baking sheet. Allow to cool and set at room temperature.

When set, break into pieces, then pulverize them to a fine powder in a coffee grinder. Store in an airtight container if not ready to use.

Preheat the oven to 300°F. Line a baking sheet with a Silpat. Using a silicon rubber stencil (see Sources, page 229), trace four 3-inch circles on the Silpat. Using a fine-mesh sieve, for each tuile, sift 2 tablespoons of the powder into each circle. Sprinkle a few rose petal pieces over each tuile, followed by ⅛ teaspoon of the chopped pistachios.

Bake the tuiles for 1½ minutes. Allow the tuiles to cool on the Silpat, then carefully remove them. Store in an airtight container until ready to use.

LEMON

VANILLA PARFAIT WITH LEMON SORBET, CITRUS *BISCUIT*,
AND CRISP MERINGUE

Few classic French desserts are as texturally exciting as the *vacherin*.
Typically a dish composed of ice cream or sorbet, baked meringue, and
whipped cream, it's all about the interplay of cold, crunchy, and creamy.
To give this classic a modern turn, we deconstructed the elements to
highlight each. This dish debuted on the menu in winter, when citrus is
at its peak; the nearly monochromatic presentation of whites and pale
yellows really does look like a snow-covered landscape at sunset.

SERVES 4

PHOTOGRAPH ON
PAGES 108–9

THE LEMON SORBET
2 ¼ cups water
2 cups sugar
1 tablespoon nonfat dry milk
1 cup fresh lemon juice

THE VANILLA PARFAIT
2 tablespoons whole milk
2 tablespoons heavy cream
2 tablespoons sugar
Grated zest of 1 lemon
¼ teaspoon vanilla extract
1 large egg yolk
1 sheet (2 grams) gelatin, softened
   in ice-cold water
⅓ cup heavy cream, whipped
   to soft peaks

THE CRISP MERINGUE
1 egg white
3 tablespoons sugar

THE CITRUS *BISCUIT*
2½ ounces high-quality
   white chocolate, melted
3½ tablespoons unsalted
   butter, softened
2 large eggs separated
1 teaspoon Trimoline (invert sugar)
   (SEE SOURCES, PAGE 229)
Grated zest of ½ orange
Grated zest of ½ lemon
2 tablespoons sugar
3 tablespoons cake flour, sifted

THE VANILLA EMULSION
⅓ cup heavy cream
½ cup sugar
1 vanilla bean, split
2 egg yolks
1 cup heavy cream, whipped
   to soft peaks

THE LEMON CURD
2 eggs
¾ cup sugar
Grated zest of 2 lemons
6 tablespoons fresh lemon juice
6 tablespoons unsalted butter

THE LEMON SYRUP
½ cup Simple Syrup (PAGE 228)
2 tablespoons fresh lemon juice

For the lemon sorbet, combine the water, sugar, and milk powder in a small saucepan and bring just to a boil, stirring to dissolve the sugar and milk powder. Remove from the heat and allow to cool completely.

Stir the lemon juice into the sugar syrup. Freeze in an ice cream machine according to manufacturer's instructions. Pack into a container and freeze until ready to serve.

For the vanilla parfait, combine the milk, cream, sugar, lemon zest, and vanilla extract in a small saucepan and bring to a boil, stirring to dissolve the sugar. Remove from the heat and slowly whisk in the egg yolk. Add the gelatin, whisking to dissolve. Allow to cool slightly, then fold in the whipped cream. Transfer the mixture to a pastry bag fitted with a large plain tip.

Wrap one end of 4 cylindrical molds that are ½ inch in diameter and 5 inches long (see Sources, page 229) with plastic wrap. Pipe the parfait mixture into the molds and freeze.

For the crisp meringue, preheat the oven to 200°F.

Whip the egg white in the bowl of a stand mixer on medium speed to soft peaks. Slowly add the sugar, whipping until firm peaks form.

Using a small offset spatula, spread thin 3-inch circles of the meringue onto a Silpat-lined baking sheet. Place in the oven and dry until crisp. Let cool, then carefully remove the circles and store in an airtight container.

For the citrus *biscuit,* preheat the oven to 325°F. Line a jelly-roll pan with parchment paper.

Combine the melted chocolate and butter in a bowl and stir until thoroughly blended and smooth. Stir in the egg yolks, Trimoline, and citrus zest.

Whip the egg whites until frothy in the bowl of a stand mixer. Gradually add the sugar and whip to soft peaks. Fold in the sifted cake flour, followed by the white chocolate base. Pour the batter into the prepared pan and bake for 12 to 15 minutes, until firm. Allow to cool on a rack.

Unmold the *biscuit* and cut out 4 rectangles slightly larger than the cylindrical molds of parfait; set aside. (Reserve the rest of the *biscuit* for another use.)

For the vanilla emulsion, combine the cream and sugar in a saucepan. Scrape the seeds from the vanilla bean and add the seeds and pod to the cream. Bring to a boil over medium heat, stirring to dissolve the sugar. Remove the pan from the heat and very slowly whisk in the egg yolks. Strain through a fine-mesh sieve into a bowl and chill for at least 1 hour.

Fold the whipped cream into the vanilla base and refrigerate.

For the lemon curd, whisk together the eggs and sugar in a heavy saucepan, then add the lemon zest and juice. Bring to a boil, stirring constantly (the mixture can easily scorch on the bottom). As soon as it reaches

a boil, remove from the heat and whisk in the butter a small amount at a time. Strain the lemon curd through a fine-mesh sieve and chill in an ice bath, then refrigerate until ready to use.

For the lemon syrup, combine the simple syrup and lemon juice in a shallow bowl.

To serve, soak each rectangle of the *biscuit* in the lemon syrup and place on a serving plate. Unmold the vanilla parfait by warming each mold with your hands, and slide onto the *biscuit.* Spoon the vanilla emulsion and lemon curd onto the plates. Break the meringues into pieces, and arrange on top of the parfaits. Finish each plate with a quenelle of the sorbet, and serve immediately.

APRICOT

ROASTED APRICOTS, BLACK SESAME PANNA COTTA,
CHERRY GRANITÉ, AND SOY CARAMEL

The flavors of Asia, especially those of Japan, lend themselves quite well to our style of cooking, both savory and sweet. The silky panna cotta in this dessert is perfumed with the sweet nuttiness of black sesame, a perfect foil for in-season roasted apricots. The cherry granité gives the dish a high-end hit of acidity, while the mellow complexity of the soy caramel provides just the right grounding. To save time, spoon the panna cotta into individual dishes or ramekins and chill until set, then place the remaining ingredients on top as a garnish.

SERVES 4

THE CHERRY GRANITÉ
1 cup cherry juice (SEE SOURCES, PAGE 229)
¼ cup water
¼ cup sugar

THE ROASTED APRICOTS
4 ripe medium apricots,
   halved and pits removed
Sugar for sprinkling

THE BLACK SESAME
PANNA COTTA
½ cup heavy cream
3 tablespoons sugar
1 tablespoon black sesame paste
   (SEE SOURCES, PAGE 229)
1 sheet (2 grams) gelatin, softened
   in ice-cold water
¼ cup whole milk

THE SOY CARAMEL
¼ cup sugar
¼ cup orange juice
2 tablespoons water
1 teaspoon soy sauce

THE GARNISH
1 shiso leaf, cut into julienne
8 Sesame Tuiles (RECIPE FOLLOWS)

For the cherry granité, whisk together all the ingredients and pour into a shallow baking pan. Freeze for 1 hour, stirring every 15 minutes to break up the ice crystals.

For the roasted apricots, preheat the oven to 350°F.

Arrange the apricots in a baking dish, cut side up, and sprinkle liberally with sugar. Place the baking dish in the oven and bake for about 10 minutes, or until the apricots are soft and caramelized. Remove the apricots from the oven and allow to cool. Carefully remove the skins, and set the apricots aside.

For the panna cotta, combine the cream, sugar, and black sesame paste in a medium saucepan and bring to a simmer over medium heat, stirring to dissolve the sugar. Remove the pan from the heat, add the softened gelatin, and, using an immersion blender, puree the mixture to ensure that there are no lumps of sesame paste. Stir in the milk and strain through a fine-mesh sieve.

Pour the mixture into twelve 1½-inch Flexipan molds (see Sources, page 229; if necessary, use twelve 1½-inch molds with dome-shaped depressions). Put the molds on a baking sheet, and freeze until set.

Remove the panna cotta from the Flexipans, put on a parchment-lined baking sheet, and refrigerate.

For the soy caramel, combine the sugar and 2 tablespoons water in a saucepan. Cook over medium heat, without stirring, until the sugar is dissolved and the caramel is a medium amber color.

Meanwhile, gently heat the orange juice and water in a second pan. Remove the caramel from the heat and slowly add the juice mixture. Return to the heat and stir to dissolve any hardened lumps of caramel, then reduce to a syrupy consistency. Remove from the heat and add the soy sauce. Let cool, transfer to a squeeze bottle, and refrigerate.

To serve, place 2 apricot halves in the center of each plate and arrange 3 panna cotta next to the apricots. Drizzle the soy caramel over and around the dessert. Place a few strips of shiso on top of each one. Scrape the frozen granité with a fork and place a small mound on top of the apricots, then garnish with 2 of the sesame tuiles. Serve immediately.

SESAME TUILES
MAKES ABOUT 10 TUILES

It's a good idea to make extra tuiles to allow for breakage; you can store leftovers in an airtight container—they go great with ice cream.

1 ¾ cups confectioners' sugar
1 tablespoon all-purpose flour
¼ teaspoon apple pectin powder
12 tablespoons (1½ sticks) unsalted butter
3 tablespoons light corn syrup
5 tablespoons water
Black sesame seeds for sprinkling

Sift the confectioners' sugar, flour, and pectin; set aside. Combine the butter and corn syrup in a saucepan and melt the butter over low heat. Whisk in the sifted ingredients and then the water. Increase the heat to medium and bring just to a boil, stirring. Remove from the heat and let cool for at least 1 hour.

Preheat oven to 350°F.

Using a small offset spatula, spread thin 2-inch circles of batter onto a Silpat-lined baking sheet. For the recipe above, make 8 tuiles, plus a few extra to allow for breakage. Sprinkle a few black sesame seeds onto each tuile.

Place the pan in the oven and bake until the tuiles are golden brown, 10 to 15 minutes. Remove from the oven and let cool for 1 minute. While they are still warm and pliable, carefully remove the tuiles, twisting and stretching them into irregular shapes. Place on a paper towel to blot off any excess butter. (Once cooled, the tuiles can be stored in an airtight container for up to 1 day.)

CHICKEN JUS
MAKES I CUP

1 tablespoon canola oil
4 pounds chicken legs
6 cups Chicken Stock (RECIPE FOLLOWS)

Preheat the oven to 500°F.

Place a small roasting pan or shallow ovenproof pot in the oven to heat for 5 minutes.

Add the canola oil and then the chicken legs. Return the pan to the oven and roast the legs, stirring periodically so they don't stick to the pan, for 20 to 25 minutes, until they are golden brown.

Meanwhile, bring the chicken stock to a boil in a stockpot.

Remove the pan carefully from the oven and pour off the fat. Transfer the legs to the chicken stock. Return the pot to medium-high heat and bring to a boil. Lower the heat to low and let simmer for 2 to 2½ hours.

Strain the chicken jus and reduce to about 1 cup; the consistency should be close to that of a sauce.

Store in an airtight container in the refrigerator for up to 5 days or in the freezer for up to 2 months.

CHICKEN STOCK
MAKES 3 QUARTS

6 pounds chicken backs
5 quarts cold water

Rinse the chicken well under cold running water and place it in a large stockpot. Add water to cover by 2 inches. Bring to a boil, then turn the heat down to a low simmer.

Simmer the stock for 3 hours, carefully skimming away any fat and impurities that rise to the surface with a ladle.

Remove the stock from the heat and strain it through a colander and then through a fine-mesh sieve, being careful to leave the sediment in the bottom of the pot. Degrease the stock again with a ladle.

Cool the stock in an ice bath. Store until ready to use: in the refrigerator for up to 1 week, or in the freezer for up to 2 months. Scrape off any congealed fat before using.

MUSHROOM STOCK
MAKES 2 CUPS

5 pounds button mushrooms
8 cups water

Put the mushrooms in a small stockpot, add the water, and bring to a boil. Reduce the heat and simmer gently for about 2 hours, until reduced by half.

Strain the mushroom stock into a saucepan. Bring to a boil and reduce by half again.

Store in the refrigerator for up to 1 week, or in the freezer for up to 2 months.

FUMET

MAKES 1 QUART

3 pounds fish bones (preferably
  from halibut or turbot)
6 cups water
3 shallots, thinly sliced
1 cup dry white wine

Soak the fish bones in lightly salted
cold water for 1 hour, changing the
water twice.

Preheat the oven to 400°F.

Drain the bones and pat them
dry. Place the bones in a shallow
roasting pan and roast for 2 minutes.
Remove the bones from the pan and
blot away any blood.

Put the bones in a wide pot and
add the water. Bring to a boil. Add
the shallots and wine, reduce the
heat to low, and simmer for 10 minutes. Remove from the heat and let
stand 1 minute.

Strain the fumet through a fine-
mesh sieve into a container. Store in
the refrigerator for up to 2 days or in
the freezer for up to 2 months.

SHRIMP STOCK

MAKES 1 QUART

1½ teaspoons canola oil
1 pound small shrimp (41–50)
¼ cup medium-diced onion
2 tablespoons medium-diced carrot
2 tablespoons medium-diced celery
6 tablespoons tomato paste
5 cups cold water

Heat the canola oil in a wide heavy
pot until very hot but not smoking.
Add the shrimp and sear until
most of the shells have turned bright
orange, about 2 minutes. Add the
onion, carrot, and celery and cook
until the vegetables soften, about
5 minutes.

Add the tomato paste and stir well
with a wooden spoon. Cook, stirring
constantly to prevent scorching,
until the paste has turned from red
to orange, about 5 minutes.

Add the cold water to the pot
and bring to a boil. Remove the pot
from the heat.

Process the stock, in batches, in a
blender or food processor until the
shrimp is coarsely chopped.

Return the stock to the pot and
bring to a simmer. Remove from the
heat and let sit for 10 minutes to
allow the flavors to infuse.

Strain the stock through a colander and then through a fine-mesh
sieve, pressing on the solids to
extract as much liquid as possible.

Cool quickly, and store until ready
to use: up to 3 days in the refrigerator or up to 1 month in the freezer.

POT-AU-FEU BROTH

MAKES 1 QUART

10 pounds oxtails
5 pounds pork shoulder,
  cut into pieces
8 quarts cold water

Rinse the oxtails and pork shoulder
under cold running water and place
in a large stockpot. Add water to
cover by 2 inches Slowly bring to a
simmer, carefully skimming away any
fat and impurities that rise to the
surface with a ladle. As soon as the
liquid comes to a simmer, drain the
oxtails and pork in a colander.

Rinse the blanched oxtails and
pork well, making sure the water runs
clean and all of the impurities have
been removed. Return the oxtails and
pork to the clean stockpot, add the 8
quarts cold water, and bring just to a
boil, skimming. Turn the heat down
to a low simmer and simmer the stock
for 4 hours, skimming frequently.

Remove the stock from the heat
and strain it through a colander
and then through a fine-mesh sieve.
Pour into a pot, bring to a boil, and
reduce to about 4 cups.

Store in the refrigerator for
up to 5 days, or in the freezer for
up to 2 months.

VEAL STOCK

MAKES 2 QUARTS

8 pounds veal knuckles and bones
5 quarts cold water

————

Rinse the veal knuckles and bones well under cold running water and place in a large stockpot. Add water to cover by 2 inches. Slowly bring to a simmer, carefully skimming away the fat and impurities that rise to the surface with a ladle. As soon as the liquid comes to a simmer, drain the bones in a colander.

Rinse the bones well under cold water until the water runs clean, making sure all of the impurities have been removed. Return the bones to the clean stockpot, add the 5 quarts cold water, and bring to a boil, skimming. Turn the heat down to a low simmer and simmer the stock for 4 hours, skimming frequently.

Remove the stock from the heat and strain it through a colander, then strain it through a fine-mesh sieve into a large bowl or other container. Skim any fat from the top of the stock with a ladle.

Cool the stock in an ice bath. Store until ready to use in the refrigerator for up to 2 weeks, or in the freezer for up to 3 months. Scrape off any remaining fat before using.

VEAL JUS

MAKES 1 QUART

2 tablespoons canola oil
6 pounds veal shoulder, cut
   into 2-inch pieces
½ small carrot, diced
1 rib celery, diced
½ medium onion, diced
About 2 quarts Veal Stock
   (RECIPE PRECEDES)

————

Heat a large stockpot over medium-high heat.

Add the canola oil and the veal. Sear the veal shoulder for 15 to 20 minutes, until golden brown, stirring periodically so the meat does not stick to the pot. Add the diced carrot, celery, and onion and cook over medium heat for 8 to 10 minutes, until soft.

Add enough stock to cover the veal and bring to a boil. Reduce the temperature to low and simmer the jus for 2 to 2½ hours.

Strain the veal jus into the clean stockpot and reduce over medium heat to 1 quart

GARLIC BUTTER

MAKES ABOUT ½ POUND

1 tablespoon chopped
   Italian parsley
½ pound unsalted butter, softened
2 tablespoons minced garlic
1 tablespoon minced shallot

————

Wrap the parsley in a square of cheesecloth and squeeze to remove excess moisture.

Whip the butter in the bowl of a stand mixer until creamy. Add the garlic, shallot, and parsley and mix well.

Transfer the butter to a plastic container and store, tightly sealed, for up to 1 week in the refrigerator or up to 1 month in the freezer.

TRUFFLE BUTTER SAUCE
MAKES ¾ CUP

1 tablespoon water
6 tablespoons unsalted butter,
   cut into ½-inch cubes,
   plus 1 tablespoon if needed
¼ ounce black truffle
Fine sea salt and freshly ground
   white pepper

To make a beurre monté, bring the
water to a boil in a small saucepan.
Whisk in 6 tablespoons butter, about
1 tablespoon at a time.

Transfer the beurre monté
to a blender. Add the truffle and
blend until the truffle is finely
chopped. Season to taste with salt
and white pepper.

The sauce is ready to be used and
can be kept at room temperature
for up to 2 hours. When reheating,
whisk in an additional 1 tablespoon
of butter if needed to re-emulsify
the sauce.

BROWN BUTTER SAUCE
MAKES I CUP

½ pound unsalted butter
1 cup Chicken Stock (PAGE 220),
   reduced to ½ cup
1 tablespoon fresh lemon juice
Fine sea salt and freshly ground
   white pepper

Melt the butter in a medium pot
over medium-high heat, then cook,
whisking occasionally, until the milk
solids are dark brown and the butter
is fragrant. Remove from the heat
and set aside.

Heat the chicken stock in a
medium saucepan and add the
lemon juice. Bring to a boil.

Remove from the heat and, using
an immersion blender, slowly blend
the brown butter into the chicken
stock. Season to taste with salt and
white pepper. Use immediately.

GINGER OIL
MAKES I CUP

4 ounces ginger, peeled and minced
½ cup canola oil

Put the ginger in a clean jar and add
the oil. Seal tightly and let stand at
room temperature for 2 hours, or
refrigerate overnight, before using.

Store refrigerated for up
to 2 weeks.

SHERRY VINAIGRETTE
MAKES I CUP

3 tablespoons sherry vinegar
1½ teaspoons red wine vinegar
¼ cup extra virgin olive oil
¼ cup olive oil
¼ cup canola oil
Fine sea salt and freshly ground
   white pepper to taste

———

Combine the vinegars in a bowl and whisk to blend. Using an immersion blender, slowly drizzle in the extra virgin olive oil, olive oil, and canola oil. Season to taste with salt and white pepper.

Transfer the vinaigrette to a jar and refrigerate, tightly sealed, until ready to use. The vinaigrette will not stay emulsified; be sure to whisk well before using.

LEMON CONFIT
MAKES 24 PETALS

5 cups kosher salt
5 tablespoons sugar
6 lemons, scrubbed

———

Combine the salt and sugar and mix well.

Trim the ends off each lemon, and quarter the lemons. Toss the lemons with half of the salt-sugar mix, coating well.

Pour a layer of salt-sugar mix into the bottom of a plastic container or jar. Layer the lemons into the container, covering each layer with more of the salt-sugar mix. Pour the remaining salt-sugar mix on top of the last layer of lemons.

Tightly seal the container and refrigerate for at least 2 weeks before using. The lemons are best after 3 months and will keep for up to a year (keep them in the salt-sugar mix until ready to use).

To use, thoroughly rinse the lemons. Cut away all of the flesh from the rind; discard the flesh. Use as directed in the individual recipe. If using as a garnish, briefly blanch the rind in boiling water before mincing or julienning.

TOMATO CONFIT
MAKES ABOUT 30 PIECES

3 tomatoes, cored, peeled, and
   cut into ¾-inch-thick wedges
Fine sea salt and freshly ground
   white pepper
2 tablespoons extra virgin olive oil
1½ tablespoons thyme leaves

———

Preheat the oven to 200°F.

Line a baking sheet with parchment paper and arrange the tomatoes on the pan. Season the tomatoes with salt and white pepper and drizzle with the olive oil. Sprinkle the thyme leaves over the tomatoes.

Bake the tomatoes for 1 to 1½ hours, until they've collapsed and flattened a bit and have browned lightly. Remove from the oven and let cool to room temperature.

Transfer the tomatoes to a container and store, tightly sealed, in the refrigerator for up to 1 week.

SHERRY GELÉE
MAKES ABOUT ½ CUP

5 tablespoons sherry vinegar
2 tablespoons water
1 sheet (2 grams) gelatin, softened
  in ice-cold water

Bring the sherry and water to a
boil in a small saucepan. Remove
from the heat. Remove the gelatin
from the ice water, squeeze out any
excess water, and add the gelatin to
the hot liquid. Swirl the pan to dissolve the gelatin.

Transfer to a small stainless steel
bowl and refrigerate until set, about
4 hours.

PONZU
MAKES ABOUT 3½ CUPS

1 cup soy sauce
Minced zest and juice of ½ orange
Minced zest and juice of ½ lemon
Minced zest and juice of ¼ lime
⅓ cup yuzu juice
1 teaspoon sugar
2 cups water

Mix all of the ingredients together
in a bowl.

Transfer to a jar or bottle, seal
tightly, and refrigerate for at least
24 hours before using.

PICKLED SHALLOTS
MAKES ¼ CUP

1 tablespoon sugar
2 tablespoons water
6 tablespoons champagne
  vinegar
1 teaspoon coriander seeds
½ star anise
1 clove
¼ teaspoon black peppercorns
1 teaspoon saffron threads
¼ cup sliced shallots

Combine all of the ingredients
except the shallots in a small pot
and bring to a boil.

Put the shallots in a small bowl
and strain the liquid over them;
allow to marinate at least 2 hours
before serving. These can be
kept refrigerated up to 1 month.

BASIL OIL
MAKES ABOUT ¾ CUP

2 cups loosely packed basil leaves
½ cup canola oil

Blanch the basil leaves in a pot
of boiling salted water. Drain and
immediately plunge into an ice bath
to cool. Drain and squeeze dry.

Combine the basil and oil in
a blender and blend to a smooth
puree. Strain the oil through a sieve
lined with a coffee filter.

Transfer to a container and refrigerate for up to 1 week.

TEMPERING CHOCOLATE TO MAKE PLAQUETTES

Tempering is a technique that gives chocolate a smooth and glossy finish, as well as a crisp "snap," and makes it slightly more resistant to melting. Any chocolate that you purchase, whether in small bars or large blocks, is in "temper" state when it leaves the factory. However, once chocolate is melted, the complex crystal structure of its cocoa butter is thrown out of temper so that chocolate melted in order to use for certain garnishes, coatings, or molding candies often must be tempered again. Tempering can be accomplished in several different ways; the simplest technique for home cooks is the one usually referred to as the "seeding method."

TOOLS NEEDED FOR TEMPERING CHOCOLATE AND MAKING PLAQUETTES

A microwave-safe bowl
A wooden spoon or rubber spatula
An instant-read thermometer
A large offset spatula
A ruler
Two plastic acetate sheets, measuring 18 by 12 inches (available from baking supply and art supply stores)
An X-Acto knife or thin paring knife

It is usually best to work with a fair amount of chocolate, about 1 to 2 pounds; this will make the process more efficient and the resulting tempered chocolate easier to work with. Any leftover chocolate can be eaten or used in another recipe.

To begin, finely chop the entire quantity of chocolate. Place two-thirds of the chocolate in the microwave-safe bowl and slowly melt in the microwave, using short, low-power bursts and stirring frequently (alternatively, the chocolate can be gently melted in a double-boiler). Keep in mind that chocolate melted in the microwave can hold its shape until stirred, so appearances can be deceptive. The chocolate should be entirely melted and the temperature should reach 110° to 115°F, no higher. Allow the melted chocolate to stand for about 10 minutes, during which

time the temperature will drop to about 100°F.

Add the remaining chopped chocolate to the melted chocolate and stir until completely melted. The chocolate should now be in temper. A quick test is to dip a small piece of parchment paper into the chocolate and allow it to set at room temperature. If the chocolate does not set to a smooth, shiny appearance within a few minutes, add a bit more chopped chocolate, and test it again.

When the chocolate is in temper, make the plaquettes: Place one acetate sheet on a sheet of parchment on a smooth, level work surface. Pour roughly 1 cup of the melted chocolate onto the acetate and spread into a thin, even layer, almost covering the entire sheet. Allow the chocolate to set just until it no longer appears wet or tacky. Working quickly, so the chocolate doesn't set too hard, mark 4-inch increments along the length of the chocolate sheet and 1-inch increments down along the sides. Using the ruler as a guideline, connect these marks to make rectangles. Carefully cut the chocolate into shapes with the small knife, applying just enough pressure to cut through the chocolate but not through the acetate.

Once all the rectangles are cut (there will be more than needed for the recipe, to allow for any breakage), place the second sheet of acetate on top of the first and place a flat baking sheet on top. This light pressure will prevent the chocolate from curling, as tempered chocolate contracts as it sets. Once the chocolate is completely hardened, remove the top sheet of acetate, store the chocolate plaquettes, still on the acetate, in a cool, dry place. When ready to serve, gently lift them off the acetate.

CRÈME ANGLAISE

MAKES ABOUT 1¼ CUPS

3 large egg yolks
3½ tablespoons sugar
1 teaspoon Trimoline
  (SEE SOURCES, PAGE 229)
½ vanilla bean
1 cup whole milk
2 tablespoons nonfat dry milk
½ tablespoon light corn syrup
2½ tablespoons heavy cream

Whisk the egg yolks, 1 tablespoon of the sugar, and the Trimoline in a small bowl; set aside.

Scrape the seeds from the vanilla bean and put the seeds and pod in a small saucepan. Add the milk and nonfat dry milk and stir. Heat over medium heat and whisk in the remaining 2½ tablespoons sugar and the corn syrup, until the sugar is dissolved.

Remove from the heat and temper in the egg yolks.

Return to low heat and cook until the crème anglaise thickens considerably, 3 to 5 minutes. Put the heavy cream in a bowl.

Remove the crème anglaise from the heat. Strain through a fine-mesh sieve into the bowl of heavy cream, and whisk. Chill in an ice bath and refrigerate until ready to use, up to 3 days.

CARAMEL SAUCE

MAKES ABOUT ½ CUP

⅓ cup plus 1 tablespoon sugar
¾ teaspoon light corn syrup
⅛ teaspoon fresh lemon juice
¾ tablespoon water
¼ cup plus 2 tablespoons
  heavy cream
½ tablespoon unsalted butter

In a small pot, combine the sugar, corn syrup, lemon juice, and water. Without stirring, cook the mixture over medium heat until the sugar has dissolved and the caramel turns a golden color.

Meanwhile, heat the heavy cream in a separate pot until warm.

Remove the sugar mixture from the heat and quickly whisk in the cream (the sugar mixture and the cream should be warm to avoid lumps from forming). Whisk the sauce over low heat until the sugar is completely dissolved and the sauce is smooth.

Remove the sauce from the heat and whisk in the butter.

Allow the sauce to cool, transfer to a container, and cover tightly with plastic wrap. Store at room temperature if using the same day or refrigerate until ready to use, up to 1 week.

SIMPLE SYRUP

MAKES ½ CUP

¼ cup sugar
¼ cup water

Bring the sugar and water to a boil in a small saucepan, stirring until the sugar is completely dissolved. Remove from the heat and let cool.

Store in an airtight container in the refrigerator for up to 6 weeks.

SOURCES

Many of the recipes in this book call for micro cilantro or other micro greens. You can buy these at a well-stocked specialty food store, gourmet store, or greengrocer.

The following items are also available at most specialty food stores:

Candied chestnuts and puree
Freeze-dried corn
Cherry juice
Xanthan gum
Verjus
Shishito peppers
Candied citrus peel
Lemon oil

Baking supply stores will offer many items that aren't in your supermarket, including:

Feuilletine
Agar-agar
Tapioca maltodextrin
Pistachio paste
Invert sugar (Trimoline)
Isomalt
Fondant
Hazelnut praline paste

Asian markets have proliferated across North America in recent years. They're worth exploring and are a good source for the following:

Yuzu juice
Fresh wasabi paste
White soy sauce

Aki nori
Bonito flakes
Green papaya
Black sesame paste
Korean hot pepper paste

Here are sources for other hard-to-find items:

Nirmala's Kitchen
www.nirmalaskitchen.com
718-361-7807
GARAM MASALA; GREEN CARDAMOM SEEDS

Kalustyan's
www.kalustyans.com
212-685-3451 or 800-352-3451
TANDOORI POWDER; HALEN MÔN
SMOKED SALT; ROSE SYRUP; ROSE PETALS;
DRIED ROSEBUDS; TAMARIND CONCENTRATE

Despaña
www.despananyc.com
212-219-5050
SQUID INK; PIQUILLO PEPPERS; CHORIZO;
HOT PIMENTON; SOLERA AGED SHERRY
VINEGAR; AJI AMARILLO PEPPER PUREE;
PIMENT D'ESPELETTE POWDER

Salt Traders
www.salttraders.com
978-356-7258 or 800-641-7258
VIKING SEA SALT

Terra Spice
www.terraspicecompany.com
574-586-2600
FREEZE-DRIED CORN; TAPIOCA
MALTODEXTRIN

Minus 8
www.minus8vinegar.com
877-209-7634
RICE WINE VINEGAR

For specialty equipment, try baking supply stores for items such as cylindrical molds. For other kitchenware, these two retailers have a great selection:

J.B. Prince Company
www.jbprince.com
800-473-0577

Bridge Kitchenware
www.bridgekitchenware.com
212-688-4220

ACKNOWLEDGMENTS

This book would not have come to life without Christine Muhlke, Nigel Parry and Melanie Dunea, and Shimon and Tammar Rothstein, nor without Ann Bramson at Artisan, Josh Liberson and Ethan Trask at Helicopter, Susan Lescher, and their respective teams, all of whom helped us document the life of Le Bernardin.

I am personally grateful to my wife, Sandra, and son, Adrien, my mum, and my family. They have stood beside me and supported me with their unconditional love.

I offer deepest thanks to my partner, Maguy Le Coze, and my entire team at Le Bernardin, including Ben Chekroun, Chris Muller, Eric "Coco" Gestel, Aldo Sohm, the Angels (Mandy Oser, Soa Davies, and Michelle Lindsay), David Mancini, Michael Laiskonis, Fernando Uruchima, Jose Almonte, Frédérique Reginensi, Carlos Tomazos, Vinny Robinson, Segundo Uruchima, and Justo Thomas. And I am grateful to everyone else who is a part of our team: the cleaning crew, captains, special events, reservationists, cooks, busboys, waiters, sommeliers, accountants, and publicists. Each of these individuals works with unfailing passion and tireless effort to keep Le Bernardin running. I thank all of them from the bottom of my heart.

I would also like to thank Gilbert Le Coze, who gave me my first shot, and my other mentors, Jean-Louis Palladin and Joël Robuchon. Thanks also to our clients, purveyors, supporters, friends, and brothers. Le Bernardin is privileged to have their great support.

This is our legacy. May it inspire you . . .

—Eric Ripert

INDEX

Note: Page numbers in *italics* refer to illustrations.